CAPTURED EAGLES

OSPREY
PUBLISHING

CAPTURED EAGLES

Secrets of the Luftwaffe

FREDERICK A. JOHNSEN

First published in Great Britain in 2014 by Osprey Publishing,
PO Box 883, Oxford, OX1 9PL, UK
PO Box 3985, New York, NY 10185-3985, USA
E-mail: info@ospreypublishing.com

Osprey Publishing is part of the Osprey Group

A CIP catalogue record for this book is available from the British Library

Frederick A. Johnsen has asserted his rights under the Copyright, Designs and Patents Act, 1988, to be
identified as the Author of this Work.

ISBN: 978 1 78200 368 7
e-book ISBN: 978 1 78200 974 0
PDF ISBN: 978 1 78200 973 3

Index by Zoe Ross
Typeset in Conduit ITC, Cambria & Trojan Pro
Originated by PDQ Digital Media Solutions, Suffolk
Printed in China through Asia Pacific Offset Litd.

14 15 16 17 18   10 9 8 7 6 5 4 3 2 1

Front cover: Fw 190 (*Topfoto*)

Back cover:
Top: Do 335 (*AFHRA*)
Bottom left: Ju 88D (*USAAF via Peter M. Bowers*)
Bottom right: Bf 109F EB-100 (*USAAF*)

Osprey Publishing is supporting the Woodland Trust, the UK's leading woodland conservation charity, by
funding the dedication of trees.

www.ospreypublishing.com

CONTENTS

FOREWORD

It is rare when a book not only covers a fascinating part of the past, but offers some critical insight for the future. A close reading of this volume will provide the reader with some useful information on why and how America gained ascendancy in the Cold War and in the space race. It also provides a basis for assessing the current state of world affairs and provokes thought on what America needs to do to maintain its place in these turbulent times.

Few subjects have enthralled the American aerospace public more than the analysis and exploitation of German technology before, during and after World War II. The amazing advances implicit in the introduction of jet fighters, guided missiles and ballistic missiles caught the imagination of US military leaders. The nation was fortunate to have General of the Air Force Henry A. "Hap" Arnold in a position to see and foster the need for scientific research for the future. Arnold was far from a scientist himself, and he was not well. But he knew how to select people and inspire them, and he created a framework that permitted the United States to avoid a "scientific demobilization" of the sort that had decimated the armed forces in the 18 months following Japan's surrender. Arnold's establishment of the Army Air Forces Scientific Advisory Group (AAFSAG), chaired by Theodore von Kármán, led the way to America's future dominance in air and space.

Arnold's initial efforts were aided by the famous Operation *Paperclip*. Its aim was to seek out valuable hardware and engineering data. However, at a time when the Nazi leaders of Germany were awaiting trial for their war crimes, a controversial decision was made that the personnel available in the German engineering community were too valuable to waste. Against considerable internal political opposition, the United States elected to import leading German engineers and scientists into the American research and development community. The results were far-reaching in every industry. The most evident example, seen today at every large airport, comprises the swept-wing transports crowding the tarmac. Yet for engineers still engaged in almost every field, the results are evident in the citations of the research they do on current subjects.

It is important to note, as author Frederick Johnsen does so well, that this shotgun marriage of German and American minds succeeded in large part because of the capability of the American partner. American scientists and engineers had done their homework and were gaining on the Germans. It is fair to say that had the war gone on another few years, American technology would have caught up with and then exceeded German achievements. But the pairing of the two scientific communities came at a critical time in what became known as the Cold War, and gave invaluable impetus to American efforts to counter the increasingly belligerent attitude of the Soviet Union. It should be noted that while the Soviet Union also acquired significant amounts of the same elements of German technology, it ultimately depended more upon its own intrinsic capabilities. It is not too far a reach to believe that this was a factor in the USSR losing the exhilarating race to the moon.

American interest in German aerial technology was far from new. The great champion of air power, Brig Gen Billy Mitchell, had surveyed the German aircraft industry after the "Great War" and directed the application of many of his findings into the tiny postwar American aviation efforts. After Adolf Hitler reestablished the Luftwaffe officially in 1935, there was intense interest in the rapid progress in which new, higher performance machines were being introduced. The United States was suffering from the Great Depression, military budgets were cut to the bone, and aviation research was grossly underfunded.

The inevitable result was that the United States Army Air Corps (USAAC) lacked planes, pilots and equipment. It was grudgingly accepted even by the press and public that both Germany and Great Britain were fielding aircraft that had a higher performance than their American equivalents. Fortunately, there were hard-working scientists in American industry and at the National Advisory Committee for Aeronautics (NACA). They remained aware of foreign developments, and in some instances paralleled them, as with Robert T. Jones' investigations into the advantages of a swept wing.

Despite the funding difficulties, and despite personal obstacles such as the lack of promotion opportunity, there existed within the USAAC officers blessed with an important insight, a grasp of the scale on which the next war would be conducted. A handful of these officers created the Air War Plan Division (AWPD), which sought to establish bombing doctrine, prioritize targets and estimate the number of aircraft required. Its estimate was stunning, for it stated that more than 61,000 aircraft would be required at a time when the USAAC had about 3,000 planes.

The estimate was uncannily accurate. It led the United States to a scale of effort that was far more than anything done by Germany or Great Britain, and was matched only by the Soviet Union. Fortunately, American industry responded to the demands of the AWPD, and reached a rate of production of about 100,000 aircraft per year by 1944. In contrast, Germany, with a truly Herculean effort despite being bombed, was able to manufacture only about 40,000 aircraft in 1944. There were enormous differences, however, in the comparative support efforts – training, maintenance, pilot proficiency and so on – where the United States had a great advantage.

When the vast disparity in size and strength became evident in late 1943, the two opponents took different paths. The United States and its allies were determined to overwhelm German air power with great numbers of contemporary aircraft. The Luftwaffe was to be destroyed not only in aerial combat, but also by the removal of its manufacturing and training basis. Germany, in desperation, turned to a fervid attempt to win by advanced technology, hoping that weapons such as the Me 262 and the V1 and V2 would turn the tide. It was a losing strategy, but the fruits of its efforts were of vast interest to the Allies. In simplest terms, a huge quantity of good technology overwhelmed a much smaller quantity of very advanced technology.

In the ongoing 21st-century contest between established nations and shadowy terror organizations, the United States is the winner at bringing advanced technologies to bear. But there is a lesson to be learned from the historical over-reliance on high technology, and on delaying the development of such technology. One must hope the defense planners of the United States are learning from the past by planning robust capabilities against everything from terrorists, to peer states, to the threat of a cyber war that would cripple modern infrastructure. These are different threats that demand different defenses. Such diversity of defense is something Germany may not have fully appreciated on the eve of World War II.

The reader can take Frederick Johnsen's look into the United States Army Air Forces' (USAAF's) relationship with German technologies as a colorful and dramatic historical snapshot in time, or as a text with lessons applicable today.

Walter J. Boyne

PREFACE

There is a compelling mystique and intrigue about the World War II Luftwaffe that continues to interest readers, researchers, modelers, and, increasingly, restorers and even replicators of full-size German warplanes. This volume represents a largely American view of the Luftwaffe, ranging from captured German aircraft under evaluation in the United States to casual G.I. snapshots of abandoned Luftwaffe aircraft in Europe.

The course of World War II and its technological developments is curious. Before the United States entered combat in December 1941, British advances in radar were the marvel of the day. In the last half of the war, German ascendancy with jets and rockets was startling. And yet, only America perfected an atomic bomb. Some would argue the capacity of America to produce thousands of great, if not perfect, aircraft and other armaments, manned by well-trained crews known globally for their innovativeness under fire, gave the Allies the final victory. This volume will not presume to call one Allied power's contributions to victory more important than any other nation's efforts and sacrifices, but it will juxtapose the advanced technologies of wartime Germany against the efforts of the United States in particular.

The absorption of German technologies and the amalgamation of German scientists and engineers into America's Cold War developments deserve reflection too. Certainly, advanced German technologies boosted and accelerated American aerospace efforts after the war. But it would be a disservice to the American brain trust extant in 1945 to presume those breakthroughs would not have come indigenously, if over a longer period of time, had there been no German technologies to study.

The wealth of documentation on German wartime technologies preserved in American archives has far greater depth and breadth than can be exhausted by one work such as this. A few examples must suffice in representing whole fields of endeavor. Pre-war assessment of nascent German aerial strength came from the visits of Charles Lindbergh to Germany in the 1930s.

Elsewhere the reader will find anecdotes about American analysis of German summer-weight flying helmets. The wreckage of a Ju 88 and its hapless crew's personal effects come in for scrutiny. The remarks of an imprisoned Hermann Göring are revealing, and the evaluation of German rockets reveals both how much we knew, and did not yet comprehend, about the impending space age. By late 1944, the air war over Europe was fast becoming a race to see if American strategic bombers and piston-engined fighters in abundance could overwhelm growing numbers of faster German jet fighters. The outcome of the war – or at least its prolongation or termination – hung in the balance. It is telling that experimental, futuristic German jet fighter prototypes were found with wings using wooden ribs and skins surmounting steel spars, so acute was Germany's paucity of aluminum late in the war. The trouble-plagued He 177 bomber is said to ultimately have been the victim of this metals shortage, its cancelation in 1944 at least in part a way to free up precious aluminum for the fighters Germany urgently needed to take on the relentless Allied bomber formations. The anecdotes are legion; let this volume serve as a glimpse into the arcane world of wartime intelligence gathering and postwar technology transfer on so many levels.

The archives remain rich for future research as well – demonstrating how pervasive the quest to comprehend German technologies was. There is a photograph extant of Howard Carter, discoverer of the tomb of King Tutankhamun, gazing at the sarcophagus with the unmistakable gleam of discovery in his eyes. Sometimes, the vast cache of documents revealing aspects of German technology and Allied intelligence can invoke that same sense of discovery. This volume preserves some of those documents intact as appendices, so that the reader may more fully appreciate the sense of revelation and discovery present in those papers.

My exploration in American archives and writings about German technologies led to another interesting observation: the Americans and the British had an ever-evolving relationship when it came to sharing technical intelligence information with each other. Sometimes collaborative and sometimes contentious, nonetheless the sum total was beneficial for the Allied cause.

A few technical points must be highlighted at the outset. If some of the images in this volume are scratched or blurry, they are included as examples of a bygone fighting force; photos that may fill in some missing puzzle pieces for discerning readers. The USAAF's understanding of Luftwaffe aircraft was continually honed throughout the war and into the postwar period as ever more encounters with German warplanes were assimilated into the body of knowledge. The photographs in this work, both official and unofficial, pace that process. From a repainted Bf 109E in the States in 1942 to a freshly bellied-in Me 262 surrounded by Americans during the death throes of the Third Reich in 1945, the images in this book bear witness to a brief time of furious combat and remarkable invention, ultimately surmounted by the indomitable spirit of the wartime American generation and their Allied peers. Wartime documents were not uniform in their use of German aircraft nomenclature, and the reader will note references to both Bf 109s and Me 109s, plus occasional capitalizations as ME; variations in nomenclature and even the spellings of German cities are artifacts of their era.

ACKNOWLEDGMENTS

Thanks are due to many people and organizations who helped increase my understanding of the Luftwaffe, including the following: Air Force Academy Special Collections (USAFA), Air Force Test Center history office, Air Force Test Center Technical Library (and Darrell Shiplett), Air Force Historical Research Agency (AFHRA), American Aviation Historical Society, Peter M. Bowers, Walter J. Boyne, Harry Fisher, Bob Fleitz, Freeman Army Airfield Museum (and Larry Bothe), Gene Furnish collection, Richard P. Hallion, Carl Hildebrandt, Hoover Institution at Stanford University, Keith Laird, Fred LePage, Richard Lutz, Museum of Flight archives (and museum curator Dan Hagedorn, archivist Katherine Williams, photo archivist Amy Heidrick, and assistant curator John Little), National Air and Space Museum (NASM), Ralph Nortell, Stan Piet, Doug Remington, Will Riepl, San Diego Aerospace Museum (SDAM), Barrett Tillman, and the University of Washington Aeronautical Laboratory (and its business manager, engineer Jack Ross).

It is not sufficient to simply list the Air Force Academy Special Collections, the Air Force Test Center History Office, and the AFHRA without elaboration; the enthusiastic help provided by Dr. Mary Elizabeth Ruwell and John Beardsley at the USAFA, Jeannine Geiger and others at the Test Center, and Archie Difante and the team at AFHRA make it a joy to conduct research. Their suggestions and the opportunities they provided opened major new avenues of exploration for this book. The collection of papers pertaining to "Hap" Arnold and his era in the USAFA is a treasure that can only be truly appreciated through serendipitous browsing.

Likewise, further words about Walt Boyne and Dick Hallion are required. Walt's study of all things aeronautical continues to grow a major body of published work, including articles and books that delve into German technology and its acquisition by the United States. His tenure as director of the National Air and Space Museum (NASM) put him in a close working relationship with some of the crown jewels of the American war booty from Germany. Much more than that, Walt has been a mentor and friend since I began my writing career, and I owe much to his good counsel. Dick Hallion is another renaissance man of aviation letters. A former chief Air Force historian and Air Force advisor, Dick's prodigious writings include analytical forays into the development of aeronautical technologies. Dick's understanding of the aeronautical journey through history makes his observations intellectual and yet disarmingly concise and cogent. He shared insights and texts with me during the production of this book, for which I am grateful.

Thanks also to my wife Sharon once again, for her exceptional transcription and proofreading talents – and her amused patience. It runs in the family – Sharon's brother, Carl Kaproth, is a master of the vast digital library network from his position in the Seattle Public Library. Carl patiently explained and excavated, finding documents that had me stumped until he used his professional librarian legerdemain to track them down.

One previous volume is a particular delight whenever I contemplate the interactions of the Allies with appropriated German aircraft. Phil Butler created a remarkable and well-illustrated trail of information in his volume *War Prizes*, published by Midland Counties Publications in 1994. It is hard to put it down once you start researching something in it. There are other worthy texts, some of which you will find in the Bibliography.

Frederick A. Johnsen, 2014

PROLOGUE

On a carefree Saturday when I was four years old, my father, aeronautical engineer Carl M. Johnsen, took me on a leisurely walk among rows of surplus warplanes, some German, at the old Grand Central air terminal near Glendale, California. We were one decade into postwar America at that time. Even back then the silent shapes of those aircraft spoke volumes. I can still hear the incredulity in my father's voice as he encountered late-war construction shortcuts on the Luftwaffe machines that would never pass muster with him. I am forever grateful for that experience. It was as if we did our own technology review right there on the tarmac while the rest of Los Angeles whizzed by in a pall of leaded-gas and high-octane smog, oblivious to the marvels in their midst.

Over the ensuing decades, that stroll through history has lingered in my mind. I cannot recall which specific aircraft we paused to ponder, but the ambience of the quiet tarmac and the faded, slumbering warplanes of a vanquished power made an indelible imprint on me. How did they come to be there, and why did we care?

CHAPTER 1

EARLY OBSERVATIONS

Even before the rise to power by the Nazis in the 1930s, German technology had earned a reputation for precedent-setting breakthroughs. Furthermore, among American air power theoreticians, Gen Billy Mitchell would ultimately gain a reputation for prescience that was at times startling. So, a vignette about Mitchell in Germany in 1922 sets the tone for what was to follow.

In February 1922, Mitchell and his assistant Alfred Verville visited Germany, where fellow American air power pioneer (and some-time Mitchell rival) Benjamin Foulois enjoyed status as a military attaché assigned to The Hague with observer taskings in Berlin. Foulois had gained the confidence of a number of World War I German aviators, including Hermann Göring. As an American observer in Germany, Foulois sent substantial documentation back to the United States, but to his chagrin, he believed it was not properly leveraged to gain an early appreciation of post-World War I Germany.

During Mitchell and Verville's visit to Berlin, Verville later recounted, Mitchell launched a diatribe one morning against what he likened as automobile engines for aircraft. According to Verville, Mitchell posited that somewhere a German scientist was already working on a new powerplant for use in the next war possibly two decades hence. Mitchell challenged Foulois, with his German contacts, to produce that German scientist.

Foulois arranged a meeting with some Germans, one of whom was an assistant to Hermann Oberth. Oberth explored early notional rocket technologies. One of his later assistants was a young Wernher von Braun, who would later credit Oberth with setting von Braun's famous career path in rocketry that culminated in the successful Apollo program for NASA.

At the 1922 meeting with Mitchell, the German assistant agreed that "automobile-style" aircraft engines would give way to as-yet unperfected turbines burning kerosene. Discussions and demonstrations next depicted future rocket engines that would burn a mixture of alcohol and something the Germans called "liquid air," Verville related. He also noted the Germans envisioned a range of 400km and speeds upward of 3,000 mph. As Mitchell's assistant, Verville was possessed of significant aeronautical acumen. According to accounts, Verville recalled how Mitchell was clearly affected by what the Germans had said and demonstrated, but this early meeting apparently did not have any effect on American policy at that point.[1] Yet history proved Mitchell's powers of prediction largely correct when it came to the development of better aircraft powerplants, strongly influenced by German explorations.

The emergence of a renewed German military aeronautical capability in the early 1930s was initially masked by various subterfuges, ranging from the location of training fields far to the east, away from casual observation, to the duplicitous use of aircraft that had dual transport and bombardment capabilities. As the decade advanced, Hitler's emboldened regime revealed more about its nascent air force. In the United States, developments in Germany initially prompted varied reactions. It has been estimated that as many as 75 percent of Americans at one time preferred isolation and noninvolvement in European confrontations in the years leading up to 1941. If postwar tellings of American history tend to make it seem everyone was united in the nation's posture toward war, such solidarity was achieved only at the expense of Pearl Harbor. An active voice in the pre-war American milieu said European wars were inevitable and interminable, and not the province of Americans. Revulsion at the still-remembered horrors of World War I trench warfare influenced American isolationism. Ironically, the American population was composed largely of European expatriates and their offspring; émigrés who showed, by their very removal to the United States, a willingness to turn their backs on their former homes across the Atlantic.

The isolationists, including some prominent members of Congress and the media, did what they could to blunt the clearly interventionist desires of the Roosevelt administration. The ebb and flow of isolationist support in the United States changed in response to world events as well as actions by the US government in the 1930s and through nearly all of 1941.

Yet even during times of ambivalence toward Europe, some Americans were early observers of German rearmament. A knowledgeable celebrity vector into the new Luftwaffe was provided by famed aviator Charles Lindbergh; he made several visits to Germany in the 1930s, where he was apparently given wide access to new aircraft and organizations.

Lindbergh had an ally for his German forays in the person of Truman Smith, who was assigned as American military attaché to Germany from August 1935 to April 1939. Smith arrived in the midst of world-shaping events. As an army officer, he had first spoken with Hitler as far back as 1922, when the future German leader had no real power. Now Smith had the opportunity to facilitate information gathering on the burgeoning Luftwaffe – information that could inform American defense policy. Smith's faculties for intelligence gathering and analysis are described by historian Dr. Richard P. Hallion:

> Generally, American military intelligence limped along in the interwar years. Most talented officers gravitated towards combat commands, and those that chose intelligence went overseas with little training and few resources. No consensus existed on collection protocols, attachés often just submitting questionnaires to foreign contacts. One notable exception to this general pattern was Maj (later Lt Col) Truman Smith, a gifted and experienced infantry officer who arrived in Berlin as Military Attaché in August 1935. Smith, who blended a military intellectual's insight with a combat officer's instincts, quickly realized he faced challenges requiring immediate resolution: his office was receiving contradictory inputs on the state of German aeronautics; and the office's air intelligence effort was at best sporadic, too-focused on preparation of an annual report that had but limited value.[2]

Col Smith later said in a sworn statement that, "it was my function while I was Military Attaché in Berlin from July 1935 to April 1939 to keep abreast of the strength, organization, and training standards of the German armed forces, to keep myself advised of all economic, political, and military activities and trends that might have a bearing upon German capabilities and intentions of waging war." Smith went on to say his findings were mostly the result of his own observations while in the field with German troops, or visiting German airfields, military installations, and factories producing war materiel. While Smith acknowledged inputs from Germans as well as US State Department representatives, his sworn statement's explanation did not mention one of his correspondents by name: Charles Lindbergh.[3]

Lindbergh's publicized visits to Germany, where he was ostensibly treated with the cordial courtesies extended to a celebrity, prompted the American aviator to offer observations on Germany to Smith, Gen "Hap" Arnold, and publicly. Lindbergh, outspokenly isolationist in his views, has been called the only person opposing Franklin Roosevelt's pre-war interventionist ambitions who had the charisma and presence to match and even outmaneuver the savvy

Roosevelt on some levels. Nor did Lindbergh's pronouncements only concern isolationism; in 1934 he was critical of the Roosevelt administration's actions in canceling air mail contracts, and it seems evident Roosevelt did not take this lightly or with pleasure, coming from one with Lindbergh's credentials.

Official correspondence from Smith to Lindbergh sometimes merged collegial chattiness with official business. In one 1937 letter sent just after the completion of Smith's important assessment of the Luftwaffe, Smith offers Lindbergh the use of the official attaché automobile to facilitate future travel in Germany. The letter also politely scolds Lindbergh for sending Smith "certain data" via mail instead of diplomatic pouch, where the security of such information was expected to be greater.[4]

A major document arising from the Smith–Lindbergh collaborations is the "General Estimate as of Nov. 1, 1937" submitted by Truman Smith, reporting on evidence of German air activities. Its opening paragraph picturesquely sets the tone: "Germany is once more a world power in the air. Her air force and her air industry have emerged from the kindergarten stage. Full manhood will still not be reached for three years." The rest of the document is a straightforward analysis of the state of German air rearmament as perceived by Smith, and influenced by Lindbergh. "The astounding growth of German air power from a zero level to its present status in a brief four years must be accounted one of the most important world events of our time. What it portends for Europe is something no-one today can foretell and must be left as a problem for future historians."[5]

Smith emphasizes several reasons for the growth of the German Air Force at that time, including:

> [t]he military aptitude of the German people … The technical and scientific skill of the race … The vision of General Göring who from the start planned a fantastically large Air Force and Air Industry and who at the same time possessed the energy to convert his plans into reality … The unified direction and execution made possible by the dictatorial nature of the German Government … The wise realization of the German air authorities at the start of their rearmament that other nations, especially the United States, were far in advance of them, both in scientific knowledge and technical skill. This humbleness of spirit has been one of the chief strengths of Germany. The old adage that self-dissatisfaction is true strength has never been better exemplified than in the German air development from 1933 to 1937.[6]

Truman Smith expressed amazement at the size of the German aircraft industry at that time. He cited 23 "known airplane concerns with their 46 identified plants, having a potential annual plane production of probably 6,000 planes." He also acknowledged:

> There is every reason to believe that the plants identified only give a part of the picture and that the truth, could it be known, would show a still higher potential production. The scale of the German airplane motor industry is no less impressive. It is ever and again the size of this industry, which forces the foreigner, – and even the American who is accustomed to think in big terms, – to pause, ponder and wonder as to the future.[7]

Smith's 1937 analysis was prescient as it remarked on German aeronautical technology growth:

> Behind this industry stands a formidable group of air scientists, with large and well-equipped laboratories and test fields, constantly pushing forward the German scientific advance. This advance is remarkable. The fact that the United States still leads in its air science and manufacturing skill must not be allowed to overshadow the German achievements between 1933 and 1937 and above all, not to lead to an underestimate of what Germany will achieve in the future.[8]

An intriguing give-and-take characterized American and German aeronautical advances from the 1920s through the immediate post-World War II era. Airfoil research and rationale emanating from Germany's Göttingen laboratories set the cadence in the post-World War I (and pre-Nazi) era. In 1932 America's National Advisory Committee for Aeronautics (NACA, forerunner of NASA) acknowledged German precedents in the development of wing airfoils. Soon, NACA's extensive catalog of varied airfoils with traits suitable for different types of aircraft would be seen as the standard, but it owed much to the pioneering efforts of German scientists at Göttingen. Meanwhile, German rocket scientists and enthusiasts were early to recognize the encouraging work of American rocketry pioneer Dr. Robert H. Goddard. Immediately after World War II, important German theory in wing shapes would once again augment the developments of the postwar NACA in the United States. Dr. George Lewis, Director of Aeronautical Research for the NACA, was predicting in 1936 that Germany would steal the march on state-of-the-art aeronautics unless the United States stepped up its investment in research and infrastructure.[9]

Smith's November 1937 report about German air power was blunt in its characterization of some other nations friendly to the United States:

"[B]ecause on November 1, 1937 the American technical level, which is but one phase of air power, has not been reached [by Germany], is no ground for the United States to adopt the British policy of smugness. If so, we shall be as doomed to the same position of air inferiority with respect to Germany, as France now finds herself in and which Great Britain just as certainly will find herself in tomorrow – unless she realizes promptly her own shortcomings." Clearly, Smith was sounding an alarm about current and impending German aeronautical prowess.

Smith's 1937 report offered observations about the intentional defensibility of the German aviation industry:

> The German air industry has been strategically located and each factory has been designed on tactical principles. Factories are located as far back from the frontier as possible and the new factories, while many, are relatively small. The principle of factory design is that there may be many separate and small buildings, each with separate powerplant and bomb and gas-proof chambers. Each is designed to operate as a complete airplane factory in time of emergency. This lay out of industry, which gives it great defensive strength against hostile air attacks, must be reckoned an important element of German air industry and air power.[10]

Interestingly, the postwar United States Strategic Bombing Survey (USSBS) noted that the German electric power system, "except for isolated raids, was never a target during the air war. An attack was extensively debated during the course of the war. It was not undertaken partly because it was believed that the German power grid was highly developed and that losses in one area could be compensated by switching power from another. This assumption, detailed investigation by the Survey had established, was incorrect."[11] The postwar surveys concluded that the German electric power situation was precarious from the beginning of hostilities, and only declined as the war unfolded. Evidence has not been located to suggest conclusively that the USAAF's disinterest in attacking German electrical power emanated from Smith's 1937 report, but the apparent divergence merely suggests even an observer as prescient as Truman Smith may have misread some of the signs, or possibly been misled by his German hosts.

In November 1937 Smith enumerated Germany's frontline combat aircraft in production as the Heinkel He 111 twin-engined bomber, considered "heavy"; the Dornier Do 17 bomber that he classified as "light"; and the Messerschmitt Bf 109 fighter. They would all be encountered in the skies over England less than three years later. The collaboration of Smith,

Lindbergh and Smith's assistant, Maj Albert Vanaman, came up with a remarkably accurate assessment of Luftwaffe strength in November 1937: "The actual November 1st strength of the German Air Force is probably from 175 to 225 squadrons. If we take a mean between these figures of 200 squadrons, we find Germany to at present possess 1,800 first line planes in units, 600 first line planes in reserve units or a total of 2,400 planes." In his research, historian Richard P. Hallion has confirmed the accuracy of these educated estimates, noting: "at that time the Luftwaffe had 213 squadrons and an approximate first-line air strength of 2,356 planes."[12]

The seminal November 1937 report characterized the skills of German aviators: "The level of flying ability reached by the German air power still leaves much to be desired, both by our standards and theirs also. While good potential pilots, the Germans must still be rated as unrefined. However, they have made great progress since 1933. The present flying of units would be better still were it not for the air force expansion." But, the report's authors cautioned, any current and momentary German personnel performance difficulties "must not be allowed to obscure the certainty that these deficiencies will gradually cease to exist. If any foreign country feels self-satisfied in the matter of the superiority of its training, it will receive a rude awakening in the not too distant future."[13]

The November 1937 report judged German air power mature enough "where it must be given serious consideration as a powerful opponent of any single nation." Citing "qualified officers" who had recently inspected the air forces of Germany, as well as of Great Britain and France, the report was blunt in its assessments: "Technically, Germany has outdistanced France in practically all fields. Germany is on the whole superior to Great Britain in the quality of her planes, but is still slightly inferior to Great Britain in motors, but rapidly closing the gap." British and French air force training levels were judged to be better than those in Germany in late 1937, but during that year Germany was seen to reduce the gap in training with those countries.[14]

Citing "a highly competent observer, well acquainted with both American and German air developments," Truman Smith's November 1937 report predicted that if the "progress curves" of both German and American air developments over the previous two years were replicated in the following two years, "Germany should obtain technical parity with the USA by 1941 or 1942." The report makes an ominous observation: "If, however, America makes a single blunder, or if some important incident, whether political or a conflict of views within the armed forces, should slow down her present development, German air superiority will be realized still sooner." Smith was succinct in his summation: "In November 1937 it appears that the development of German air power is a European phenomenon of the first diplomatic importance. The upward movement is still gaining momentum."[15]

Smith's seminal 1937 report qualifies some of its attached lists of German Air Force units, strengths, and factory locations with the notation that secrecy made it difficult to judge if all such tallies were complete and up to date. Of interest is a map showing that German aircraft motor construction plants tended to be located deep in Germany and somewhat concentrated. This situation appeared corroborated later as the war unfolded, causing the USAAF to make a conscious decision about delaying a campaign against German aero engine production until sufficient aircraft were on hand to permit safe and recurring long-range missions to that part of Germany to cripple motor production, as will be seen later.

If Truman Smith did not readily name Charles Lindbergh at the time the November 1937 report was drafted, it is interesting to note that in the 1950s, while writing about his air intelligence activities in Germany two decades earlier, Smith gave "special reference to the services of Col Charles A. Lindbergh."[16]

Lindbergh's access to German airspace in the late 1930s seems, in hindsight, surprisingly unfettered, unless Germany's intent was that the American aviator should see many Luftwaffe fields as he transited the country in his own aircraft. In late October 1937, Charles and Anne Lindbergh flew from Germany to their residence in England, affording the opportunity to overfly at least six Luftwaffe airfields, at which Lindbergh observed and reported to Truman Smith the presence of various fighters, trainers, and Do 17 bombers. Over the following year, Lindbergh lobbied a number of American policymakers as he continued to express concerns over the growing might of German air power. He indicated concerns that France could not effectively defend against a German attack, and he expressed some doubt about Great Britain's abilities at defense, although he gave the country higher marks than France. He presumed Russian aircraft construction to be effective, yet inferior to the manufacturing abilities of the United States. All of which, he told Joseph P. Kennedy, the US ambassador to Great Britain, suggested a European war could damage all combatants and lay Europe open to the spread of communism. Lindbergh also urged USAAC Gen Henry H. "Hap" Arnold in November 1938 to visit Germany to learn firsthand how the Luftwaffe and industry were developing.

As Germany expanded its grip on portions of the European continent by the fall of 1940, the availability of raw materials for aircraft construction – mainly aluminum and steel – appeared assured with access to Hungarian bauxite resources and Silesian aluminum plants and coal deposits. This was reported by Truman Smith in September of that year as he once again endeavored to provide an updated forecast of German aviation growth in the coming year. Using the information available to him, Smith posited in September 1940 that Germany would produce a minimum of 42,000 aircraft of all types between September 1, 1940 and September 1, 1941.[17] German records indicate the number was closer to 12,000 for that time period.[18] But if Smith's estimates were based on capacity, he could not have known for sure the political and strategic decisions that went into the actual construction effort for that period.

The intrigue of life for an American in Germany in the 1930s was embraced by Truman Smith. His proactive efforts to quantify German military growth and strength provided a basic guide that appears to have subsequently informed target priorities after the United States became embroiled in the European war. Perhaps the ultimate irony of the isolationist counsel that Smith's newfound friend Charles Lindbergh gave to all who would listen came on December 11, 1941 when Hitler, only days after the Japanese attack on Pearl Harbor, removed all ambiguity by declaring war on the United States.

For his efforts at creating a picture of German rearmament, Col Truman Smith was later awarded the Distinguished Service Medal. The citation for that award summarized his contributions:

> As Military Attaché to Germany during the fateful period from August 1935 to March 1939, Col Smith accurately reported Nazi Germany's rapidly growing military strength and intentions and greatly facilitated the efforts of the United States Army to keep abreast of German organization, tactics, and equipment. His reports stimulated action and were in a measure responsible for the manner in which the Army developed its plans to build up the military strength of this country. Upon the return of Col Smith to the United States his intimate and expert knowledge of the enemy was of importance to the formulation of Allied strategic plans.[19]

If Germany and Japan won early victories in part due to their stunning, decisive offensives, the air of invincibility the Axis powers projected in 1942 was sobering, and in need of studied evaluation. By 1942, the Royal Air Force (RAF) had shown the Luftwaffe could be thwarted, yet the depth and breadth of the German Air Force was far from mapped by the Allies at this early stage of the war.

CHAPTER 2

MID-WAR UNDERSTANDING

The ongoing evaluation of German aircraft included a detailed subset of information gleaned from the various data plates and tags affixed to aircraft during production. In the fall of 1942, a dozen USAAF officers received air technical intelligence training in the methodology of crash investigations of enemy aircraft. From the RAF, an expert identified in some reportage only as Sqn Ldr Colley taught the USAAF men how to extract performance information about enemy aircraft, including temperature ranges and other mechanical functions, from the various instructional data plates affixed to engines and other assemblies. One of the Americans in attendance was William D. McGarey, who subsequently went to the Air Ministry in London where he became conversant in the markings applied to German ball bearings retrieved from battle. McGarey's analysis contributed to the targeting and prioritizing of specific German ball bearing plants in 1943. Later in the war, Maj McGarey served in the South Pacific, where it is said he personally retrieved approximately 1,000 data plates from downed or abandoned Japanese aircraft, yielding a treasure of information about the locations of manufacturing plants worthy as targets for USAAF bombing.[1]

Other pieces of intelligence could be gathered from downed or captured German aircraft, the air intelligence students learned. Unit markings painted on German aircraft were intended to clarify the order of battle for the Luftwaffe; when interpreted by the Americans and British, the same useful information helped the Allies comprehend German air unit operations.[2]

The USAAF was still refining its intelligence-gathering rationale when one of its fighters protecting Iceland collided with a reconnaissance Ju 88A-1 on October 18, 1942. The resulting wreck of the Junkers bomber provided a windfall of information that was logged as "Crash Report No 2" by the USAAF's Intelligence Service. According to the report, the Ju 88 fell to earth at 64 degrees 15' North Latitude and 21 degrees 30' Longitude. The bomber evidently frequented the region, for it carried on its rudder small painted maps of Iceland and Norway, according to the USAAF intelligence report.[3]

The three German fliers aboard perished. The report unemotionally recorded: "Crew appeared to be between 23 and 30 years old." They were two second lieutenants and a sergeant. Their effects included clues about them: a certificate from Reconnaissance Group 120; a map of southern Norway; a railroad timetable for the towns of Stavanger, Sandnes, and Ålgård; Danish and Norwegian cash in small amounts; and the daily trappings of lives abruptly ended.[4]

Once the USAAF had removed everything it could from the crash site, "due to the inaccessible location, it was recommended that the main parts of the aircraft be burned." From the wreckage, two large aerial cameras were turned over to the RAF, as were various aircraft and component data plates, a generator, all radio equipment, one oxygen breathing apparatus set-up, two pieces of armor plate and one piece of bullet-resistant glazing.

The Americans reviewing the pieces noted the frequencies two radio receivers had been tuned to at the time of the crash. Some radio antenna hardware appeared to be identical to installations used on four-engined Fw 200 Condor long-range reconnaissance bombers. The report recorded: "The workmanship and materials in these radio sets appears to be of very high grade."[5]

The report listed basic construction and characteristics of the Ju 88, including several assessments:

Fuel and Tankage:
    Gasoline 87 octane.
    One tank in bombay [*sic*] of approximately 12 cu.ft.
Cause of Crash:
    Tail assembly appeared to have been shot off.[6]
    Aircraft broken into four primary parts.
Armament:
    1 x MG 131-13 mm.
    Link belt fed.
    Ring sights.

Ring mounting.

Ammunition:

13 mm on cap AP.40 2a avu.

on cap HE.41 1 avu.

on fuze 1532 eds 41 181.

on cap HE.39 14E P345.

on fuze AA.56.

Order of loading 1 AP, 12 HE.

Armor Plate:

Area of cockpit was well surrounded with armor plate approximately 1/4" thick.

Crew:

3, all dead.

Leading Edge:

Pulsating de-icing devices on all leading edges.

Internal Equipment:

Cameras were installed in bombay [sic].

These with radio equipment were sent to Air Ministry, UK

General Remarks:

Entire bombay [sic] was occupied by camera equipment. The fact that only one gun was found indicates that the aircraft had been lightened to increase the range.[7]

The equipment and mission of the downed Ju 88 in Iceland elicited more interest than the battered airframe itself in the fall of 1942. Before a year had elapsed, a flyable Ju 88 would be delivered into American hands by the RAF, who obtained it from Romanian defectors.

German setbacks in North Africa, Sicily, and Italy in succession left a trail of Luftwaffe aircraft carcasses behind the retreating German forces in the Mediterranean in 1943. It was during this year that the United States, often with the substantial assistance of the British, acquired several flyable Luftwaffe warplanes in the Mediterranean.

By the spring of 1944, a variety of Axis aircraft had been flown and probed in the United States for months. (In fact, the very first German aircraft to be flown at Wright Field was a Bf 109E, courtesy of the RAF, arriving at the Ohio base in mid-May 1942. It bore the RAF-assigned serial number AE479.)

On March 10, 1944 Brig Gen Frank O. Carroll, chief of the Engineering Division at Wright Field, listed in a memo the German and Japanese aircraft at that base, with the number of hours each had been flown at Wright Field up to March 6, 1944:

Ju 88D 43-0650 (Presumed to be an Americanized version of its German *Werk Nummer* or *W.Nr.*)	53 hours
Ju 88A 43-00227 (Presumed an Americanized version of its *W.Nr.*)	36 hours
Me[8] 109F EB-100	8 hours
Me 109G EB-102	0 hours
Fw 190 EB-101	11 hours
Fw 190 EB-104	4 hours
Zeke EB-200 (Japanese Mitsubishi A6M fighter)	0 hours
Hamp EB-201 (Japanese Mitsubishi A6M fighter variant)	22 hours [9]

Brig Gen Carroll explained problems faced with the planned operation of captured Axis aircraft:

Every enemy airplane we have received is usually short of something, or something has been broken in shipment, and in most cases we have had to manufacture the repair parts to get the airplanes in commission. Also some of these foreign airplanes appear to have such poor mechanical characteristics that it is difficult to get our people to release them. For instance the brake system on the Japanese airplanes appears to our people to be absolutely hopeless, and even on the Fw 190 we have had a lot of trouble to get the brake system to operate satisfactorily.

Spare parts were a problem at this stage in the war, Brig Gen Carroll noted:

Our supply of spares for the fighter types of German airplanes is extremely limited due principally to the obvious fact that German fighters are rarely brought down over Allied territory. However, we will do the best we can on furnishing any spares, and if absolutely necessary will try to manufacture minor parts to keep the airplanes flying.[10]

Before Wright Field could release the enemy aircraft to Eglin Field for testing, Brig Gen Carroll said, "there has been a small amount of flying required to meet a directive from Washington to obtain flight photographs for the Training Aids Division and Public Relations."[11]

A month later, on April 8, 1944, a letter from Eglin Field's Materiel Command Liaison Officer recorded experiences with a Ju 88 (presumably the D-model, FE-1598 – 43-0650), and Bf 109F EB-100, Bf 109G EB-102, and Fw 190 (probably) EB-101 at the Florida base:

> Several flights have been performed in both the ME 109G and ME 109F. Considerable trouble has been encountered regarding the operation of the propellers on each of these aircraft. Particularly difficult has been the maintenance of these propellers so that they will operate in the automatic position. The enlisted personnel given instructions in the maintenance of ME 109-type aircraft were not instructed regarding the maintenance of fuel injection systems because the system was not available at the time training was given. If there is any additional information regarding this type system, I request that it be forwarded to the Proving Ground Command most expeditiously.[12]

The Eglin officer said of the two Bf 109s: "The operating limits of the rpm are somewhat in doubt ... and the boys feel that they are not getting maximum performance." He noted the propeller of the Fw 190 "was received at this station in a considerably rusted condition," among other problems. "The Sub-depot at Eglin Field is attempting to take both the propellers and assemble one (1) good one. One of the blades runs considerably out of track, as of this date, and effort is being made to make this correction."[13]

Despite the lack of spare parts, and the condition of some of the enemy aircraft sent to Wright and Eglin fields during the height of the war, the USAAF worked diligently to quantify the performance and describe the essence of enemy aircraft at its disposal. An Aircraft Evaluation Report on a captured Me (Bf) 109F (the USAAF tended to use the "Me" instead of "Bf" designator regardless of the model of 109 fighter being studied) is as diligent as one would expect from a domestic flight or maintenance manual, let alone one compiled on a captured enemy fighter. Printed in July 1943, the report was prepared by Wright Field's Engineering Division of the Materiel Command.

Interestingly, in the summer of 1943 the Engineering Division report stated: "The 'ME-109F' [sic] is comparable to our Bell 'P-39D' or Curtiss 'P-40E' but is smaller and lighter than either. General characteristics include low wings, single engine in the nose and retractable landing gear. Armed with two small caliber machine guns and one cannon, the 'ME-109F' is a formidable weapon." The USAAF evaluators described three known sub-variants of the F-model: "Sub-types 'ME-109F-1' and 'ME-109F-2' both have Daimler-Benz 'DB-601N' engines but the armament of the '109F-1' consists of 2x7.9 mm machine guns and 1x20 mm cannon, whereas, the '109F-2' carries 2x7.9 mm and 1x15 mm guns. Sub-type 'ME-109F-4' is powered with the Daimler-Benz 'DB-601E' and is armed with 2x7.9 mm plus 1x20 mm guns." The evaluation report[14] listed comparative performance data for different Bf 109Fs compared with the P-39D Airacobra and P-40E Warhawk:

Type	Maximum speed	Time of climb to 15,000ft	Service ceiling
Bf 109F-1 & F-2	371 mph at 22,000ft	5.0 min	37,500ft
Bf 109F-4	390 mph at 20,000ft	4.8 min	39,000ft
P-39D	368 mph at 13,800ft	6.0 min	32,100ft
P-40E	361 mph at 15,000ft	7.2 min	30,000ft

Combat anecdotes from the Mediterranean Theater of Operations (MTO) tended to flesh out what these statistics show: P-40s could miss a victory if a Bf 109 climbed to a higher perch than the P-40 could reach in a timely fashion. But the rugged diving speed of the P-40, and its ability to out-turn a Bf 109, could be leveraged into victories over Axis adversaries within the P-40's operating altitudes.[15]

Wright Field evaluators pored over their Bf 109 examples and described what they saw in detail in their Aircraft Evaluation Report:

The fuselage shell is made in two halves aft of the cockpit, joined at top and bottom with two longitudinal rows of rivets. Each half shell is composed of cylindrical sections of aluminum skin with integrally formed Z-section rings. These sections are lap-jointed and riveted along planes perpendicular to the thrust line ... [The wing is] of single-beam construction using stamped aluminum alloy ribs. An auxiliary trailing edge spar supports the metal flap and fabric-covered aileron. The attachment to the fuselage is by three bolts ... [The vertical fin and horizontal stabilizers are] conventional fully cantilever construction. The elevator and rudder are fabric covered.

The F-model marked the first Bf 109 variant to use an unbraced horizontal stabilizer. What the Wright Field testers probably did not know was that earlier F-models suffered a series of mysterious crashes until it was determined that the original unbraced stabilizer needed to be modified to preclude a fatal phenomenon where vibrations, exacerbated by the engine at certain settings, could tear the tail apart in flight.

A large rounded propeller spinner mated closely to a new streamlined cowling on the F-model. The Wright Field examiners noted in their report: "The Messerschmitt fuselage is remarkably clean and bulletlike. The engine is compactly mounted in the nose and is inclosed [sic] in easily removable cowling. Protuberances that mar the clean lines are cut to a minimum by partially submerging the coolant radiators in the wing." This was another new feature on the F-model that the USAAF studied and diagramed in the evaluation report. With coolant radiators partly inset into the lower surface of the wing, drag was less than on previous models. Thoughtful routing of air made this configuration feasible:

> Each flap is divided into two sections: the outer section is a modified split arrangement serving the additional purpose of controlling the airflow through the internally mounted wing radiators. At the front edge of the radiator is a hinged plate linked with the trailing edge flaps to open with them. This plate picks up the boundary layer on the underside of the wing, bypasses it around the radiator, and discharges it at the trailing edge. This form of boundary layer control causes smoother flow through the radiator, thereby reducing the area required for proper cooling.

The Bf 109F's three-bladed propeller was listed in the report as "infinitely variable in pitch and has a governor that limits the rpm in proportion to the throttle setting. The automatic governing mechanism can be disconnected and manual operation used for feathering, etc."

The USAAF report noted distinctions in the F-model's wing. Especially visible were rounded wingtips, a difference that combat fliers needed to note:

> One of the best means of identification of the original 'ME-109' planes, the square wing tips, has been changed in the later "ME-109F" series. The tips are now well rounded, the wing leading edge is slightly swept back and the trailing edge rather sharply swept forward. Automatic slots, operating independently, are fitted on the leading edge of each wing panel. The ailerons are externally mass balanced and are fitted with metal tabs, adjustable on the ground.

Along with notations about the wing design, the Wright Field evaluators commented on the Bf 109F's main landing gear:

> The main landing gear struts of the "ME-109F" are simple cantilever members pivoted at the fuselage in such a manner that they may swing out and slightly back into the wings when retracted. This system permits the changing of wing panels without removal of the landing gear.

But the ease of maintenance that this arrangement provided gave the Bf 109 a narrow landing gear spread, a compromise also noted in the USAAF report: "The narrow tread landing gear would tend to make recovery from a ground loop more difficult than would be anticipated with a wider tread gear." The evaluators said the main wheels, when extended, were "sufficiently far ahead of the center-of-gravity to permit severe braking without nosing over." Compared to the typical American fighter of the era, the Bf 109 had one particularly visible difference according to the report: "The vertical [tail] surfaces appear very small."

The pilot of the Bf 109 sat just ahead and above the fuselage fuel tank: "One L-shaped self-sealing fuel tank is installed immediately behind and under the pilot's seat. The weight of tank and fuel is taken by a specially strengthened panel of the fuselage and the walls are kept from bulging by plywood panels." The report also noted the ability of the Bf 109F to carry an external drop tank. Normal fuel load was placed at 102 US gallons; maximum fuel capacity was 182 US gallons. This points up a crucial difference in perceived fighter requirements between Germany and the United States. The Bf 109F's fuel capacity was dwarfed later in the war when the Republic P-47N was introduced for long-range Pacific escort work, boasting a maximum fuel capacity of 997 gallons. American fighters needed range to take the war to the enemy from distant bases.

If part of the Wright Field inspection and quantification of the Bf 109F was to see what might be learned about German design tenets from this glimpse of enemy technology, there was also an urgent need to comprehend the Messerschmitt's combat strengths and weaknesses to give Allied airmen information on effective tactics to down the German fighter. Particular emphasis was placed on understanding the Bf 109F's protection from stern attacks, the most likely fighter-versus-fighter scenario:

> Protection for the pilot's body is provided by plates immediately behind the seat: the upper 1½ feet are 8 mm thick and the remainder is 4 mm. The pilot's head and shoulders are protected by a curved piece of armor 10 mm thick

attached to the cockpit inclosure [sic]. A section of bullet-resistant glass 2¼ inches thick is mounted on the windshield directly in front of the pilot.

The report also noted another armor device: "Additional armor has been found on '109-F' airplanes recently inspected. This is in the form of a laminated dural bulkhead placed approximately 6 inches behind the fuel tank. Total thickness of the 30 laminations used is about 7/8 inches." The stopping power of this laminated bulkhead was the topic of a British test, the results of which were shared in the Wright Field Bf 109F evaluation report:

> The British have carried out tests on one of these bulkheads with the following results: from 100 yards range dead astern, .303 inch and .5 inch incendiary ammunition will not penetrate the dural bulkhead. At this range 20 mm HE/I (high explosive/incendiary) is still effective for penetrating the bulkhead and igniting the tank. At 200 yards range, the effect of the interposition of the dural bulkhead is that at 5 degrees off dead astern .303 A.P. (armor piercing) is completely ineffective against the pilot, but .5 A.P. in about 30 percent of cases will pass through the bulkhead and will penetrate the 8 mm pilot's armor, even if it has to pass through the tank below fuel level. Twenty mm A.P. will still be effective in penetrating the pilot's armor … [Tests showed] that US .50 caliber M1 incendiary ammunition is capable of penetrating the dural plate effectively.

It was a grim, simple fact that all combatants had to acknowledge and accommodate in some fashion: incapacitating the opposing pilot would decide the fight.

Discussion of the Bf 109F's armament clustered in the nose of the fighter included this anecdotal reference: "German prisoners claim that centralization of guns in the nose permits better aim in turns and at long range." But the emergent USAAF single-engined fighters, the P-51 and P-47, continued their use of wing-mounted machine guns outside the propeller arc. This removed the need for synchronization gear. If long-range accuracy was an issue, some pilots heeded the advice to move in close "and when you think you're in close, get closer" to ensure hits. The Wright Field report briefly discussed Bf 109F deployment and tactics:

> The "109F" is being used by the German Air Force in all theaters of operation as a standard pursuit ship; however, they have been concentrated particularly in North Africa while the Fw 190 has to some extent replaced the Messerschmitt in the European Theater. A bomber version (external rack) is

sometimes employed and is usually escorted by fighters to insure the accomplishment of the mission without having to jettison the bombs to fight … [Reports of combat tactics] indicate that Messerschmitt [109] should be highly regarded in respect to rate of climb and altitude performance. Maneuverability of the 'F' series, although greatly improved over the older series, is still not quite as good as the Spitfire at higher altitudes or the "P-40" at lower altitudes.

A closing anecdote was offered in the report: "The following excerpt may give some idea of what may be expected in action. It is taken from combat reports of British pilots flying Kittyhawks (P-40E) in Africa. 'The Messerschmitts attack from high altitude making use of all available sun and cloud cover and then zoom away. They have proven most vulnerable at the top of their zoom when they are almost stalled.'"[16]

LEARNING ABOUT THE LUFTWAFFE OVER OHIO

Ralph Hoewing, who retired from the US Air Force (USAF) as a colonel in 1967, was afforded a rare opportunity fresh out of flying school in late 1942 when he was selected to report to Wright Field to become a test pilot. The frantic pace of wartime test activities often forced pilots like Hoewing to jump from one test to the next without learning the outcome or application of the program just finished. Vignettes from Hoewing's test flying career offer glimpses into the wartime world of USAAF test pilots, and the aircraft they sampled.

When Ralph Hoewing reported for duty as a brand-new test pilot at Wright Field's test facilities near Dayton, Ohio, he flew any and all types of aircraft. In 1943, testing was split into bombers, fighters, and cargo aircraft groupings. Hoewing first was put in fighters, then in bomber test to work on the B-29 program among others. Acknowledged as chief of the first USAAF flight test training facility as early as 1944, Ralph Hoewing's subsequent experiences included attendance of Great Britain's Empire Test Pilots' School in 1945. This aided him as first commandant of the nascent USAAF test pilot school at Wright Field.

Bf 109

Hoewing's work in fighters included flights in German and Japanese examples at Wright Field. Wright Field had a Messerschmitt Bf 109 for flight evaluation. (Wartime USAAF records, including test pilot Ralph Hoewing's flight logs, called it an Me 109; contemporary German records may have used the terminology Bf 109.) Ralph Hoewing's first flight in the captured Bf 109 brought a surprise. He considered most foreign fighters, including the Bf 109, to have cramped cockpits. The Messerschmitt's unusual side-hinged canopy was a heavy structure unlike those on American fighters. "First time I flew it I didn't get the canopy latched. I took off and got a couple miles south of base," Hoewing recalled. A burble of turbulence put momentary negative loading on the Messerschmitt, allowing the canopy to swing upward and over on its side-mounted hinges, scraping Hoewing's head as it lifted open and wrenched free, departing in the slipstream. "They located the canopy a few days later … fortunately it wasn't damaged too badly and they put it back on the plane," he said.

When he first flew the Bf 109, the idling speed of its Daimler-Benz engine was set high; so high that Hoewing and the Messerschmitt floated along the Wright Field runway on three separate passes, unable to land. On the fourth approach to landing, Ralph killed the ignition switch and brought the German fighter in for a deadstick landing. Mechanics at Wright Field subsequently adjusted the idle speed lower, Hoewing remembered.[17]

LOST IN A FOCKE-WULF Fw 190 OVER ENGLAND

As previously noted, Ralph Hoewing went to England in 1945 to attend the Empire Test Pilots' School. Having flown a captured Focke-Wulf Fw 190 at Wright Field, he felt confident he could ferry an Fw 190 the British needed moving from Farnborough to Oxford; no British pilots with Fw 190 experience were immediately available. But the rationale of the German fighter was different enough from American types that it took concentration to operate the aircraft. Reaching down to disengage the landing gear downlock on climbout from Farnborough, Ralph took his eyes from the windscreen long enough to see the landing gear safety mechanism on the cockpit floor lock into place – and long enough for the German fighter to enter solid cloud cover. The instruments of the Focke-Wulf were, to the point, foreign. Scanning the German panel, Hoewing determined how to read a combination turn-and-bank indicator and artificial horizon. Watching this and a vertical speed indicator, he kept the German warplane climbing, wings level, until he popped out of the overcast.

Now a new problem beset Ralph – a higher overcast obscured the sun, and that made dead reckoning impossible for him. The German compass markings were confusing, and the very real possibility existed that Ralph would fly the reciprocal heading of the westerly one he intended, and could wind up over continental Europe by mistake. It was the summer of 1945 and

European combat was over, yet nonetheless Ralph Hoewing had no desire to add an epilogue to the story of "Wrong-Way" Corrigan, the American aviator who ostensibly got lost and crossed the Atlantic by mistake. Hoewing correctly divined which way the foreign compass pointed, and flew to a hole in the undercast, dropping down to find a landing field not far from his intended final destination.

Ralph Hoewing noted some strong points in the enemy fighters he tested, but afterward he opined: "No doubt in my mind, ours were superior to all of theirs."

QUESTIONING THE ENEMY

The combat acquisition of German airmen and their aircraft usually involved a protocol to extract the most useful information from the circumstances. In the Mediterranean Theater of Operations (MTO), Headquarters, Twelfth Air Force sent out a memorandum on April 12, 1944 that spelled out what should take place when enemy aircraft and airmen were apprehended[18]:

> The interrogation of captured enemy air combat personnel and examination of captured enemy documents and effects are the functions in this theater of the Combined Services Detailed Interrogation Centre (CSDIC). Its staff of American and British specialists includes mobile teams which operate in Italy.

The memorandum said only CSDIC officers with CSDIC passes that matched other identification cards were to conduct interrogations. The sequestration of captured enemy airmen was described:

> While awaiting the arrival of authorized interrogators, prisoners will be kept incommunicado under guard; officers, non-commissioned officers and private soldiers being kept separate. Where possible, officers should be placed in solitary confinement. Personal effects and documents will be taken from prisoners immediately upon capture and will be held for delivery to the authorized interrogation officer.

Documents found, but not in the possession of a captured enemy, were to be forwarded to Headquarters, Twelfth Air Force. The notification of enemy captures to higher headquarters was to include information about the detainees' injuries, if any.

Aircraft were magnets for G.I. souvenir hunters, and the Twelfth Air Force memorandum was succinct in this regard:

Captured enemy material or crashed enemy aircraft will be placed under guard and immediate notification of its location and the circumstances surrounding its capture will be sent to the Assistant Chief of Staff, A-2, Headquarters, Twelfth Air Force. Pending the arrival of an authorized representative of the Technical Intelligence Section, no personnel will be permitted to take souvenirs, or otherwise tamper with the captured enemy material, nor will it be moved unless it is blocking a highway, or railway, or is obstructing an airfield.

Photo albums are filled with snapshots of military members clambering over downed German aircraft, some of which have had the painted-on swastikas cut out of their vertical fins. Whether this happened to the chagrin of official intelligence gatherers, or only after the teams had departed with their information, is a fact largely lost to the ages.

The Anglo-American cooperation in acquiring and assessing air intelligence information in the MTO in 1944 included a standing request for a wide variety of items individual airmen might be carrying at the time of their capture. Documentary items of interest included "maps, sketches, orders, technical manuals and instructions, code sheets/books, war diaries, diaries, newspapers, notebooks, service records, payroll/paybooks, shoulder straps, badges, and any other insignia, decorations, identifying marks of individual uniforms and pieces of equipment, post cards, letters, photographs, records of headquarters and post and telegraph offices, telephone exchanges, banks, police stations, municipal and government offices, brothel tickets, identity discs, and anything of a similar nature." The net was cast wide as Allied intelligence teams sought to learn anything of value about the enemy.[19]

V1, AMERICAN STYLE

One of the most ambitious and blatant uses of captured German technology was an American effort to reverse-engineer the Fieseler Fi 103 pulse jet-powered V1 "Buzz Bomb". Even as the Allies decried the seemingly random and blind way in which these unpiloted weapons plunged down upon England in 1944, the notion of copying the device was unfolding. American industry was in a position to undertake this effort that summer; certainly, factories worked multiple shifts to produce arms, but American plants were not threatened with bombing and the attendant disruption that harassed German workers by that time. With characteristic American confidence, the notion of replicating V1s was undertaken on a short schedule. Engineer Ezra Kotcher, whose forward-thinking stewardship and advocacy helped the Bell X-1 supersonic research aircraft program become a reality after the war, was an engineer at Wright Field in 1944 when the notion of building copies of the V1 was hatched. Kotcher, part of the American V1 project that was known by the alphanumeric designator MX-544, kept in his papers a detailed chronology of events. From this it is evident the project was expected to mature from concept to launch in less than five months.[20]

The first description of a German V1 was received from USAAF G-2 intelligence on June 17, 1944, according to this chronology. On July 4, USAAF officers, including Gens Carroll and Gardner met, and agreed to discuss the idea with manufacturers the following day. (This notation most likely referred to Grandison Gardner, a member of the Joint Committee on New Weapons and Equipment from Eglin Field and Franklin O. Carroll, chief of the experimental engineering section at Wright Field.) The following day, two significant decisions were reached: America would reverse-engineer the V1, and Northrop would produce an original flying bomb, the JB-1, somewhat in parallel. On July 6, Gen Carroll hosted a meeting with representatives from the USAAF's Power Plant Laboratory, Aircraft Projects Section, and Equipment Laboratory during which it was decided the Fighter Branch would be project office for the American buzz bomb. The US version was given the nomenclature JB-2. The JB- prefix stood for "Jet-propelled Bomb."

A week later, on July 13, 1944, recovered parts of a V1 arrived by air at Wright Field. On July 17, a conference was held with manufacturers including Ford, Northrop, Hammond, Bell, and the firm of Jack & Heintz, known for producing aircraft components including starters, motors, automatic pilots, and other parts. At this meeting, the construction of 3,000 buzz bombs was discussed. The next day, this total was raised to 18,000, at least in discussion. The chronology recorded: "Engineers from Republic, Ford, Jack & Heintz arrived [at] Wright Field to duplicate buzz bomb." On July 19, as the American buzz bomb effort accelerated, a decision was made to construct a 2,000ft launch track at Muroc Army Air Base (later to become Edwards Air Force Base). On July 20, according to the chronology, the Assistant Secretary of War for Air and the Assistant Chief of Air Staff, Materiel, Maintenance and Distribution inspected the retrieved German V1 parts.

By August 1, 1944, Wright Field's Power Plant Laboratory staff had made their first successful start and continuous run of a buzz bomb pulse jet engine. On August 7, a directive was issued for construction of 1,000 buzz bombs and 500 engine spares. On the next day, a test in the Wright Field Five-Foot Wind Tunnel was completed. Administratively, the MX-544 project was reduced from Secret to Restricted category on August 14. Production was underway; between August 14 and 28, Jack & Heintz achieved satisfactory results with its intended control equipment for the copied buzz bomb by flying the gear in a Beech C-45 aircraft for testing and validation. During this time, on August 15, a conference at Northrop produced the decision to build the 2,000ft track at Muroc for launch dolly testing along with two 500ft tracks at Eglin Field; one would be level, and the other 500ft track would be inclined, to accommodate actual launches.

The Massachusetts Institute of Technology (MIT) harnessed its scientific brain trust and laboratories to help the war effort. For the buzz bomb project, drawings and data were given to MIT's Radiation Laboratory on August 22 to enable that laboratory to consider guidance methods for the Americanized weapon. To understand the available power of the buzz bomb's pulse jet engine, wind-tunnel tests of a running engine were conducted on August 28. Measurements showed the engine had a gross thrust of 875 pounds at 400 mph, This was calculated to be the equivalent of 900 hp. When aerodynamic drag was deducted from the statistics, the net thrust was characterized as 450 pounds. Fuel flow was said to be 2,900 pounds an hour.[21]

Although the simple pulse jet engine of the V1 could run without forward velocity, due to its clever design and use of one-way shutters to alternately let air in and block the combustion chamber for thrust, it was considered inefficient for self-started takeoffs. Hence the Germans built inclined ramps about 150ft in length that were difficult to conceal. The German variants used a catapult system driven by steam produced by chemical reaction to accelerate the V1 to takeoff speed. American versions would use a separate rocket-powered dolly that would fall free as the V1 was airborne. Both countries made provisions for air-launching buzz bombs mounted beneath the wings of conventional bombers.

The brisk pace of American buzz bomb development saw the team obtain 30 large Tiny Tim air-to-surface rocket motors to install on the Northrop rocket booster sleds by September 4. But this was a one-time acquisition, and looking ahead to further needs for sled booster rockets, the MX-544 team solicited help from Monsanto to produce a rocket with a two-second 9,500-pound capability. Four days later, on September 8, 1944, an engineering inspection and successful trial runs were made on the first American domestically produced buzz bomb copy at the Republic Aviation plant, less than three months after the load of V1 parts arrived in the United States for inspection. A logistics decision by the MX-544 development team caused an order with Northrop for 100 additional launching dollies on September 12 to match the volume of Monsanto rocket deliveries, enabling the launching of 40 buzz bombs a month. Also at that same time in September, according to Kotcher's chronology, the test track at Muroc was reported to be completed.

As US ordnance experts studied the German V1, they opined on September 13 that the skin thickness of the German warhead was too thin for safe transportation. They also decided to use a mechanical arming method to avoid the potential for an electrical short in the existing system. The V1 was becoming "G.I." during its rapid reverse-engineering process in the United States. By September 14, discussions were underway to learn about production schedules for creating as many as 25,000 American buzz bombs at a production rate of 5,000 monthly. Out in the sparse Mojave Desert at Muroc, by September 18, testers said they were successful with the dolly or sled, reaching 385 ft/sec in 1.4 seconds with an overload weight of a half ton. They reported very little wear on the sled slippers. (American rocket sleds typically used smooth steel "slippers" to ride on railroad-style tracks.) Milestones were met almost daily as Monsanto satisfactorily fired the first two-second rocket motor on September 19; two days later, they were asked to develop a one-second rocket intended for use on a short 200ft launching track – even the buzz bomb's means of getting flying speed was being Americanized.

The number two buzz bomb was shipped on September 23 to Wright Field for tests in the 20ft wind tunnel; tests were to begin by month's end. On September 27, word was received of the capture of a German launching ramp as the Allies pushed into France; this ramp was to be replicated by the MX-544 project team. The American launching site was being prepared for a first test launch tentatively set for October 7, 1944. In an effort to do what later public relations professionals would term "managing expectations," that first launch, according to the Kotcher chronology, was only to be open to Air Technical Service Command and necessary contractor personnel by invitation "since it is so uncertain as to the outcome."

In actuality, the first American JB-2 launch occurred on October 12, 1944 at Eglin. Even given the stark throwaway simplicity of the overall V1 design, its complete replication by reverse-engineering in one day less than three months since the arrival of German parts at Wright Field must stand as testament to the importance American planners placed in this German weapon, as well as to the amazing adaptability and fleetness of the American engineering enterprise. The collaboration of Republic Aviation, Ford, Jack & Heintz, Northrop, and airframe subcontractor Willys-Overland resulted in a remarkably quick turnaround on this ambitious project.

There was talk of building 75,000 JB-2s for mass use in the impending invasion of Japan, but only about 1,000 were completed by war's end. Although some of the JB-2s may have been en route to the Pacific when atomic bombs abruptly silenced the war, no American buzz bombs were launched in anger. As with so many German technological advances, the copied V1 was an accelerator of indigenous American surface-to-surface missile programs in the Cold War 1940s. After the war the US Navy launched Loons, as the American buzz bombs were called, from ships and submarines as well as shore ramps, and the new USAF as a separate armed service resumed JB-2 activity at Holloman AFB in New Mexico, near the vast White Sands Proving Ground ranges. Postwar Loon flights enabled improvements in radio-control guidance systems far beyond the rudimentary devices for control installed in operational German V1s.

Originally, the JB-2 used the same mechanical counter to estimate distance to the intended target. The device looked like a miniature propeller that spun in the slipstream of the V1 (or early JB-2) in flight. Its revolutions were counted down toward zero on a mechanical counter fitted with four numerical drums inside the vehicle. When zero was reached on each disc according to plan, a number of functions were initiated, including arming the weapon, and a complex sequence of events that ensured the rudder was streamlined aft and the tailplane was aerodynamically altered by the deployment of spoilers on its underside, causing the craft to dive – hopefully into its intended target. Setting this mechanical device was accomplished by knowing how many revolutions the small propeller should make while the V1 or JB-2 covered a given distance to the target. Simple and useful to a point, this system would ultimately give way to more sophisticated radio control in postwar American testing.[22]

The USAAF contemplated air-launching JB-2s as an operational possibility when the devices were under consideration for the impending invasion of Japan. A test detachment flew to Wendover Army Airfield, Utah, in 1945 to launch JB-2s that were carried two at a time beneath the outer wing panels of a B-17G Flying Fortress. Among the aircrew testing JB-2s at Wendover was a young captain named Glen Edwards, whose promising postwar flight test career was tragically cut short in the crash of a YB-49 Flying Wing jet bomber. But the end of World War II shelved the USAAF's interest in JB-2s and the contract was terminated with about 1,200 finished. (Later, a brief renaissance of interest in USAF JB-2s would help improve subsequent indigenous missile programs.)

If the USAAF and its industry team showed intrepidity in reverse-engineering the V1 and Americanizing it in short order during the summer of 1944, it was the US Navy that gave the United States the ultimate service from these clearly copied missiles. The US Navy was prescient at the end of World War II to the fact that future wars could not be won with the same equipment, or even evolutionary iterations of equipment. New technologies and new methodologies needed to be embraced and perfected. The US Navy saw a role for itself in bringing seaborne surface-to-surface missiles that could hit an enemy far inland. Agreed, the sputtering JB-2 (navalized as the KUW-1 and still later the LTV-N-2, and called "Loon") was hardly a strategic world-beater. But the US Navy leveraged its supply of ex-USAAF JB-2s by making purposeful experiments in launch and guidance technologies. Two submarines, USS *Cusk* and USS *Carbonero*, were modified with the installation of a Loon launching track on the deck aft of the conning tower. A large watertight canister just behind the track housed a partially disassembled Loon. Both submarines demonstrated the ability to surface, assemble the missile, launch it, and submerge. By 1950, the US Navy's finesse with the Loon included guidance systems that could be handed off to shore stations following launch, or operated by the now-submerged submarine, directing the Loon in one instance on a course that was more than 100 miles, splashing the missile near its intended target site, a rocky prominence in the Pacific Ocean.[23]

From the US Navy's use of its ex-USAAF JB-2s in the early Cold War period came salient refinements in the ability to control the path of surface-to-surface missiles that would yield benefits to newer, purely American missile designs like the US Navy's Regulus variants as well as the USAF's operational Matador, Mace, and Snark. The cumbersome early test launches of Loons from the decks of surfaced submarines showed the US Navy two things: the ability to move missiles around the high seas submerged was a tactic worth developing, and a means would need to be devised to make even the launch take place while the submarine was submerged and less vulnerable to detection and destruction. The outgrowth was the Polaris, Poseidon and Trident family of nuclear-capable missiles that could be vertically launched from a submerged submarine.

NOT ALWAYS ALLIED ABOUT THE V1

The presence of V1s raining down on England in the summer of 1944 occasionally put Anglo-American cooperation to the test. Issues that surfaced in high-level message traffic in the files of war leaders such as "Hap" Arnold included the sharing of intelligence information and the best means of thwarting the V1s. By February 1944, it was well established that the Germans were building rocket-launching sites in coastal France, with England as the obvious target. Britain's intelligence-gathering mechanism learned a year earlier, in 1943, about German unpiloted aircraft weapons falling in Scandinavia and on test ranges in occupied Poland that were operated by the Luftwaffe. Evidently not all of the British knowledge was shared with the United States quickly, in what has been called an exception to the usual high level of wartime cooperation between the two Allies.[24]

In the spring of 1944, Gen Grandison Gardner received an urgent telephone request from "Hap" Arnold to come up with answers on how to locate and destroy the sometimes-concealed V1 launch sites in France. British drawings of a site were en route to Gen Gardner, and Arnold told him he had days, not weeks, to devise effective ways to neutralize the sites. Gardner wryly figured he had 13 days in which to accomplish this task, since that was technically less than "weeks." Gardner commissioned the construction of an initial frame-and-cloth mock-up of the site at Eglin Field, where vast test ranges allowed the replication of the so-called V1 "ski site" facility based on best estimates from reconnaissance photography. He also created a concrete replica of the site to gain an appreciation of bomb damage potential. But the world of intelligence gathering can be imperfect. In a February 26, 1944 letter to Gen Arnold, a British air marshal, who had recently visited the Eglin replica site with Arnold, said the latest British information now suggested too much concrete reinforcement had gone into the American replica of the V1 facility, and this might skew bomb damage assessments. This British letter to Arnold said recent photo-reconnaissance following a RAF Mosquito bomber low-level attack on an actual ski site showed that 500-pound bombs were effective. Before the first V1 launched toward England, the USAAF was suggesting low-level attacks by fighter-bombers would be the best way to take out the German V1 sites.[25]

The remarkably quick development of a replica structure at Eglin for the purpose of bombing trials in the spring of 1944, coupled with at least some British post-mission analysis of actual ski site bombing, argued for low-level strikes. But this became a point of contention between British and American planners when some British military leaders, including Air Marshal Trafford Leigh-Mallory, commander of the Allied Expeditionary Air Force for the Normandy invasion, insisted on using Eighth Air Force strategic heavy bomber assets to attack V1 launch sites, to the chagrin of the USAAF. The detriment, from a USAAF standpoint, was a diminution of the Eighth Air Force's relentless pursuit of German target priorities both in support of the invasion and as part of the greater strategic war against German combat capabilities that had been so carefully devised over the years of fighting. "Hap" Arnold urged Leigh-Mallory to use fighter-bombers, but in the end some redirecting of heavy bombers occurred.[26]

By mid-March 1944, one USAAF assessment of Operation *Crossbow* (the destruction of V1 capabilities) bombing sorties estimated 1,000 500-pound bombs were expended for every direct hit on a V1 site. "Most of the Fortress operations have been in the nature of 'practice' bombing," reported Brig Gen Thomas White, an intelligence officer, to "Hap" Arnold. Flak was increasing over *Crossbow* targets in the spring of 1944, yet the missions were considered only worth partial combat credit, to the dismay of the crews flying these sorties.[27]

Gen Samuel Anderson commanded Ninth Air Force's Ninth Bomber Command (Medium) during the *Crossbow* era, and he recalled in 1970 how his twin-engined bomber crews learned to increase their chances of hitting the elusive V1 sites, hidden in forested areas and generally hard to see from altitude:

> Leigh-Mallory wrote me a letter and said that my command was by far the most effective in bombing those targets. It was a problem in identification. What we did, we could pick those damn things out in photographs, you see, whereas the man flying at 12,000 ft couldn't pick them up soon enough. Now, what we did was study the photographs and pick an offset aiming point, which we know the bombardier is going to be able to identify in time to get lined up on it. So, we didn't actually aim at the ski sites, very rarely, because they didn't show up in time. We aimed at an offset bombing point, aiming point, which we had fixed, and which we had briefed all of our crews and ourselves on.

In this way, the bombardier would make his bomb run on a readily visible landmark that was known, via photo-reconnaissance, to be a precise distance and heading from the real V1 target site. The bombsight would be set up to account for that offset, so that when the bombardier released while keeping the visible landmark in view, the bombs would actually travel to the hidden V1 site. Gen Anderson, who was subsequently awarded the Distinguished Service Medal for his technical proficiency with the medium bombers of the Ninth Air Force, said, "there is not one bit of reason to take your planes and your crews over there, and risk the planes, risk the lives of your crews if you don't put the bombs on target. That's the sole purpose."[28]

In addition to the medium bombers, if the temporary diversion of some B-24s and B-17s to support Operation *Crossbow* was vexing to the Americans, worse still was an idea broached at a British Chiefs of Staff meeting on July 3, 1944. The notion suggested was that a public announcement be made that continuing use of V1s by the Germans would result in the obliteration of selected towns in Germany. Arguments against such a plan included the observation that this would create an appearance of negotiating with the enemy, plus some felt the German command cared little if German civilians died as long as the V1 attacks were evidently effective. And, any such targeting of German towns for reprisal efforts would take needed bombers away from targets of military significance.[29]

This first suggestion of threatening German towns with obliteration was evidently followed by the notion of using gas warfare as a reprisal. Gen Dwight D. Eisenhower, Supreme Allied Commander of the Allied Expeditionary Force, quickly reiterated his emphatic intent not to be a party to retaliation or the use of gas. "Let's, for God's sake, keep our eyes on the ball and use some sense," he chided.[30]

The specter of gas warfare, so reviled by combatants in World War I, caused the Allies to take some preparatory steps during World War II. Interestingly, photographs surface in official USAAF historical documents showing storage of gas warfare containers in places like North Africa and England. If German agents knew of these supplies, their mere presence had to be cause for caution by the enemy, rather than engendering a cavalier approach.

In early February 1944, "Hap" Arnold received a memo citing a special report on German secret weapons that said the enemy was capable of launching bacteriological warfare with agents identified as "N" and "X" that could be dispersed from pilotless aircraft. The sobering report said there was no method of detection, and decontamination procedures were not known. In preparation was a special filter to equip all US gas masks in the United Kingdom by May 1, 1944, and 400,000 doses of an antidote for agent "X" were expected to be available by that time as well. Fortunately, gases and bacteriological agents remained only threats during World War II.[31]

In May 1944, a few weeks before the notion of using gas warfare to retaliate for V1 attacks, representatives of Supreme Headquarters Allied Expeditionary Forces (SHAEF), including USSTAF's Brig Gen C. P. Cabell, created plans limiting the retaliatory use of gas by air attack if the Germans initiated the use of gas warfare. The sole measurement of whether or not the Allies should use gas in retaliation was said to be based on the effectiveness of doing so versus using other available weapons. Gas would not be used by the Allies on civilian populations unless first introduced by the Germans against Allied civilians; the possible use of gas by the Germans against military targets would not trigger unrestricted Allied use of gas warfare. While the SHAEF representatives largely put strings and conditions on the use of gas warfare, they also agreed that if all restrictions against Allied use of gas were ever lifted, the decision to use gas should be made at the level of the air forces commander who normally made choices regarding proper bombs and fuses for specific targets.[32]

As the war advanced during the post-Normandy summer of 1944, coastal V1 sites were overrun, rendering continued bombing unnecessary; the concept of retaliating with gas warfare for continued German rocket-bomb attacks was moot. But the summer's problems of vengeance weapons, be they rocket bombs or gas warfare, kept the USAAF actively engaged in neutralization as well as intelligence gathering.[33]

The RAF quickly found a proactive way to disrupt V1s in flight by intercepting them early in their one-way sortie with fast fighters (including Gloster Meteor jets) and deftly knocking the robot bombs off balance by tipping a wingtip with the wing of the British fighter. Antiaircraft batteries also began to take the measure of V1s.

When larger, faster, rocket-propelled V2s entered the equation, the radio control system of this more sophisticated weapon was targeted by Allied jammers. In this effort, the USAAF sometimes supplied the RAF with jamming equipment. The RAF's No. 100 Group was mentioned in a cable from Lt Gen Carl A. Spaatz, commander of Strategic Air Forces in Europe, to Gen Arnold on July 22, 1944; at that time, No. 100 Group was carrying out research missions to determine which radio frequencies promised the best possibilities for jamming the anticipated V2 missiles. Intelligence suggested the use of V2s against England was imminent, but the first actual operational launch was aimed at Paris on September 8, 1944, followed shortly by V2s targeting England. Specially modified B-17G Flying Fortresses, operated by the RAF as Fortress IIIs, probably took part in V2 jamming efforts.

The development and deployment of these so-called robot bombs by Germany in 1944-45 came at a price for both sides. The Allies suffered deadly and random bombings in England and on the Continent, but correspondence between senior USAAF officers in early 1945 shared the observation that Gen Eisenhower evidently believed the cost to the Germans, in materiel and labor, was a drain that helped the Allies gain ascendancy over the Luftwaffe.[34]

CHAPTER 3

ATTRITION VERSUS TECHNOLOGY

The menace, both real and potential, imposed by the Luftwaffe's expanding deployment of jet- and rocket-powered fighters and bombs caused concern in upper USAAF circles. USAAF chief Gen "Hap" Arnold instructed the USAAF's Evaluation Board to aid in development of techniques to combat what was considered an imminent threat from German jets in the summer of 1944. Arnold also wanted USAAF specialists to evaluate a captured V1 in order to build test vehicles. He indicated it did not matter to him whether the American robot bomb was a copy of the German V1 or some amalgamation of German and American design ideas. (Ultimately, the US reverse-engineered the captured V1 in short order, as described in the previous chapter.) Arnold envisioned a more surgical use of robots against precision targets like bridges, instead of the indiscriminate way in which German V1s fell on England, and he asked the USAAF Evaluation Board to study whether American robot bombs would be effective in Europe or the Pacific. Gen Arnold's interest in robots and rockets included concerns over German deployment of rockets that might eventually reach the United States. "We must use everything in our power to prevent any such occurrences," he instructed. V2s had not yet fallen from the sky in anger, but Arnold was aware of radio-controlled designs that he believed had to be thwarted. He pondered the efficacy of dropping large quantities of aircraft drop tanks filled with gasoline on German launch sites.[1]

Information about impending German jet fighters bothered USAAF planners as early as April 1944. One paper presented to a concerned Gen Arnold the following month suggested that fighter tactics by USAAF "standard" (propeller-driven) fighters should include a scenario wherein "the standard fighter should force the fighter into the slow speed bracket where the standard aircraft should be superior in maneuverability, acceleration, deceleration, rate of climb, and initial rate of dive." Arnold quickly rejected the report in a memo in which the USAAF chief said the notion of forcing a jet to slow down "is the same as saying that the horse that finishes last in a race will force the horse that is winning the race to slow down until the last horse catches up and wins the race." Arnold continued: "The jet propelled airplane has one idea and mission in life and that is to get at the bombers, and he is going by our fighters so fast that they will barely see him, much less throw out a skyhook and slow him up."[2]

Across the Atlantic at VIII Fighter Command in England, some pragmatic ideas prevailed. Gen William E. Keppner, chief of that command, figured he was the first general officer to fly a jet in the US when he earlier sampled the Bell XP-59 Airacomet at Muroc Army Airfield in California's Mojave Desert. "So I knew something about a jet," Gen Keppner recalled in a 1970 interview. "It couldn't make sharp turns, things like that," he remembered. "One day a bomber outfit reported that here was an airplane that didn't seem to have any props, and flew like the devil and threw out a lot of black smoke, and went faster than anything they had seen before. So I went over and talked to them. I said: 'Boys, you have just seen your first jet.'"[3]

In a July 15, 1944 letter to USAAF Lt Gen Barney Giles, USAAF deputy commander, Keppner acknowledged "I am somewhat concerned about the possibility of the GAF [German Air Force[4]] appearing with 'jets'." Keppner added "...it is possible they will have speed equal to those that are reported for our own, and if so you know what that will mean, because such speeds permit a fighter to make or break contact." An old fighter pilot slogan embraces the notion that "speed is life." Now, in the mid-summer of 1944, Eighth Air Force fighter pilots showed signs of concern that German jets would soon use speed to the enemy's advantage, dictating the rules of engagement based on the laws of physics. Keppner had concerns, but he was far from defeatist as he contemplated the introduction of German jet fighters into the combat arena. He believed tactics could be developed to hamper the jets' freedom of action. Keppner informed Lt Gen Giles that he sought access to Allied jet fighters to enable his own fighter pilots to develop tactics against the fast jets. "It may be that we can find out something," he said. "Anyway, we will be in there pitching and never say quit regardless of whatever surprise is sprung."[5]

METEORS STAND IN FOR MESSERSCHMITTS

In July Keppner requested three of the nonoperational American jet fighters be sent to England so he could get his fighter pilots practicing against them. When US jets were not forthcoming for Keppner's plan, he "went to the British and I asked them to borrow four of their jets." The RAF was operating Gloster Meteor jet fighters then, and Keppner wanted to make some tests using a B-24 bomb group. His efforts led to a tactic whereby P-51s would bracket a jet and "we'd then practice like the coyotes did, in running down a deer. One of them would run him and when he [the German jet] started to make a turn, he was committed to that; this other [USAAF] fellow would cut in for an intercept," he explained. Keppner said the USAAF's coyote herding technique, plus lurking for slowed-down jet fighters in their airfield traffic patterns, cost the Luftwaffe as many as 240 German jets downed.[6]

Lt Gen Spaatz wrote to Gen Arnold on September 3, 1944 with intelligence information about the emphasis Germany placed on jet fighter production. Spaatz's remarks included the following:

> Although our information is somewhat spotty, it is apparent that the enemy is making every effort to get these fighters operational and in production. We expect to meet each of these fighters at an early date in forces as large as one group. The most disturbing feature of the enemy program except the obvious performance superiority of these fighters, is that all evidence points toward production in small, dispersed and underground facilities.[7]

The underground facilities and work areas in forests were already comprehended long before American G.I.s found such plants during the Allied sweep through Germany in the following year.

Spaatz, who is frequently acknowledged as a masterful air leader, reported to Arnold that all known German jet fighter test and training airfields, as well as targets related to jet fuel, engines, and airframes, were being attacked. Changes in gunnery were being introduced in an effort to counter the high-speed jet threat, as were improved tactics for USAAF bombers and fighters. Improved effectiveness of H2X radar for bombing through overcast was seen as a way to conduct bombing in bad weather that seemed to blunt the jets' advantage. But Spaatz had to contemplate a drastically changed scenario in the skies over Germany if enemy jet fighter strength reached numbers too high for current bombing tactics to tolerate. He told Gen Arnold the courses of action under consideration for such an eventuality included limiting the range of bomber penetrations to increase the available density of close escort fighters, reverting to previous plans that relied on elaborate diversionary missions to throw the Germans off guard, turning to night bombing or bombing through overcast, using long-range fighter-bombers, and employing robotic aircraft and American versions of buzz bombs.[8]

A chilling harbinger of attacks that would come later against bomber formations was a spate of Me 262 interceptions of photo-reconnaissance aircraft around August 1944. Traditionally, high and fast recon aircraft used speed and altitude to evade destruction over Germany. But in the late summer of 1944, Spaatz reported, of ten recon flights sent over Munich by Mediterranean Allied Air Forces (MAAF), six were attacked and three were downed by the jets, whose capabilities negated the piston-engined reconnaissance planes' previous performance advantages. Spaatz opined to Arnold in his September 3 letter:

> At present I am more concerned about the fate of photo reconnaissance than strategic bombing ... The Fifteenth Air Force intends to experiment with fighter cover for PR [photo-reconnaissance aircraft] in formations of one to four escorts per photo airplane, but if the enemy makes determined effort to stop our [recces], I feel that the only solution will be reconnaissance by our own jet fighter airplanes. I recommend that early consideration be given to a PR version of the P-80.

The fast new Lockheed P-80 Shooting Star was America's best jet design that was still not available for combat.

An important part of the USAAF's war against Germany was the dissemination of knowledge gained about new German weapons with the American crews who would face them in combat. In his September 3, 1944 letter Spaatz advised Arnold that reports and presentations on German jets and rockets given to operational bomber units by the USAAF Board had been of great value:

> These reports and lectures have helped dispel the uncertainty in the minds of our crews prior to meeting these new enemy aircraft. We found the reports forecast so accurately, and in detail, the performance of the rocket and jet fighters that they have reflected an increased measure of confidence from operating commands. These and other reports received recently have changed the attitude of combat units from indifference to reliance on the recommendations of the Board.

In the same letter to Arnold, Lt Gen Spaatz produced a list of projects he believed needed the highest priority to counter the looming German jet threat:

a. Increase production of P-51 airplanes to the maximum in order to provide all escort groups of the Eighth and Fifteenth Air Forces with our best long range fighters. [Here is unequivocal evidence of how Lt Gen Spaatz felt about the P-51 and its contemporaries.]

b. Accelerate the H2X equipment program and improve the training program so that we can reach authorized strength in operating and maintenance personnel, H2X sets and maintenance equipment at the earliest possible date. [This indicates Spaatz's interest in masking his heavy bombers as much as possible with darkness or obscuring with clouds to diminish jet fighter effectiveness.]

c. Accelerate development, production and training on improved BTO [bombing through overcast] equipment with an eventual goal of one per heavy bombardment airplane.

d. Improve the performance of our heavy bombers by accelerating the changeover to more powerful engines and improved armor plating and fire proofing of engine nacelles.

e. Accelerate the program for improved gunnery equipment to include higher speed turrets, the new simplified K-13 and K-15 computing sights, and stabilized turrets. [The K-13 computing gunsight was adaptable for use in everything from B-17G chin turrets to Martin top turrets on B-24s and waist guns on both types of heavy USAAF bomber in Europe. Its computations simplified the gunners' chores, and especially if this could be coupled with faster tracking turrets, gunners might be able to better defend against German jets.]

f. Increase the rate of fire from heavy bombers by perfecting and producing the high cyclic rate of .50 caliber machine gun. [This probably references longstanding efforts to develop a .50 caliber machine gun with a rate of fire well in excess of 1,000 rounds per minute. The work was underway as Spaatz wrote this letter, and a successful newer .50 caliber weapon, the M3, was not standardized until April 1945 – too late for use in the European war against German jets.]

g. Develop more powerful guns such as the .60 caliber and improved 20 mm for fighters and bomber nose and tail turrets. [Longer ranging and harder hitting big bore weapons could be expected to force jets to keep their distance, but in the end, the standard M2 .50 caliber aircraft machine gun remained the standard armament of B-17s and B-24s in Europe.]

h. Improve our fighter gunnery by installing the K-14 gyro sight in all fighters and emphasize deflection shooting in our training programs. [A proactive acknowledgment of the need to adapt tactics to meet the high-speed threat.]

i. Most important of all is to put long range jet fighters into the field at the earliest possible date.

Some of these recommendations were in the pipeline and were implemented to greater or lesser degree; others, like the faster-rate .50 caliber machine gun and the hoped-for .60 caliber weapon would not be delivered, although the faster-firing M3 .50 caliber machine gun became a postwar standby. Clearly, Lt Gen Spaatz sought proactive measures to meet the specter of high-performance German jet fighters based on the information available to him at the time.

Gen Arnold's reply to Spaatz included word that the fast P-51H variant of the piston-engine Mustang fighter was being emphasized for quantity production, while some P-47s would have night capabilities. Both of these developments were seen as valuable to protect USAAF bomber formations against German jet activity.[9] The P-51H's top speed of 487 mph bested the P-51D then in European service by 50 mph, but no H-models reached the European Theater of Operations (ETO) during combat. Arnold put the most value in the potential of the P-80 jet fighter, but this did not arrive in time to see combat in World War II.

The P-80 was America's first viable combat jet fighter; the earlier P-59 was a vital step in discovering the capabilities of jet-propelled warplanes, but its performance was not enough of a leap to warrant combat use of P-59s. The P-80 would change this perception, although not in time to affect the outcome of World War II. While the Germans placed great store in the production and fielding of jet and rocket aircraft, the USAAF chose to be more deliberate, using tried-and-true piston-engined aircraft to carry the fight while jets like the Lockheed P-80 Shooting Star matured at home. Even as the earlier P-59 was in development in the skies over southern California, Lt Gen Barney Giles, the USAAF's deputy commander who had a penchant and an ability for developing USAAF operational policy, said in a 1970 interview that he "did everything that I could to discourage diverting any of our manufacturing plants into [producing the P-59 jet fighter]". Mostly, and with Giles' urging, his boss, Gen Arnold, kept fighter production geared toward P-51s and other piston-engined workhorses while development continued on America's second jet fighter, the more capable P-80. Giles reflected, "In terms of jet fighters, it would be a long time. We should win this war, and then prepare for the next one."[10] Message traffic from 1945 plus interviews decades later tend to present a picture of urging development of the P-80 for possible combat use, while leveraging existing production fighters in massive numbers that, along with bombardment tactics, could overwhelm even a technologically superior Luftwaffe.

Later in 1944, fighter escorts of four to six aircraft were mounted to support photo-recce missions over Germany, as Lt Gen Spaatz had postulated.

If it was difficult to stop an Me 262 with a Mustang, it was not impossible. The first victory over a jet in the MTO was credited to the teamwork of 31st Fighter Group Mustang pilots Roy L. Scales and Eugene P. McGlauflin, both lieutenants, when they trounced an Me 262 on December 22, 1944.[11] Some Fifteenth Air Force reconnaissance aircraft were modified with the installation of tail-warning radar to improve their chances against interception.

Mediterranean Allied Air Forces (MAAF) commander Lt Gen Ira C. Eaker, who had aviation accomplishments reaching back to 1918, had the might of Twelfth and Fifteenth air forces under his command in October 1944 when he wrote to Lt Gen Giles:

> I have noted the German's claim that he is concentrating on jet- and rocket-propelled fighters. If this is true, and there seems no reason to doubt it, I believe our best antidote, aside from all-out attacks on the factories building these planes, is to have available on forward airdromes by April 1st several groups of our own jet-propelled fighters. Would it not be possible for you to concentrate on jet fighter production and the formation of groups equipped with this type and have them available here by early spring?[12]

Lt Gen Eaker acknowledged the general lack of range and endurance for jets of the era, as well as the threat posed by the enemy:

> Obviously these planes with their present range would not be satisfactory as accompanying fighters for our heavy bombers; they would have to be put on the most forward airdromes and operate as interceptors against enemy rocket formations or for furnishing target support for our heavy bombers ... The little we have seen of these [German jet] planes leads us to believe they would be a very bad weapon provided the enemy employed hit and run tactics against bombers, making fullest use of their speed to escape our accompanying fighters.

In the same letter, Lt Gen Eaker told Lt Gen Giles he had also urged Lt Gen Spaatz to embrace German jet fighter plants as high priority targets.

Early in January 1945, the Eighth Air Force's director of intelligence, Col George W. Jones, Jr., warned Lt Gen James H. Doolittle, commander of the Eighth Air Force, of the peril in future months from expanding production of the Me 262. The Jockey Committee, one of several intelligence-based Allied organizations, had apparently concluded the Me 262 was on the cusp of large-scale production. Estimates varied from April 1 to June 1, 1945 as the period when Germany could throw 500 jets into the fray. When the

Junkers engine plant near Strasbourg, in the far eastern Alsatian region of France, was overrun on November 23, 1944, one of the intelligence dividends was information indicating production of the Me 262's Jumo turbojet engines was planned to reach 200 per month by July 1945.[13]

The clamor for bomber attacks on German jet factories in late 1944 and early 1945 could not be answered independently by the USAAF. The war against Germany, in the air, on the ground, and still at sea, involved joint effort by British and American armies, navies, and air forces as well as other Allies. Systemic differences in opinion about the efficacy of area attacks versus specifically targeted attacks bred a host of advocates for differing bombing priorities. When the Eighth Air Force began its build-up and early missions in 1942 from England, these differences were apparent. Realizing the importance of a thoughtful rationale for conducting daylight strategic bombardment as a means of bringing the war with Germany to a victorious conclusion, the USAAF imported a number of civilian scholarly analysts to sift through mounds of intelligence information and help formulate bombing policy for the Americans. Known as the Enemy Objectives Unit (EOU) from October 1942 onward, this group advocated for relentless bombing pressure on target systems that would do the most to cripple Germany's ability to wage war, as opposed to a broader view of harassing interdiction and area bombing that seemed to offer vague promises of German capitulation that the EOU questioned. The EOU was but one voice in the sometimes cacophonous chorus of opinions about targets, but it did furnish rationale of use to the USAAF. Even as German ground forces made some surprising offensive moves in January 1945, the bombing proponents were paying attention to what a later Central Intelligence Agency (CIA) historian would call "the ominous but tardy German development of jet aircraft".[14]

Computations produced an estimated figure of 3,250 sorties over three days required to successfully neutralize six known above-ground jet plants as well as underground facilities near Nordhausen.[15] But in the final days of the European war, arguments were made for using the heavy bombers to strike marshalling yards, although some bombardment advocates (including the EOU) chafed at what they considered an inefficient use of resources. Ultimately, sprinting ground forces made most of the railyard sorties moot. The EOU, it is said, "felt it was intrinsic in the nature of strategic bombing that the heavy bombers should end the war not with a bang but with a whimper."[16]

An overview of USAAF missions flown over western Europe from January 1, 1945 to the war's end in May depicts the split nature of Eighth Air Force efforts as the conflict played out. Heavy four-engined B-24 and B-17 bombers made some attacks on marshalling yards, while still carving out sorties targeting the production of jets and their components, as well as petroleum – another longstanding strategic target set. During the spring of 1945, some Ninth and Eighth Air Force assets would move onto the Continent, and the heavy bombers of the Eighth would occasionally recover at Continental airfields under Allied control when weather made large-scale return to England dangerous. This Continental migration was boldly challenged by the Luftwaffe on New Year's Day when a German force estimated at 700–800 warplanes struck at Ninth Air Force airfields and 2nd Tactical Air Force airfields in the vicinity of Brussels, Belgium and Eindhoven, in the Netherlands, and to some extent near Metz, France. The German attack cost 127 operational Allied aircraft in a single day. Allied fighters and antiaircraft batteries claimed large numbers of German attackers destroyed. Though not a jet battle per se, the vigor and strength of this effort by the Luftwaffe had to be sobering to USAAF planners concerned with the emerging jet menace. On January 18, most of a force greater than 100 B-17s supported by three fighter groups had to divert for landings on the Continent when cloud cover made recovery in the United Kingdom unwise. Parking strategic bombardment assets within reach of the Luftwaffe had to be vexing for the USAAF.[17]

January 29 saw Eighth Air Force bomber raids on unspecified German aircraft factories, and on February 16 the companion Ninth Air Force sent its medium bombers after a turbojet component factory in Solingen. The German jets would not flourish unchecked. The Eighth kept the pressure up on March 4, striking an identified jet aircraft plant at Schwabmünchen as one part of a multi-target 1,000-plane raid. A factory making castings for jet aircraft at Hildensheim was targeted by the Eighth Air Force on March 14. Careful scrutiny of markings on parts from crashed or captured German jets could yield clues about where vital components were made. Five days later, on March 19, a force of more than 1,200 heavy bombers from the Eighth Air Force went after targets including airfields and jet aircraft plants at Neuburg an der Donau, Asbach-Bäumenheim, and Leipheim. The Americans were challenged by more than 100 German fighters, including 36 jets in formation – the largest jet concentration to date.

The race to defeat Germany before the jets could gain an upper hand was in full motion, with both sides comprehending the strategic issue raised by growing numbers of German jet fighters. The jet count of March 19 paled in comparison to more than 50 German jets noted on April 7, along with 100 piston-engined fighters that challenged a huge force of more than 1,200 Eighth Air Force heavy bombers. The fighters downed 15 bombers, losing some jets to the protecting USAAF fighters. Two days later, the target list included as many as ten jet airfields for the Eighth Air Force heavy bombers to hit. It was an old trade-off; bombing jet airfields was a defensive move intended to give the bombers greater security, but it lacked the offensive clout of a strike on a target system like oil. The next day, the Luftwaffe put up a jet force estimated by the USAAF to be 60 jets. If strangulation of German petroleum was crippling the piston-engined Luftwaffe, the coal-oil burning jet fighters were less constrained as they rose in greater numbers to meet mighty armadas bent on their destruction. As late as April 19, the Eighth Air Force encountered German jet fighters. [18] By April 26, according to some accounts, the fragmented Luftwaffe amassed at least 95 Me 262s at Munich.[19] On May 7, 1945 the German High Command surrendered unconditionally, effective two days later. The German jet menace was laid to rest.

WHEN TO STRIKE

During the war years an emerging rationale for American target selection suggested items that were built quickly to replace similar items that were lost quickly were best targeted at the construction point, while items that were built more slowly to replace items that were lost more slowly were best attacked in service. This translated into better efficiency attacking submarines at sea instead of under construction, and airplanes at the factory rather than on operational airfields. (The overall danger of the Luftwaffe ultimately made it a target in the air as US fighters sought out their German counterparts, even as American bombers went after aircraft plants or vital subassemblies such as engines.) When German fighter aircraft were identified in 1943 as a high priority target for the strategic bombers, attacks on airframe manufacturers were considered less fruitful than attacks on aircraft engine builders. But that year, the Eighth Air Force was not yet prepared to attack Berlin, where significant aero engine factory capacity resided. US rationale said that attacks which targeted only part of the engine capacity would be less effective because of Germany's ability to shift production to factories not under attack, so prioritization of German engine plants was delayed until all of Berlin was regularly accessible in early 1944.[20] This delay on attacking engine plants was noticed by Albert Speer, Germany's powerful Reichminister of Armaments and War Production. When interrogated by the Combined Intelligence Objectives Subcommittee (CIOS) in 1945, Speer expressed criticism of the Allied attack priorities that did not target engine manufacturing earlier; he was not in a position to know the rationale that led to this decision. A September 1945 CIOS summary report said Speer "was critical of the initial blows on the airframe industry, believing that air engine manufacture was much more vulnerable. He expressed surprise that the Allies did not concentrate on the latter type of target at an earlier date."[21]

The art of timing strategic bombing campaigns was informed by statistical computations suggesting that the impact of attacks on the German ball bearing industry would not be fully felt by the military for at least five months due to inventory in the logistics pipeline. This data could be used to extrapolate the impact of targeting systems on future anticipated events like the invasion of Continental Europe from the west by the Allies. On June 10, 1943 Operation *Pointblank* was codified as policy that targeted German fighters and ball bearing production for the next nine months.[22] It can be seen how USAAF strategic bombing was not a reactive tool applied in the heat of the moment, but rather worked from a list of target priorities intended to provide lasting and real benefit to the Allied war effort by comprehending which target systems would hurt the German war machine the most.

The ongoing wartime study of the Luftwaffe by the USAAF, as well as the RAF, was boosted by a formerly private English company that was requisitioned into wartime service and known as the Central Interpretation Unit. A later American history credited the Central Interpretation Unit's Flg Off Constance Babbington Smith with making that agency especially useful:

> From 1941 to the end of the war she brought craftsmanship, enthusiasm, and a creative imagination to the analysis. This was of particular importance because the aircraft industry has shallow roots; both the locations and the processes of production were under continuous development and alteration, and the many important changes could be followed with precision only by the study of air photos.[23]

The US Embassy's Enemy Objectives Unit in London prepared a report in October 1944 that analyzed available data on German fighter aircraft production compared with average daily Luftwaffe sorties, and derived targeting recommendations for VIII Fighter Command. The intellectual, analytical and mathematical effort seen in reports such as this reveal a nuanced contemplation of targeting priorities. The study said, in summary: "Evidence on the present condition of the GAF [German Air Force] indicates that training schools for fighter pilots have now become possible targets of some value for strafing or bombing by Allied fighter forces."[24]

The unit's report said German single-engined fighter activity since the beginning of 1944 "has not been commensurate with first line strength and during the last two months the ratio of daily sorties to strength has declined even more noticeably." The report cited figures showing German single-engined first-line fighter availability had risen from a low of around 1,800 "after the battle of Normandy" to a level of 2,300 aircraft by October 1944. However, the Luftwaffe was not leveraging the availability of this increased number of fighters. According to the unit's report, average daily German fighter sorties were off from a level of about 900 to 550, and were "running about 200 below 1943 in spite of higher first line strength."

The report concluded that the statistics documenting this decrease in sortie rates "corroborate other information that the main factors limiting sef [single-engined fighter] effectiveness are now: 1) oil, and 2) a shortage of experienced pilots, rather than production or first line strength." The report continued: "As part of a counter GAF program from now until the Spring of 1945, therefore, it has been recommended that the strategic air forces continue to press their attacks on oil, and that the fighters be given the GAF fighter training establishments as a secondary target system for harrassing attacks."

The sources in the Enemy Objectives Unit report painted a picture of expedient desperation on the part of the Luftwaffe in coping with a shortage of fighter pilots in April and May 1944:

> To remedy the growing shortage of fighter pilots, the GAF High Command shifted a great number of pilots from bomber, transport, and other units to conversion courses for fighter pilots. By the time of the invasion, the pilot force was back to adequate levels although the quality was still unsatisfactory. After the battle of Normandy, however, the shortage of experienced pilots again became a problem and has continued down to this date, partly due to the greater rate of wastage.

The report analyzed German actions with its fighter training schools, and the outcome of attacks on them:

> In August [1944] the GAF High Command closed down all of the first half of the "A" Schools ... and put the student pilots into the "paratroops". These paratroop units were assigned to the Army and were actually used almost entirely as infantry. Instructors from these schools were sent to conversion schools to become fighter pilots. In other words the Germans were attempting to get every man into an activity where by December he could be used in first line strength for an all-out defense of the Reich. Those student pilots above the level of the first half of the "A" schools were allowed to continue training, on the principle that they would be ready for operational *staffeln* by the end of December.

The wartime view of German pilot training is fascinating: "As far as is known the first half of the 'A' schools have never been reopened, partly because of the petrol shortage and partly because of the need to put all able bodied men into first line Army units." The report assessed lead times for fighter pilot production: "Even if these schools have been partially reopened, there remains about a two month gap in the pipeline of student pilots coming up through the system, which probably cannot be remedied by any further speeding up of the program." The report forecast this gap to be felt by December 1944, with the GAF beginning to "run out of the men converted from bomber and transport pilots," causing "an even more serious drop in the supply of experienced pilots. Any delay or casualties that can be inflicted on the training program now will aggravate the situation and directly affect the fall in effectiveness of the German single-engined fighter force."

The unit's report included a list of 17 known German fighter schools and nine fighter pools including map coordinates. It offered: "If you feel that these would make feasible targets for the fighters, either for strafing during returns from escort or for special fighter bombers or strafing missions, our office can do some further target analysis on them, furnishing photographs and building identification charts, and additional information on the units present." Whether or not this information was fully exploited by the USAAF fighter units, the report demonstrates the methods in which information was amalgamated and interpreted to present a picture of German fighter pilot capacity, and ways to hinder it.

Ar 234 SUBTERFUGE

Germany tried to counter the Allied intelligence-gathering activities about its aircraft production by assigning bogus names to aircraft plants. Additionally, the nascent Arado Ar 234 Blitz, or Lightning, jet bomber received the code name Hecht (Pike), the same designation earlier given to a glide bomb project. Two early test versions of the Ar 234, fitted with reconnaissance cameras, were dispatched to Juvincourt, France, in the latter half of July 1944, where they launched successful and unhindered reconnaissance sorties over Allied airfields and the artificial harbor at Aisnelles-sur-Mer to keep a watchful eye on the Allies entering France. Flying well above 30,000ft, the fast jets did not orbit or remain long enough for successful interceptions. The preproduction Ar 234A models were supplemented at Juvincourt with a pair of production Ar 234Bs that year. These B-models would make the first jet reconnaissance flights over the United Kingdom.[25]

Even as the Me 262 jet fighter was receiving most of the attention from USAAF planners, on December 21, 1944 Capt Donald S. Bryan dived on a pair of fast-flying Ar 234Bs with his P-51, scoring hits on one of the jets before it accelerated out of range. On Christmas Day near Liège, an RAF Hawker Tempest V flight engaged an Ar 234B, again scoring hits before the German jet accelerated to freedom. Other engagements between Allied piston-engined fighters and Ar 234s continued into early 1945. On March 2, 1945 Ar 234Bs of *Kampfgeschwader* (KG) 76 busied themselves attacking Allied tanks and troop concentrations in the vicinity of Düren, Germany. Diving attacks said to be in excess of 500 mph rendered the Blitz bombers impervious to Allied fighters and difficult for antiaircraft tracking. But the Ar 234s had to slow down to land, and British fighters broke through a screen of defending Bf 109s to down two of the Blitz bombers and damage a third for the loss of two Tempest Vs and a Spitfire. The USAAF's longstanding policy of neutralizing the Luftwaffe included a B-24 mission against the airfield at Achmer on March 21, 1945, followed by Mustang ground attacks. Ten Ar 234s lay in ruins after the American attack, and eight more of the German jets were damaged.[26] It was a curious time, with fast Arados doing limited damage to the Allies even as slower Allied fighters impeded the German jet pilots' freedom of movement and ultimately overwhelmed the jet bombers by sheer numbers.

The USAAF weighed a gamble in January 1945, as intelligence specialists predicted the war could be won with existing conventional US fighters if Germany could be defeated by the end of June 1945. But if Germany had any ability to last longer than that, a very real possibility existed that Luftwaffe jet fighters would be available in sufficient quantity to throw Allied air supremacy into jeopardy.[27]

Even as European USAAF commanders clamored for new P-80 Shooting Star jets to counter the German jet threat, in February 1945 Lt Gen Giles told Lt Gen Spaatz that the production tempo of P-80As would increase from one aircraft in that month to 39 by December. Giles predicted the first 30 P-80As would be needed for testing and training in the United States; beyond that number, Spaatz and Eaker should expect Shooting Stars for the ETO and the MTO. The P-80 now enjoyed the same high-level priority for production as the B-29 Superfortress, which was viewed as the implement vital to winning the air war with Japan. Meanwhile, tests were underway to see if a piston-engined P-51 could be fitted with an internal JATO (jet-assisted takeoff) unit to provide intermittent thrust as high as 540 mph at 24,000ft. This hybrid would not meet the test of war; standard P-51s would remain the top fighter at the end of hostilities with Germany.[28]

The paper trail within the USAAF on countering German jet attacks is intriguing for the high-level attention the topic received. One might expect colonels to delegate defensive planning to officers under their command, and while this probably happened in the execution of such plans, nonetheless, the highest-ranking general officers in the USAAF were sharing ideas and tips on how best to combat the jet threat. On January 26, 1945 Lt Gen Barney Giles wrote to Lt Gen Carl Spaatz and offered detailed ideas on air base antiaircraft defense against German jet ground attacks. Lt Gen Giles agreed with an earlier cable from Lt Gen Spaatz expressing concern about airfield jet attacks:

> I think, too, that the Germans, when they have sufficient numbers of jet-propelled planes, will employ them in heavy attacks against our airfields rather than dissipate their power against scattered frontline objectives. Thus, the problem will become more rather than less serious ... It is my opinion that of the available defensive measures, antiaircraft fire, especially that produced by 40mm guns and multiple mount machine guns, offers the most promising means of effective defense until our own jet-propelled aircraft are available. To use our present comparatively slow fighters primarily for defense purposes is to curtail our offensive power.[29]

Lt Gen Giles wrote that the Air Force Board would study available antiaircraft weapons to ensure they were capable of handling high-speed jet targets, "but from the best advice I have received, I believe that antiaircraft weapons, providing they have been suitably modified, will be satisfactory." In the letter, Giles suggested Spaatz ensure his antiaircraft airfield defenses were using M-9 electrical directors (which could also be linked to radar sets, if radar was available). He continued:

> Further, the 40mm automatic weapons should be equipped with the high-speed traversing gears; these are available in limited quantities in your area and more are on the way ... Against low altitude, high speed targets, the antiaircraft must have sufficient warning so that their guns can be pointed in the direction of the target's approach. Tests have shown that the AA OPs should be at least ten miles out from the gun sites.

Each antiaircraft fire unit could only engage one jet at a time, and a jet target would have to be passed from one fire unit to another if not downed by the first unit. Giles noted:

To do this successfully and to engage targets simultaneously antiaircraft defenses must be concentrated and in depth. My antiaircraft advisers state that they consider a minimum of one gun battalion, one automatic weapons battalion, and one-half a searchlight battalion is required for the adequate defense of the average sized airfield.

In the letter, Giles referenced tests conducted against American jets at Palmdale, California, near Muroc Army Airfield where P-59s and P-80s flew.

Ultimately, logistics played a role in countering the perceived German jet menace. Retired Lt Gen Henry Viccellio Sr., chief of the Fighter Section of the Commitments and Requirements Division at USAAF headquarters when jets were a wartime issue, remembered in a 1970 interview: "A lot of people wished, of course, that we had jets. But by the time they came out, we had such a gigantic numerical superiority (in non-jet aircraft) that everybody realized they really weren't going to be able to do anything about the situation anyway."[30]

Maj Gen Donald J. Keirn, wartime chief of the USAAF's Powerplant Laboratory, recalled the gist of an observation he said was made by "Hap" Arnold late in the war: "Along towards the end of the war ... we didn't have a good ... combat jet, and I know Arnold made the comment: 'Well, we would have one if it was apparent that we needed it. But we've got the war about wound up'."[31]

Years after the war, Lt Gen Giles reflected on the USAAF's decision to overwhelm Germany with aircraft and armaments already in full production rather than lose any production tempo by emphasizing American jets:

The main thing was to get that war over with as fast as you could, completely swamp [the Germans]. When the Germans came through with those jets, we talked it over, long and fast about what we should do, about building jets. The decision was made to build up the airplanes that we had in production [such as P-51s], keep building arms, keep the groups fully set up, keep organizing the thing, and completely swamp the German air force with what we had, and not go into the jet business.[32]

The specter of German jet fighters with speeds far in excess of USAAF piston-engined fighters of the day caused USAAF top leadership to take notice in 1944 and to proffer suggestions for dealing with the threat posed by the jets. As the war pushed into 1945, the success of Allied bombing campaigns against German petroleum production had the effect of grounding much of the conventionally powered Luftwaffe for lack of gasoline. But the German jets remained at least somewhat viable due to their use of J-2 coal-oil fuel. The USAAF was not forced into night bombing to avoid the available German jets, and piston-engined fighters found ways to down the speedier jets. But the mere existence of German jets in 1944 caused the USAAF to focus on them with contingency coping plans.

Me 262s MULTIPLIED

Data available in the postwar analysis of the European war showed upward trending production of Me 262 jet fighters:

Month	Production total
Aug 1944	5
Sep 1944	19
Oct 1944	52
Nov 1944	101
Dec 1944	124
Jan 1945	160
Feb 1945	280

It was a hard-fought race to the finish, but logistics and production favored the United States.[33]

There were other demons keeping the USAAF's leadership on the alert during the war with Germany. In his role as the ultimate steward of American strategic bombardment policy, Gen Arnold is said to have worried over the possibility of Germany perfecting a proximity fuze for detonating antiaircraft explosives. Use of such a fuze was envisioned to be either via traditional flak artillery fired from the surface, or alternately as a bomb fuze for weapons that would be dropped by Luftwaffe aircraft flying higher than the heavy bomber formations. Gen Earle Partridge, former deputy commander of the Eighth Air Force, characterized the potential destructiveness of German flak had they perfected a proximity fuze: "They would have given our formation a drubbing from the ground ... if their antiaircraft artillery had been fitted for the proximity fuze, we would have had a rough time indeed."[34]

For the week ending February 17, 1945, Lt Gen Spaatz received a weekly activity report from USSTAF which stated that the intelligence community believed it was virtually impossible for Germany to reach production of a proximity fuze in less than six months. With the European war's outcome increasingly hopeful for the Allies in less than that time, this estimate was received with relief. "Hap" Arnold's chronicler Murray Green said, "Arnold was very much afraid of the proximity fuze in German hands because it would have been a potent weapon against the bomber box [formation] in the hands of German fighters."[35]

Lt Gen Spaatz, knowing of "Hap" Arnold's concerns about the enemy perfecting a proximity fuze, interrogated Reichsmarshal Hermann Göring about it on May 10, 1945 during a two-hour grilling of the former Luftwaffe chief by several general officers and others who were invited. Spaatz asked Göring: "Have you any knowledge of a proximity fuze?" Göring replied, "Yes, in three or four months there would have been production." Spaatz wondered if the Germans had shared proximity fuze designs with the Japanese. "I do not think so," Göring said, "because it was not yet in production and we never gave them anything unless it was in production. The Japanese have had the designs of the Me 262 for some time."[36]

The nearly completed German proximity fuze, like the only partially realized jet fighter force, was a potential disaster avoided only by Germany's timely capitulation. The era of massed bombardment formations that was brought to its epitome by the Eighth Air Force over Germany would soon become untenable in a postwar world equipped with better defenses.

USAAF planners contemplated the need for US airfields in Germany and surrounding European countries during the occupation period, which seemed increasingly inevitable in the spring of 1945. Although elements of the German army and air force showed occasional resilience that year, the momentum favored an Allied victory. In mid-March 1945, USAAF planners envisioned a presence of combat aircraft in and around Germany "to maintain the required air threat and otherwise fulfill their responsibilities for participation in the enforcement of the terms of surrender of Germany." So many years after the war, it may seem odd that Americans in the spring of 1945 believed Germany might not go quietly in surrender. A March 15, 1945 planning document discussed training and basing requirements to ensure that "the entire Occupation Air Force can be kept at peak efficiency, ready to strike at any time as a single force against Germany." Nor was the need for occupation bases made strictly on military requirements, as the March 15 document noted:

[T]here will be important psychological advantages in encircling Germany with mutually supporting strategic air bases located in various surrounding Allied countries. The establishment of such bases will impress upon the minds of the German people the fact that the United Nations are still united in contributing to the enforcement of peace in Europe. Through the years of war, the power of Allied strategic air bombardment has been a symbol to the

German people of overwhelming Allied might. The continuing threat of this special form of attack against Germany will be a weighty reminder to the German people of the dangers of any effort to thwart the strict enforcement of the terms of surrender.[37]

The March 15 memorandum included requirements for Very Heavy Bomber (such as B-29 Superfortress) airfields. Interestingly, the postwar demarcation of Germany and the ensuing compartmentalizing of East Germany by the Soviet Union altered the basic posture on US security in the region. The American occupation forces quickly administered the destruction of Luftwaffe assets not required for technical study, and the growing threat posed by former ally Russia affected the nature of US air forces that would be kept in Europe. In addition to American fighter units to be based in and near Germany, only a few bomb groups were kept in Germany into 1946. The emphasis, especially during and after the Berlin crisis of 1948–49, was on placing some nuclear-capable B-29s close enough to give the Soviets pause, while keeping the bombers far enough distant to protect them. Rotating B-29 training operations to the United Kingdom served this need.

Developing in late 1944 and still valid as the war drew to a close in 1945, the Allies delineated the need to dismantle Luftwaffe administrative structure quickly. A directive stated: "There will be an early dissolution of the ... Air Force, and all general staffs, reserve corps, military academies, military training, administrative agencies performing military functions." The directive specified all manner of German aircraft communications and meteorological systems were to be taken under control and safeguarded. Furthermore, "all German or German controlled aeronautical experimental, development, and research establishments, testing stations, or laboratories [are] to be seized, taken under control and occupied." Documents show the impending demise of the Third Reich was anticipated, and plans were underway for dealing with a vanquished Germany.[38]

The specter of German jet fighters was all the more menacing in light of the Luftwaffe's demonstrated use of large cannons in some of its aircraft employed as bomber interceptors. The damage that could be inflicted by a single round of 30mm ammunition was demonstrated on airframe hulks by the British, and the results were shared with the Air Technical Section of USSTAF on June 12, 1944. In several photos, the overwhelming catastrophic damage caused by one round of German Mk 108 30mm ammunition was sobering. In one view, a Halifax wing section smokes profusely; its structure looks disturbingly similar to that of a USAAF B-17. In another image, the impact location on the aft fuselage of a derelict Spitfire no longer exists.

1

2

3

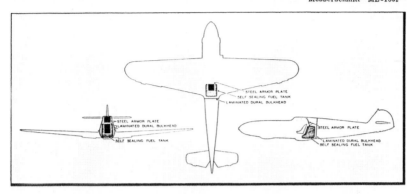

OFFENSIVE AND DEFENSIVE EQUIPMENT

8

9

10

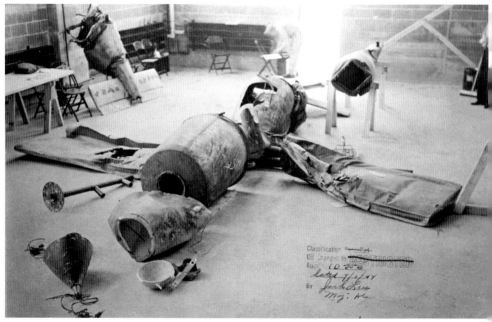

11

12

13

14

15

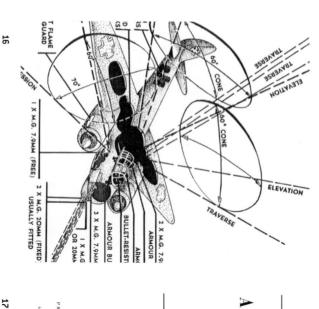

T FLAME GUARD

...SSION

1 X M.G. 7.9MM (FREE)

2 X M.G. 20MM (FIXED) USUALLY FITTED

3 X M.G. 7.9MM

1 X M.G OR 20MM

ARMOUR BU...

ARMOUR-RESIST...

ARMOUR

ARM...

2 X M.G. 7.9...

60° CONE   60° CONE

TRAVERSE   TRAVERSE   TRAVERSE

ELEVATION   ELEVATION

60°   70°

AIRCRAFT EVALUATION
REPORT

U. S. ARMY AIR FORCES, WASHINGTON, D. C.

GERMAN

MESSERSCHMITT-109F

PREPARED BY MATERIEL COMMAND, ENGINEERING DIVISION
WRIGHT FIELD, DAYTON, OHIO

APPROVED BY THE OFFICE OF THE ASSISTANT CHIEF OF THE
AIR STAFF, INTELLIGENCE, WASHINGTON, D. C.

PRINTED BY THE AIR SERVICE COMMAND

19

20

21

24

25

26

29

30

31

32

33

34

35

36

37

38

39

40

41

42

A Blenheim bomber fuselage is buckled and useless. Clearly, hits equaled destruction. The cat-and-mouse struggle between USAAF heavy bombers and Luftwaffe fighters was constantly in evolution, and if the Luftwaffe could grow its modern fighter presence, the Eighth Air Force would be increasingly imperiled. All this was not lost on USAAF planners who sought, and largely succeeded in achieving, the destruction of the Luftwaffe's effectiveness with means that ranged from petroleum starvation, to factory targeting, to frequent and recurring airfield suppression.

Nor did the intelligence gathering stop with weapons; Luftwaffe personal flying gear was the object of a September 1944 USSTAF study that characterized a German summer-weight knitted flying helmet and throat microphone:

> The helmet itself is simple in design and can be easily and rapidly produced. The earphones are of very good quality and reception excellent. The Laryngaphones are very good and the arrangement of fastening is much better than the American. Once the German Laryngaphone is set in place around the vocal cords it will not slip about as the American does. The German Laryngaphone however is thicker and not very comfortable but it does give excellent results.[39]

The wartime American intelligence gathering and interpreting enterprise in Europe was remarkable for its sophisticated approach as well as its rapid maturation. From the overt entry of the United States into the European conflict in early 1942, a generally inexperienced and relatively unsophisticated USAAF information-gathering operation had to quickly embrace the rationale for global intelligence, the need for which varied greatly from operational theater to theater. In the European war, especially initially, American efforts relied heavily on the British model. Differences in force structure precluded a simple copying of the British intelligence system, yet American information files are filled with British intelligence documents shared with their American partners throughout the war and into the occupation of a defeated Germany. Early strategic bombing operations conducted by the Eighth Air Force beginning in the summer of 1942 quickly revealed the importance of up-to-date intelligence on their German adversaries. Useful information ranged from descriptions of lucrative targets, to anticipated antiaircraft defenses. The Eighth Air Force was executing for the first time the strategic bombing doctrine it had been championing for years, and the need for theater-specific reconnaissance manifested itself. Lt Gen Ira Eaker later reported that when he brought the nascent Eighth Air

Force to England in 1942, almost no target information or other valuable information on Luftwaffe strength and disposition was available in the United States. The USAAF would have to catch up quickly.[40]

Leading up to America's entry into World War II, the exploitation of intelligence information has been characterized as fragmented in the US. The concept of intelligence as a vital study of enemy war-making capabilities, and strategic ways to hinder those capabilities from the air, was gaining credibility in the USAAF, but the service needed to learn a lot, and quickly, once America entered the war. The unified analysis of seemingly disparate pieces of intelligence information would quickly gain emphasis during the war. Such early weaknesses and a lack of information sharing between American armed services prompted the quick post-Pearl Harbor creation of groups including the Joint Strategic Committee and the Joint Army–Navy Planning Committee which augmented the Joint Intelligence Committee in January 1942. That March, the War Department reorganized to create three autonomous commands – Army Ground Forces and Army Air Forces plus Services of Supply (later Army Service Forces). With this reorganization came authorization for traditional Army G-2 Intelligence to increase its USAAF staffing (A-2, or Assistant Chief of Air Staff, Intelligence). The needs and efficiencies of USAAF intelligence gathering led to the March 1943 alignment of air intelligence functions into five divisions: Operational Intelligence, Informational Intelligence, Counter Intelligence, Combat Training and Liaison, and Historical. But the A-2 USAAF intelligence operation sometimes felt subordinated by the traditional G-2 intelligence service of the Army, especially early in the war. Air intelligence officers clamored for more access more quickly to the information they believed was needed to make informed and timely decisions. British observers noted in March 1942 that, on occasion, three different conclusions were arrived at by A-2, G-2, and British intelligence experts on the same topic. This information helped clear a path for Gen Arnold to authorize USAAF A-2 officers to go on temporary duty with the British Air Ministry for the purpose of expediting useful bombardment targeting information, aviation technical data, and other useful ETO information. The incubation of sophisticated USAAF intelligence on German topics was at work.[41]

The USAAF intel organization was charged with the responsibility of keeping the USAAF commander, Gen Arnold, apprised of the latest developments while also keeping theater commanders informed so they could make decisions about strategy and tactics. The Operational Intelligence Division's target information function prepared air estimates and air objectives. Air estimates were broadly focused studies of German economic and industrial systems considered important to Germany's ability to wage war. Air objective folders gathered images and data on specific likely military and industrial targets. The folders were an aid to mission planning and crew briefing. The intelligence was distilled still further, giving bomber aircrews target charts showing specific information such as landmarks to assist in acquiring and bombing the target.[42]

The bustling intelligence community serving USSTAF later in the war was a growth industry. In 1942, USAAF officers relied heavily on British intelligence. Though American information gathering grew during the war in Europe, the evidence points to a strong element of British information used to the advantage of the USAAF throughout the war. For American information about Germany, Eighth Air Force, working closely in league with the British Air Ministry, was the key source. Yet intelligence on targets in North Africa and elsewhere in the Mediterranean fell more to an American A-2 presence without the level of British help available in England. Interestingly, by September 1942 USAAF intelligence products made in North Africa included studies of neutral Spain. A-2 chose to be proactive in learning about Spain in case that country would end its neutrality by joining the Axis powers after the Operation *Torch* Allied landings in northwest Africa. Spain chose to remain neutral.[43]

MORE AND BETTER INTEL OFFICERS

As the USAAF embraced the need for more and better-trained intelligence officers, the school for such officers in the United States was established in April 1942, with initial students chosen from among civilians who had shown themselves adept at varied professions. These experienced, and often older, students were commissioned into the service with little military background. Some were chosen to become instructors for later classes at the school. The need for increasing numbers of intelligence officers coincided with some difficult birthing pains for the school, as the students who were tapped to be instructors were often the top students, who really wanted operational assignments. As the need for more students grew, the newer and larger classes were composed of officers, a few of whom did not always embody the professional enthusiasm of the first classes of civilians, and morale at the school slumped. An upward trend in school morale and output was noted in 1943 with the alignment of the intelligence school under AC/AS Intelligence and away from the more generic Technical Training Command. Experience gained in more than a year of war showed up in the school in the form of instructors with previous field experience, plus a stream of real-world intelligence material with which to train the students.[44]

More than 9,000 intelligence officers were graduated by the USAAF during World War II. The expanding global war effort saw various combat commands clamoring for more intelligence officers, although at other times these new intel officers occasionally found themselves underutilized, placed in other administrative slots. But some units, like the Eighth Air Force, recognized both the need for trained intelligence officers and the need for even more theater-specific training once new intel officers arrived in England. The VIII Bomber Command Intelligence School had begun as early as May 1942, with the USAAF in England quickly realizing the magnitude of the intelligence issue. The nature of American daylight bombing operations was said to provide more opportunities for intelligence gathering and interpretation than did night RAF operations, making it important for Eighth Air Force to cultivate a larger corps of intelligence officers with theater-specific knowledge. It has been said that the resulting cooperation between American intelligence officers and their British counterparts represents an outstanding level of synergy. In the first year of war for America, 1942, reliance on British intelligence structure was vital. The British had the mechanism in place to deliver real-world intelligence on German topics, and the Americans benefited by learning from their British hosts. As the European war progressed, the USAAF assumed responsibility for more of its own intelligence gathering and interpretation, but not in competition with the British and not in isolation. The presence of American officers in British intelligence organizations, and the assignment of British officers to USAAF intelligence offices, outlasted the notion of indoctrination of new officers, and was in fact evidence of a remarkable level of cooperation. In areas like signals intelligence, the Americans continued to rely on the British capability, there being no need to try to duplicate its efficacy.[45]

If Anglo-American cooperation was a hallmark of intelligence gathering in the war against Germany, some specific areas nonetheless required uniquely American solutions. The whole USAAF concept of daylight precision bombing as opposed to night saturation bombing placed different demands on the collection and exploitation of information about Germany and its potential targets. Eighth Air Force daylight mission accuracy was enhanced by the development of perspective maps that gave bombardiers and navigators clear replicas of what they should be seeing en route to a target, instead of using only the traditional high-oblique view of a normal map. Landmarks could be emphasized on these maps where they might be harder to find in the clutter of a black-and-white aerial reconnaissance photograph. Perspective map drawings showed the target from distances of seven and 15 miles, and six different approaches at 26,000ft in altitude. The perspective maps were the creation of a former architect and draftsman who became an intelligence officer in the Eighth Air Force, Capt Gerald K. Geerlings. If such detail was of no use to nocturnal RAF bombers, it was useful in broad daylight. Similarly, Eighth Air Force planners came to realize the British use of target intelligence for night missions was less specific than that required to determine the most significant precision daylight targets. For target development and analysis, the USAAF developed more detailed rationale on the impact the destruction of targets could have on German war-making capability. This included specific locations and vulnerabilities that could be exploited. Sometimes, the desired intelligence came from creative sources. An Eighth Air Force attack on an occupied Renault factory making military transports for Germany made use of detailed plans of the plant that showed the locations of specific production functions. Those plans were held by the company's insurer in the United Kingdom.[46]

USAAF intelligence activities, especially in the first half of the war, sometimes suffered from a lack of available trained personnel in adequate numbers, congestion in shipping that created logistical hurdles to be surmounted in sending German aircraft and materiel to the United States for study, shifting priorities, and the ravages of souvenir hunters and looters.[47] The USAAF frequently was the beneficiary of German aircraft delivered by British captors during the war.

Even as the USAAF nurtured its German aircraft analytical skills, another of its major intelligence tools – photographic reconnaissance – owed much to the sophisticated model developed in Great Britain and shared with selected USAAF officers in 1941 before the United States entered the war. If precision daylight strategic bombing was a distinctly American enterprise, it was underpinned by varied levels of British intelligence activities that informed the Americans and helped the USAAF work with the best and most recent data possible. The USAAF did not work in a vacuum in Europe.[48]

CHAPTER 4

POSTWAR SPOILS

"Hitler said it was no good to bomb American planes because more of them would come like bees," the imprisoned Reichsmarschall Hermann Göring explained, in answer to a question from Lt Gen Hoyt S. Vandenberg, Ninth Air Force commander, during his May 10, 1945 interview with high-ranking American military leaders. Though some of Göring's comments in his interview may have been called self-serving, there is a fundamental truth to this observation. As Germany scrambled to develop and field weapons with a high degree of technical superiority, they were simply overwhelmed by the sheer volume of American warplanes. The end of the war promised an unusual new synergy as the Americans sought to leverage their legendary industrial capacity by absorbing promising new Luftwaffe technologies now laid bare with the fall of Germany.[1]

The sinews of war became the curiosities of peace as Americans carted quantities of German aircraft back to the United States in 1945. The USAAF's Air Disarmament Division, created in October 1944, executed a two-fold plan that saw some examples of German aircraft technology saved for examination, while silent fields of former Luftwaffe combat aircraft were summarily scrapped to prevent their use again.

The rapid, wholesale destruction of the Luftwaffe was in some respects more symbolic than strategic; how could a defeated Germany possibly resurrect itself with the weapons that just recently lost a war, in an age when new technologies rapidly outmoded the operational aircraft of 1945?

SYSTEMATIC DISARMAMENT OF GERMANY

The reduction of the German war machine to remove any offensive capacity was not an afterthought. The Allies each had an interest in seeing this accomplished expeditiously. Root causes for the rise of fascism in post-World War I Germany were debated, but in the grip of 1944 combat on the Continent, at least some consensus existed for the rapid demobilization of Germany following the expected victory. What was uncertain was the duration of fighting within Germany as the Allies advanced. Even as the war raged ever closer to Berlin, the Allies had to initiate disarmament policy for the German territory and assets already acquired. That disarmament had two main thrusts: the destruction of Germany's war-making capability, plus the selective gathering of pieces of German technology that might be of use to the victors. The United States delineated a specific Air Disarmament policy; all of this was unprecedented in previous wars. The summer of 1944 was aging on the calendar as the Americans and British made inroads into German-held French territory. The first notional USAAF interest in German aviation equipment was the seizing of technologies and equipment for study. As the magnitude of Luftwaffe equipment became apparent, the second role of air disarmament – the destruction of the bulk of the Luftwaffe – became manifest.[2]

Disarming the Luftwaffe required a working knowledge of the German Air Force and its equipment. In Britain in 1944, the Eighth Air Force Composite Command and its Combat Crew Replacement Centers were charged with the responsibility of teaching replacement aircrew members about the Luftwaffe. The knowledge of the Composite Command instructors made them the natural choice to become the cadre for Luftwaffe disarmament. The training operation moved, on October 8, 1944, from Eighth Air Force to USSTAF, taking the name Air Disarmament Command (Provisional) at that time. Typical Wing, Group and Squadron structure emanated from the new command. The Air Disarmament Command had four major areas of responsibility:

1. The physical separation of war materiel from the personnel of the Luftwaffe, including supervision of Luftwaffe compliance with surrender terms, and the supervision and control of German Air Force units and personnel until they could be given to Allied ground forces for ultimate disposition.
2. The administration of Luftwaffe personnel and units until they were given over to ground forces for discharge.
3. The gathering of intelligence about the materiel, operation, and administration of the German Air Force.
4. The seizure, security, inventory, operation, maintenance, and disposal of all Luftwaffe war materiel and structures.[3]

The personnel of the USAAF's air disarmament operation spent time in England familiarizing themselves even further with what little captured German equipment was available. Identification of German aircraft, and uniforms, was emphasized. Courses in German language, German history, and the psychology of the German people were held. The air disarmament mission was given to Ninth Air Force Service Command on January 23, 1945, accompanied by the deactivation of the Air Disarmament Command. As the disarmament teams continued preparations for heading to the Continent, technicians were identified who had specific experience, such as armament and ordnance, radio and radar, medical, weather, photography and personnel equipment. To help the USAAF teams as they encountered Luftwaffe equipment, catalogs were created that explained German nomenclature and other useful information. Photos of German equipment, sometimes depicting the only damaged battlefield pick-ups then available, were included to help field teams identify what they encountered on the Continent. Special attention was given to booby traps, and this proved vital as a number of German aircraft had been rigged with destructive devices. The intelligence sections of both Eighth and Ninth air forces made it possible for the targets section, created in November 1944, to map out a plan for disarmament teams to use, providing the team with sites of military importance such as factories, airfields, and warehouses. Useful information on target sites of interest came from British sources as well as from interviewed German prisoners, some of whom proved willing to discuss specific locations.[4]

By March 1, 1945, 1,500 targets of interest had been catalogued for the disarmament teams. In the context of air disarmament, "target" meant a site to be visited by a disarmament team, with any German military assets properly secured pending Allied use or destruction. This orderly list of targets was rendered incomplete that month when American ground forces aggressively swung north, occupying territory that would fall under the Soviet Zone later. This change of events happened when German resistance weakened unexpectedly once the Allies crossed the Rhine River. Though beneficial in the overall prosecution of the war, this rapid advance demanded quick action by disarmament teams to identify targets of interest in the newly occupied territory. The disarmament teams had but a few weeks to prepare target lists for this newfound opportune region. Moreover, this territory proved to be especially rich in German air assets, much of which could easily have been overlooked had not the disarmament teams expanded their target roster to cover this windfall. The disarmament specialists believed the areas that later became Soviet-occupied territory could not have been exploited so thoroughly by the Americans without the advance descriptive work done in haste by the disarmament targeting specialists. Likewise, technologies – especially radar and radio – were found in Austria and Czechoslovakia when American forces rushed in.[5]

The prosecution of the war on the Continent in 1945 was fluid, and posed planning problems for those who were charged with the responsibility of securing and assessing German technologies. Early in the year, Germany's Rhine defenses slowed the Allied advance from the west, leading to a temporary stagnation of available new intelligence targets for exploitation. But the defeat of these German defenses and the accelerating offense in April and into early May created a new set of problems for intelligence inspectors as well as Army units charged with the responsibility of safeguarding captured German assets. As the war rolled forward, an intelligence report later observed:

> the combat elements which were charged with the seizure and safeguarding of intelligence targets were also faced with major problems. The necessity for protecting extended lines of communication, moving supplies and equipment, handling vast numbers of prisoners, and sustaining the offensive, imposed heavy burdens. The burden of military operations required that CIOS [Combined Intelligence Objectives Subcommittee] demands made on the combat elements, for transportation, administration facilities, and personnel for guard troops, be kept to the minimum.[6]

The logistics of finding, securing, evaluating, and moving or disposing of German materiel was made more difficult than had been anticipated because Allied bombing had caused so much relocation and dispersal of known or expected sites. The CIOS report explained: "During early 1945 it became increasingly apparent that many targets would not be found at their original locations, nor would they be conducting their expected activity due to wholesale evacuation and bomb destruction." Pressure from advancing Russian Army units on the Eastern Front contributed to the general dislocation of German intelligence targets as well. The rapid denouement of the European war necessitated some changes in how intelligence targets were handled, and for CIOS this meant consolidating earlier target listings into seven groups, one of which was the Air Force Group (another, for example, was the Navy group). Group 4 targets – those in the Air Force Group – included five subtopic areas: Jet Propulsion, Aircraft, Aircraft Engines, Instruments and Equipment, and Bomb Sights. Elsewhere, Rockets and Rocket Fuels, and Directed Missiles were in Group 2 along with Artillery and other army weapons. This division reinforces postwar employment of German rocket scientists in the United States, initially under the auspices of the Army, and later with the nascent NASA.[7]

CIOS represented one aspect of the overall intelligence efforts against Germany. As the work of American and Allied organizations continually shifted from intelligence gathering to mass dismantling of the German war machine in the summer of 1945, CIOS was dissolved on July 13, 1945. CIOS considered one of its achievements to be giving the American and British scientists information on German state-of-the-art technology to permit the Allies "to measure the relative status of British and American technical achievements as contrasted with those of Germany."[8] The discovery and exploitation of German technological breakthroughs by the Allies is immense. Anecdotal descriptions of some of the interesting items with aerospace applications will help to plumb the depth and breadth of this enterprise.

CIOS reported that "German radar development was generally less advanced than similar work in the United Kingdom and United States." Nonetheless, some German developments caught the attention of the Allied investigators:

> The "Schornsteinfeger" project of radar camouflage is of definite interest. German scientists were discovered to have developed various types of anti-radar coverings which would prevent radar detection. These coverings were applied and used operationally in coating submarine "Schnorkels". Still further applications were contemplated by German experts engaged on this project.[9]

The USAAF had already noted that painted aircraft tended to produce a smaller radar signature than did natural-metal aircraft, yet late in the war the Americans opted for bare-metal aircraft for a variety of other reasons. But the Germans were deliberately developing coatings to thwart radar detection – employing stealth technology decades before it was in vogue.

German improvements to continuous wave transmission navigational aids yielded greater accuracy and range than the Allies had previously achieved. German wartime developments in infrared night-vision devices exceeded Allied efforts, the CIOS report noted, and "their technique was in advance of that of the Allies." To make Allied interdiction of German vehicles more difficult, the report explained:

> infrared was used for night vision to permit night driving of military vehicles, and night sighting and aiming of weapons under conditions of total black-out. Another application was in infrared searchlights used for the protection of harbor entrances. An entire German combat element had been equipped with infrared and trained in its use for employment on the Eastern front.

(American development and use of infrared rifle scopes saw the fielding *c.* April 1945 of about 150 T3 carbines equipped with infrared scopes to combat nocturnal Japanese raids on Okinawa, but major developments in infrared technologies continued after the war, including adaptation for aircraft use.) Foretelling postwar American upper-atmosphere experimentation with captured V2 rockets, the CIOS summary noted: "German scientists had conducted extensive ionospheric investigations. The bulk of their research data has been obtained by Allied scientists."

Guided-missile development in Germany proved a boon to postwar Allied work, the CIOS noted: "Much valuable information on the use of electronic control telemetering equipment in guided missiles of all kinds has been obtained." In fact, "the exploitation of intelligence concerning German directed missiles and rocket development was one of the primary objectives of CIOS." Though accounts vary on the way in which German rocket scientists were ultimately infused into American postwar efforts, the CIOS report held its own victorious version:

> It was not until the entire Peenemünde staff, together with most of their files and much of their equipment, were seized at dispersal points in southern Germany that the full story of German V-weapon research and development became available. The resultant intelligence has proven to be one of the most significant and important discoveries in the European Theater.

Presciently, the opinions of unnamed German rocket authorities were cited in the 1945 CIOS report:

> German authorities responsible for this work have expressed the opinion that the V1 and V2 were crude and elementary weapons. They have compared the present state of directed missile design with the technical status of the aircraft industry on the eve of World War I. These same authorities confidently predict that a continuation of present research in this field for another decade would change the strategical and tactical concepts of modern war.

The CIOS report gave tantalizing accounts of German missile efforts and theories, including:

> the latest model of the A-9 which was capable of a 3,400 mile per hour speed and a range of 2,400 miles. The A-9 was an improved development of the V2 or A-4, and was equipped with wings thereby enabling it to level off at a height of 70,000ft. One model of this missile was equipped with a Lorin tube which provided propulsion at the peak of the trajectory [probably a reference to a true ramjet, invented by Rene Lorin].

The A-9 thus equipped was forecast to have a range of 2,400 miles. While purely theoretical at that point, the A-9 and derivatives were expected to be able to attain altitudes of 60 miles and speeds of 7,300 ft/sec – these were intriguing notions at that time. The German designers of these missiles said improved radio control would give them an accuracy of plus or minus 150ft – far better than that of traditional V2s and V1s, and very lethal especially in the context of nuclear weapons delivery, which the Germans were contemplating. The CIOS report showed little restraint in its description of German guided-missile plans:

> German scientists engaged in directed missiles envisaged important commercial applications of the long range missile. Experiments had already been conducted on piloted models. Missiles capable of trans-Atlantic crossings in approximately 40 minutes were found on design boards and scale models were undergoing wind tunnel tests. Amazing performances were considered practical because of the lessened atmospheric resistance and gravitational pull in stratospheric regions.

This passage in the CIOS report is most illuminating for the high expectations it suggests, rather than any actual proven technologies it represented at that stage in the discovery of German missile work. Even though largely theoretical in 1945, the promise of German rocket scientists would be actualized in the United States in the following decades.

The CIOS report contemplated German development of nuclear weapons, which were not brought to maturity in Germany, yet were in work at war's end:

> Of particular significance were the statements, made by German experts in the rocket and controlled missile field, that much of the priority accorded their work by the German High Command was in anticipation of the use of atomic explosives. These authorities stated that KWI [probably a reference to the Kaiser Wilhelm Institute of Physics] had repeatedly assured Hitler that an atomic explosive would be available for use within a comparatively short time. During the last months of work by the Peenemünde staff, V-weapons were designed with much smaller warheads. Quite possibly this trend was in anticipation of the successful development of a German atomic explosive.

The supposition that German atomic warheads would be smaller than conventional explosives seems counter to the large size of early US atomic bombs, but the discussion of combined German atomic bomb and missile developments remains intriguing.

German aircraft survival and safety gear came under scrutiny, and some praise, from the CIOS in its report:

The field of German aero-medical research was the subject of energetic investigation by United States and British specialists. The emergency oxygen bail-out system employed by the Luftwaffe in high altitude flying was regarded as of particular interest. This system permitted the use of the same oxygen mask by the pilot after leaving the plane. The device consisted of eight tubular bottles of oxygen connected in series by means of high pressure tubing. A three-way switch was employed which provided for normal supply, automatic disconnection prior to bail-out, and switching to the bail-out or emergency supply prior to parachute descent. As a result of this method, delays and complications arising from the necessity of changing masks prior to leaving the plane are eliminated.

German ejection seats pioneered the industry at the time: "The Germans had developed ejection seats to permit pilots to leave high speed aircraft without injury. This equipment operated with a cordite charge which expelled the pilot from the cockpit so that his body was prevented from coming in contact with the tail surface or vertical fin of the plane." German parachutes incorporated developments that ultimately led to the importation of their design, and designers, to the United States. The CIOS document stated:

Much information was obtained concerning new types of parachutes developed by the enemy. These types included the non-pendulating parachute which was designed to equalize air turbulence on either side of the 'chute and thus avoid the possibility of accidental collapse and failures [such failures could occur in conventional parachute designs] ... Another development was the shock-free parachute consisting of a small pilot 'chute of air permeable construction to cushion the initial shock of release prior to opening of the main 'chute. A third type of parachute is known as the ribbon 'chute; this design provided for variable air orifices so that the rate of descent can be controlled.[10]

With denial of petroleum to Germany being a major part of American air offensive strategy, it is not surprising that German scientists excelled at developing new and perhaps more efficient means of extracting usable fuels from available materials. German shale-oil distillation was one such exploration, as was hydrogenation of solid fuels. Allied investigation determined that some, but not all, of this German fuel technology had been shared with Japan. "Intelligence obtained by CIOS investigators concerning this interchange of information, including details of locations and capacities of Japanese plants, was promptly communicated to the proper authorities for use in the air offensive against Japan," the CIOS report noted.

CIOS documentation on German jet engine developments included high-speed ducting improvements: "An important design feature for which full data has been obtained is that of a center rod placed in the air duct. This device minimized pressure build-up and eliminated shock waves." Also discussed was the unfinished German DFS 346 rocket-powered research aircraft. Claims were bandied about stating it would have a top speed of 1,250 mph (although in a subsequent incarnation in the postwar Soviet Union, it never exceeded 560 mph in a test program beset with mishaps). Nonetheless, the DFS 346 was the result of German desires to use a real aircraft in free air to validate or dispute the results of high-speed wind-tunnel testing, something NACA advocated in the US even for slow-speed tunnel comparison verifications. The CIOS summary also noted German developments in fuel and water injection for turbojet engines. NACA studied water injection in turbojets later, in 1947.

Among the claims made by the CIOS was the acquisition of a listing of names, addresses and technical specialties for "approximately 15,000 of Germany's leading technical men." The depth and breadth of postwar American use of German specialists in science and industry was great. In the September 1945 CIOS summary, more than 400 reports were listed as published by CIOS at that time. These include wide-ranging topics other than aviation-related ones, but also include such titles as *Aeronautical Activities and Darmstadt, German Controlled Missiles, Lechfield Airfield, Interrogation of Bruckmann and Hagen on B.M.W. Jet Engines, Discovery of the Luftwaffe Archives, Messerschmitt Production Plans with Special Reference to the 262 Program, Radar and Controlled Missiles*, and many others of interest.[11]

The 1945 CIOS summary of its intelligence findings is interesting for the technical developments it catalogs as well as for the way in which it characterizes some of these technologies. Coming so soon after the acquisition of this German information, it appears that the CIOS report may have inadvertently added to the mythology surrounding German technical genius by repeating some performance claims that later were found to be wanting. Nonetheless, it is a document that captures many of the diverse German developments of interest to the Allies.

Disarmament reconnoitering teams followed in close proximity to the advancing armies on the Continent, sometimes even outdistancing the infantry. These advance disarmament teams assessed what kind of follow-on work would be required to process the German assets at a given target site. The air disarmament specialists had color-coded lists of Luftwaffe items to be treated in different ways. The Red List explained what items were wanted for technical intelligence. The Blue List tallied German materiel that American forces could immediately put to use prosecuting the war. (Jury-rigged 285-liter German fighter drop tanks were tried on some USAAF P-47s on the Continent with plumbing modifications made by the 10th Air Depot Group. Anecdotally, some Ninth Air Force P-47 pilots said they dropped captured German firebomb canisters, filled with US jellied gasoline.) The Brown List noted materiel that the occupying forces deemed necessary for local German use in occupied territory.[12]

The 54th Air Disarmament Squadron (ADS) was just getting comfortable with its Continental base at Ochey in eastern France in early April 1945 when orders came to move across the border into Darmstadt, Germany. The squadron took up residence in a recently abandoned Luftwaffe base. While some of the men worked on making their new German home as comfortable as possible, others crossed back into France to attend a school on booby traps – an important topic for men who would be called upon to investigate enemy equipment. The rapid advance of the Allied armies into Germany prompted another move for the 54th ADS 85 miles farther into Germany at Mosbach. The latter was the unit's first operational base, with numerous intelligence targets in the area including an underground aircraft engine factory. The squadron inspected 27 intelligence targets in April 1945, including at least four underground or tunnel sites. Aircraft engines, including turbojets found near Acholshausen, were among the cache. The finds also included a dozen Bf 109 fighters near Nassig. Elsewhere, buildings and a tunnel warehouse were uncovered that contained aircraft parts including wings, symptomatic of the German dispersal programs that helped keep aeronautical production alive in the face of relentless Allied bombing. In the last month before German capitulation, American disarmament teams were getting a quick real-world schooling on what to expect in the coming summer.[13]

The 54th ADS began its labors in April with the dismantling of an Me 262 at the airfield at Giebelstadt for shipment to England. At Giebelstadt, "the squadron was first subjected to enemy air action," a squadron summary history recorded. "Three of the members of the squadron wandered into uncaptured territory, much to their surprise. No casualties were suffered but no time was lost in leaving that area."[14]

Around this time, the squadron delved into Bf 109 dispersed production around Wertheim, as explained in an official squadron overview: "The main effort was spent on unravelling the ME-109 complex at Wertheim.

The Mannheim ME-109 plant had been bombed out, so the remains had been dispersed around Wertheim. Here it was a matter of locating machine shops in breweries, barns, etc." German fighter production showed a surprising resilience and staying power, even in the face of overwhelming bombardments.[15]

May 1945 saw the traveling 54th ADS leave its civilian homes in Mossbach for relocation to Augsburg, Germany, where the Americans set up quarters in a large administrative building of the Messerschmitt company. The official history of the 54th ADS for May 1945 explains the move in the jargon of the day: "After a good deal of work on our part, with the assistance of Krauts obtained from AMG [Allied Military Government] we had things fairly organized, including showers."[16]

The move to Augsburg was described in a summary report on the 54th: "This move was made difficult by the number of other army vehicles on the road following the final drive into the redoubt area. Traffic was further snarled by the masses of displaced persons on the move." German roads in the last gasps of the European war were scenes of urgent movements, sometimes slowed by the sheer volume of people with somewhere else to be as Germany collapsed.[17]

At the Messerschmitt headquarters, the men lived in a facility that was itself a lucrative intelligence target. The squadron historical overview noted: "Without leaving the squadron area, there was an abundance of work. Documents were located in the building, covering all phases of activity of the ME Corporation. Contracts with Japan, experimental data on the ME-163 and ME-262 aircraft, plans for new underground factories and complete data on the Enzian Flak Rocket were uncovered." Squadron interpreters screened these documents and passed significant papers on for further use.[18]

The 54th's target list for May 1945 included everything from advanced jet aircraft to repatriated Allied fighters in German markings. Highlights of the list kept by the squadron include:

> Me 262s near Autobahn between Augsburg and Ulm; Airfield near Bad Worishofen (P-47 and Spitfire with Kraut markings.); Farm near Waltershofen used as warehouse for AC parts ... Me 262 fuselages near Dinkelscherben ... Jet engines near Loungen (target of opportunity.); Experimental airfield at Lechfeld. (Me 262s were put in flying condition by our mechs.) ... Experimental test field near Neuburg for Me 262s ... Farm buildings containing AC engines near Ostendorf; ME parts factory at Baumenheim; Me 262 in the Dershing vicinity; ME testing laboratory near Garmish; Airfield with surfaced runway near Landsberg ... Jet aircraft in vicinity of

Odelzhausen; Radar installation in vicinity of Ortlfing; Aircraft near
Rohrenfels ... Radar installation and radar training school near Tander; Radar
installation near Turkenfeld.[19]

The 54th uprooted again on June 2, 1945 for the town of Mühlacker. The
official history for that month noted: "We were all quite happy to be leaving
the large, drab, grey building in Augsburg. Living conditions were far from
good, though we did have showers. For the most part however, men of this
organization shall never forget that place as future days will find them
recounting those memories of just where they were and what they were doing
the day the war ended." In Mühlacker, the Americans interacted with some
occupying French units. In an entry in the unit history that appears to have
been subsequently edited, the text originally read: "We have had several of
the French troops as guests at our movies, hoping that such acts of friendship
will create a better feeling of good will all the way around." The word "better"
has a line through it in the archival copy. When a squadron change of
command took place on June 20, a banquet welcoming the new commander
was held. "Ice cream, cake and wine were served in abundance to all members
of the outfit," the squadron historian observed.[20]

The 54th ADS overview history stated:

It was at Muhlacker that most of the actual disarming was accomplished.
Scrap was removed from numerous targets along with aircraft engines and
other accessories in usable condition. Scrap collecting points were established
and one Brown List Collecting Point set up. Rail cars were unloaded of GAF
equipment ... A final aerial reconnaissance was made of the entire area.[21]

The June squadron history endeavored to capture the wonderment the men
felt when they inspected an experimental Messerschmitt target site at
Lechfeld, about 20 miles from the squadron's erstwhile home at Augsburg:

This might be called a target of opportunity and special operation. The Technical
Team was dispatched under the supervision of M/Sgt. Freiburger, team
commander. The team was composed of the following members of this
organization: S/Sgt. Medved, Sgt. Brumfield, Cpl. Erickson, Cpl. Zurliene, S/
Sgt. Higgins, Cpl. Connors, Pvt. Dunn, Cpl. Olsonoski, Pvt. Strows and Sgt.
Baldachino. Their mission was to learn as much as possible from the German
mechanics about the new jet engines as well as see that everything operated
smoothly, in the reparation of the ME 262s, preparing them to fly. The boys
started to work on ten jet ships that were fairly intact. There were eight ships,

single seated fighters, one two seated job obviously used for instructional purposes and one fighter, the only one of its kind in existence that was equipped with a 50 MM cannon that protruded approximately six feet out in front of the propellerless nose. This fighter was also capable of carrying thirty rounds of 50 MM ammunition. During the course of events that followed at Lechfeld, S/Sgt. Higgins discovered and neutralized a TNT charged, fifteen pound booby trap under the cockpit seat of one ship. Sgt. Brumfield, Cpl. Olsonoski and Cpl. Erickson, our own 54th Air Dis. Sqdn. mechanics were taught by the German mechanics how to start and taxi the jet ships, and were authorized to do so, certainly a thrill for men who had been away from engines for such a long time. On the 10th of June, the ME 262s accompanied by German pilots and mechanics departed from Lechfeld for the States via Paris and Cherbourg where they were to be shipped back by way of aircraft carrier. Sgt. Freiburger and the rest of the boys sort of hated to see them be taken away after the days of ceaseless, untiring effort they had expended in getting them ready to fly. But the job was done, and now they had to be content with rejoining the organization to launch forth on ever new and different Air Disarmament projects.[22]

At least one German Messerschmitt pilot participated in the preparations and movement of the Me 262s from Lechfeld, including training USAAF pilots in a two-place Me 262.

The 54th ADS visited other targets in June, and listed a brief reference to finding an "air cooled 48 cylinder engine at Mannheim." The life and work of air disarmament team members in Germany in the summer of 1945 carried overtones of world events that weighed on the minds of the men. Many anticipated the expeditious completion of disarming Germany would result in sending the men to the Pacific, where war against Japan still raged. Uncertainty over the future of the war was resolved for the men of the 54th ADS on August 14, 1945, at the unusual time of two hours past midnight, according to the squadron history, when the signal to fall into formation was followed with news that the war against Japan had been won. The squadron bar served drinks as the jubilant troops toasted everything from their gallant Pacific compatriots "to the final return of this outfit to the Zone of the Interior" (the United States), as reported in the unit history:

> One could sense for the first time a wave of happiness, an obvious let down of tightened, jangled nerves that seemed to engulf the spirits of all, giving them new hopes and visions of civilian life and cars – wives, sweethearts, parents and friends – all that they had hoped and prayed for in their many months of overseas service. Looming up in the far horizon was home.[23]

The celebratory troops may be forgiven if their work output when daylight rolled around was lighter than normal. "Squadron activities were few and very limited that day," the squadron history recorded, adding: "no one cared – they were happy and all were completely relaxed. Only one day was lost, however, during the celebration. Capt Lepine had previously pre-determined the completion of our targets on the 15th of September. Not a rush job, but one that required steady and ceaseless effort for its fulfillment, so the boys went back to work." For some of the men, overseas service had already exceeded three years. The August squadron history noted:

> The 27th of the month was a happy and long awaited day for 23 members of our unit, when they, including our first sergeant, Charles W. Harasmisz, received orders to depart for the United States, destined to become civilians within a short while. Each man had over 86 points[24] and many had sweated over three years in the ETO.[25]

In four ambitious months, the target list of the 54th ADS showed a shift from refurbishing high-technology German jet fighters to more mundane inspections of factories and at least three scrap dumps as the formerly fierce Luftwaffe was increasingly erased from the countryside.[26] Its tasks finished, the 54th finally relocated to Nellingen, where it stood down. Men with 70 or more points were destined for the US Zone of the Interior; those with fewer than 60 points were transferred to the 492nd Service Group, and those men in between – about 30 in number – were "parceled out to the other squadrons or to Group Headquarters to help in the closing out of the group," the history overview explained."[27]

The US zone of occupation in Germany fortuitously had a fairly even distribution of targets of interest to the air disarmament teams. Part of the thorough scouring of Germany for Luftwaffe assets by US air disarmament specialists was made possible by dividing the US zone into a northern sector administered by the 1st Air Disarmament Wing (Provisional) headquartered in Fulda, and a southern sector handled by the 2nd Air Disarmament Wing (Provisional) based at Kaufbeuren. The air disarmament structure placed four groups and ten squadrons under the wings to administer America's portion of the disarming of the Luftwaffe. A difference in organization between the USAAF and the Luftwaffe meant flak guns and materiel were Luftwaffe obligations in Germany, but their American antiaircraft counterparts were in the ground army. The USAAF air disarmament units received the use of two army antiaircraft units to aid in the identification and disposal of German flak components, including any promising technologies requiring export home for study.[28]

The tons of equipment and documents earmarked by the United States for its further research required substantial logistics chains to manage the gathering and transfer of the materiel out of Europe. The Air Disarmament Division and the Ninth Air Force Service Command (AFSC) established depots at several German airfields and aircraft plants for this purpose. The 10th, 42nd, 44th and 45th Air Depot units began crating and shipping German items in May 1945. To the 10th and 42nd Air Depot units went aircraft and engines, specifically. In addition to priceless aircraft and other pieces, the Allied disarmament effort had to contend with thousands of routine Luftwaffe supply items, some of which had civilian applications in war-torn Germany. Nearly 34,000 tons of Luftwaffe materiel were distributed to the German population by the occupying Allied governments.[29]

With the Allies occupying various parts of Germany, a system of cooperation was instituted, although its uniformity of application may never be truly known. The United States pored over German assets in areas it initially held, even though they would ultimately become the jurisdictions of other Allies. When the transfer of zones to other Allies took place, the Americans knew that some valuable war materiel remained untapped by the USAAF's air disarmament teams. The British, French, and Americans agreed in principle that each country would first meet its own technology needs in its zone, and then inform the other two western Allies of the availability of any excess examples. A history of the air disarmament program said the closest and longest liaison took place between the Americans and the British. The flow of materiel was said to be more from the American Zone to the British, and some Americans documenting air disarmament said this was an indication of the thoroughness of the American disarmament efforts.[30] Pointedly, such liaison between allies was never established between the Americans and the Russians.

For the French, disarmament took on a different perspective. As the postwar French Air Force needed aircraft immediately, they used some German warplanes, including Ju 88 bombers, to fill gaps until other types could be acquired or built. A run of Fw 190s was assembled from parts in France, but some of these proved to be of inferior quality and their service in postwar France was limited. A USAAF air disarmament history published in 1946 noted that "the French are requesting certain serviceable material for the maintenance of their own air force."[31]

With VE Day, a systematic review of intel target locations was undertaken by USAAF disarmament teams. About 3,000 targets were checked by the Americans in zones later to be handed over to the Russians, French, and British for occupying. From June to November 1945, 9,000 targets in the US Zone of occupation were catalogued and indexed.[32]

The availability of Luftwaffe prisoners, especially in the area administered by the 2nd Air Disarmament Wing, was embraced by the Americans as a potential labor pool. It was noted that Germans could be used for disarmament tasks that were considered dangerous to the person performing the job. The 55,000 German military members initially in the custody of the 2nd Air Disarmament Wing included a preponderance – 40,000 – who were processed fairly routinely and turned over to the ground forces for discharge into civilian life. As many as 11,500 of the remainder were transferred to other jurisdictions; some also were known to have escaped. Those who remained were considered difficult cases, such as SS members who were handed over to USSTAF. The job of dispersing the 55,000 Germans was finished by August 1945.[33]

The relocation of German items of technological interest to the United States was handled by USAAF Air Depot groups – the 10th, 42nd, and 45th – who operated packing and crating centers where German materiel was sent. The nature of this work saw the 10th and 42nd Air Depot groups concentrate on complete examples of German aircraft and engines, while the 45th was to handle all kinds of Luftwaffe materiel. The task of the 45th Air Depot Group was made complicated not only by the large variety of German materiel it was expected to process, but also by the fact that turnovers in field personnel in 1945 meant a large volume of everything from flying clothing to radios to aeromedical equipment was summarily sent to the 45th's area, with important identifying paperwork sometimes lost in the shuffle. The chaotic acquisition of so much German materiel was eased by the assignment of more technical specialists to the 45th Air Depot Group's area as early as May 1945.[34]

Airfields stocked with German warplanes meant Luftwaffe ordnance was encountered regularly by disarmament teams. Field teams, not necessarily expert in bomb disposal, reported their findings to the Material Control Section, which had the only assigned bomb disposal experts. The experts indicated those bombs that held technical interest, and they marked them accordingly. Then it was a matter of engaging the services of ordnance crews and equipment in the area to safely move the heavy bombs for shipment to the United States. More than 400 tons of German aerial bombs were earmarked, crated, stenciled, and loaded on train cars for movement.[35]

The work of disarming the Luftwaffe was characterized by a steep learning curve for the men who initiated the effort. After the fall of Germany, some disarmament personnel appeared to have less zeal for the work remaining in the uncertain time between VE and VJ days. Looking ahead to deploying disarmament teams to the Pacific, some units kept their high-time members – those closest to being rotated back to the US for possible discharge – in Germany, so the men with more time remaining to serve would be groomed for Pacific duty. With victory over Japan secured by August, this policy was changed and many men in disarmament units in Germany were scheduled for rapid redeployment to the United States. All this jockeying in the period of only months in 1945 uprooted trained disarmament men and had a negative effect on the expeditious disarming of the Luftwaffe, some said, although the effort, in hindsight, looks to have been remarkably efficient. In August, the headquarters of the Ninth Air Force Service Command, including the Disarmament Division, relocated from Luxembourg City to Erlangen in Germany, placing it nearer to the ongoing action.[36]

As the major wave of air disarmament subsided into the early fall of 1945, the American disarmament units were told to conduct thorough searches of their areas of responsibility for any Luftwaffe material that might have been overlooked; they were to be on the lookout for small targets that might have gone undetected in previous sweeps. For each village and town in the area of responsibility, the air disarmament teams obtained certificates from the burgomeister (or burgomaster) that all Luftwaffe equipment and installations in each burgomeister's area of responsibility had been reported to disarmament units. The burgomeisters were additionally put on notice that they were responsible for reporting any Luftwaffe items discovered later.[37]

The air disarmament teams had reason to be thorough in their searches, and in the demands they placed upon the German burgomeisters. More than once, disarmament teams found items including aircraft engines stashed in barns or otherwise hidden; some Germans hid items to preserve them for the Allies in the frantic closing days of the war when technologies were being destroyed by other Germans who did not want them falling into enemy hands. On some other hidden items, the rationale for their concealment may never be fully known.

Into this winding-down phase of air disarmament, two officers were assigned to track down other items of technical interest as required by USAAF evaluators at Wright Field. Their task – combing Germany in an effort to find the items sought by Wright Field specialists – was all the more difficult since the major tasks of air disarmament and disposal had already been conducted.[38]

In the waning days of air disarmament in Germany, an effort was made to use specialized German machinery to make ribbon-type cargo parachutes before packing up the parachutes and the manufacturing machines for shipment to the US. In yet another beneficial technology transfer, these parachutes and their German designer became postwar residents of the United States, where further iterations yielded parachute designs that influenced cargo drops as well as American space capsule recovery years later (see Chapter Six.)

COUNTING THE WAR BOOTY

The Air Disarmament Division made a list as of March 30, 1946 that depicted its Herculean efforts over the previous year. Luftwaffe equipment described as "new or secret ... of research or experimental value" amounted to 1,894 tons in weight, shipped to Wright Field and other research sites in the United States. The tonnage included aircraft and missiles such as the Me 262, Me 163, V2, V1, Horten flying wings, Ar 234, Bachem Natter, Henschel Hs 293 remotely controlled jet-propelled flying bomb, and Fritz X 1,400kg remotely controlled bomb. Some of these devices, including the Henschel Hs 293, had been captured in the field earlier in the war, but the postwar gathering of so much hardware, documentation, and German technicians must have added depth useful to American researchers. The Air Disarmament Division's 1946 history opined: "These and other similar items returned for study and experiment are contributing greatly to the advancement of Air Force research in new and improved aircraft for civilian and military use as well as other weapons of war."[39]

Another huge tonnage tally – 294 tons – of operational German military equipment was redistributed to US armed forces by Air Disarmament units. Materiel deemed surplus to Allied military needs, and not of an operational military nature, was made available for civilian consumption in Europe. This amounted to 33,787 tons. Not surprisingly, the vast bulk of the processed Luftwaffe equipment, representing a huge 1,077,000 tons, was reduced to scrap. This included about 50,000 tons of neutralized flak guns and equipment given to Army ground forces for safeguarding and disposition.[40]

A particularly demanding task involved the interpretation and culling of significant documents from thousands of tons of otherwise meaningless material at Air Disarmament Document Centers. When the task was finished, 180 tons of documents were saved for later study. Highly trained interpreters, working in league with Air Disarmament technical experts, made the choices. The majority – 146 tons – migrated to the Air Documents Research Center in London, while 14 tons went directly to Wright Field, and other amounts were sent to different facilities in Europe.[41]

To gather so much material, Air Disarmament teams in the US zone in Germany inspected 248 airfields; 1,192 factories; 112 research and experimental facilities; 4,896 flak installations and gun sites; 1,395 air parks, depots, and storage sites; and 1,289 targets aggregated as Luftwaffe headquarters facilities, hospitals, schools, radar and radio sites, and also sites that proved to be false targets. Additionally, the US Air Disarmament forces visited 4,000 sites outside the American zone of occupation, scoring many useful finds especially in the Brunswick, Magdeburg, and Hannover areas where large aircraft assembly plants and research facilities were fertile grounds.[42]

WATSON FOUND THE GOOD STUFF

Col Harold E. Watson led a team of Air Technical Intelligence specialists on a scavenger hunt in Europe to procure examples of German aircraft, powerplants, and equipment in 1945. Forever known in aviation history as "Watson's Whizzers," this USAAF team rounded up jet-powered Me 262s, a huge Junkers Ju 290, a Ju 388L, and various other German warplanes.[43]

Imagine the fantastic adventure of entering the first German summer with no war in half a decade, and encountering airfields, hangars, forest hideouts, and even caves hiding some of the most advanced warplanes ever devised. The scene was awash in contrasts as stark as recent evidence of livestock being used to move ultra-modern jet aircraft to conserve gasoline. Filled-in bomb craters in airfields seemed ever more dated as new grass sprang up in the summer of Allied victory. Catbirds, redwings, and European robins cast their songs from the nearby woods with nothing to shatter their newfound peace. Some local residents were amenable to helping the Allies gather the spoils of war. For other Germans, the only recently abated bombardment was still too fresh, too damaging. Some even acknowledged a more charitable disposition toward the Americans than the British because of perceptions that American daylight precision bombardment confined civilian collateral damage much more than did British nocturnal area raids.

Into this first summer of German peace came the Americans – curious, sometimes apolitical, and perhaps just a bit brash. Col Watson sent out two groups: one to gather piston-engined aircraft and non-flying rockets and jets, the other to glean the cream of the flyable jet crop. Efforts to acquire German warplanes had not waited for VE Day; as soon as the Allies were overrunning German airfields on their drive east, the USAAF began tagging Luftwaffe airplanes for further study. Harry Fisher, a USAAF enlisted man who participated in the appropriation of a number of piston-engined bombers before the end of hostilities, recalled racing to apply improvised US star-and-bar national insignia in an effort to shield the captured bombers from strafing by Allied fighters in the area. Some members of American technology assessment teams reported German sniper fire in their early pre-VE Day efforts. Another issue that occasionally imperiled the German technology was the penchant of Allied soldiers to take souvenirs from enemy aircraft, sometimes to the detriment of the airplane's value as a specimen for study.

Two flying arrivals of intact Me 262s were of special interest. Before the war was over, on March 31, 1945, Messerschmitt pilot Hans Fay made the first flight in Me 262A number 111711, a product of an assembly plant at Hessental. Fay sped over the lines, defecting and landing at Rhein-Main

Airfield near Frankfurt, Germany. This was the first fully operable Me 262 the Americans had. Though airworthy, it was unpainted except for basic national markings. Its aluminum skin was reticulated with geometric lines representing filler that covered seams and rivets, all of which would have been overpainted with camouflage before the jet's intended delivery to an operational Luftwaffe unit. Number 711 came to the United States for flight evaluations aboard a merchant ship separate from the later batch of Luftwaffe machines rounded up in Germany. It retained its unfinished German markings in Ohio, flying a dozen times before an inflight engine fire prompted its American pilot to bail out safely. Number 711 crashed near Xenia, Ohio, on August 20, 1946, with fewer than 11 hours of evaluation flying in its American flight log.[44]

Men of the USAAF's 439th Troop Carrier Group were interested to see one of only two glass-nosed Me 262A-2a/U2s overhead at war's end, its pilot ready to surrender. This unusual variant replaced the normal gun package nose with a clear plastic and wooden station for a bombardier, equipped with a gyro-stabilized Lotfe 7H bombsight. The installation was intended to give the Me 262 bomber variants better accuracy as they approached small targets at high speeds. Joe Obendorf of the 439th watched the German jet's arrival, and recalled how the pilot gave a dazzling impromptu air show before lining up to land the jet in front of the Americans. Obendorf remembered his group commander was already looking forward to flying the Me 262 when the pilot made a wheels-up landing at the end of his performance. The group commander approached the bellied-in Messerschmitt with his service .45 pistol drawn, not sure what to expect from his initial contact with the German pilot, Obendorf said. Whether or not this belly-landing was deliberate, it has been recorded that some Luftwaffe pilots intentionally crash-landed or ground-looped their aircraft as a last act of defiance when landing to surrender at the close of hostilities.

With a cache of Me 262s at Lechfeld, Germany, in May 1945, Watson sent a team to prepare as many as could be made airworthy for a ferry flight to Cherbourg, France. This meant training USAAF fighter pilots in the nuances of the German jets, and bringing mechanics up to speed on how to care for the exotic Messerschmitts. A number of the Me 262s on the airfield were damaged or incomplete. The Watson team soon learned not all the damage was from combat or sabotage; Army engineers attempting to clear the airfield had evidently presumed the Me 262 was to be towed via an attach point on the nosewheel strut. But the complete towing arrangement required cables stretching back to the main gear to relieve the load on the nosegear strut.

Messerschmitt personnel helped educate the Americans, and before long USAAF pilots were test flying the German jets. A ritual ensued following a pilot's first jet hop, in which the propeller blades on the metal insignia of his USAAF uniform were snapped off, indicating he was now a jet pilot.

The logistics of moving prized German aircraft from a landing field at Cherbourg to the aircraft carrier that would ferry them across the Atlantic involved deliberate planning. The Me 262s each were marked to show jack point locations from which specially constructed slings and fittings could be mounted to enable the jets to be crane-lifted onto smaller barges for delivery to the waiting aircraft carrier. Curiously, this venture to ship German war booty to the United States was made possible by the availability of a British aircraft carrier, HMS *Reaper*. The logic of using *Reaper* was its status as a Lend-Lease escort carrier, manufactured in Tacoma, Washington, for Great Britain in 1944. Its journey across the Atlantic in the summer of 1945, freighted with German war materiel, would be HMS *Reaper*'s last military cruise before decommissioning and sale as surplus.

The aircraft carrier was expected to carry nine Me 262s, an Arado Ar 234 jet bomber, a Heinkel He 219 nightfighter, a Dornier Do 335, an Fw 190, plus other aircraft and crated parts to keep them flying once in the United States. The Messerschmitts made ferry flights to Melun, France, for delivery to the aircraft carrier in Cherbourg harbor. One of the USAAF pilots noted his surprise at how fast the countryside reeled past; his visual map navigation checkpoints came quickly in the speedy jet.

As Watson's team was rounding up aircraft to send to the United States, in June 1945 Bell test pilot Jack Woolams asked the colonel for permission to come to Germany to locate German specialists for reconstituting an operational Me 163 at Lechfeld.[45] Bell Aircraft, already committed to the rocket-powered X-1 project, had great interest in rocket propulsion. The logistics of arranging such a test in Germany argued against it, and instead Bell was later sent an Me 163 in the United States, although powered flights were not undertaken. Woolams was given access and instruction on other Luftwaffe aircraft still in Germany that summer, and he wrung some of them out for test pilot reports then, rather than waiting on a slow shipment of aircraft to the United States.

Woolams recalled barnstorming around France, Germany, Denmark, Belgium, Luxembourg, Holland, and elsewhere in Western Europe in a USAAF C-47 with about a dozen US military pilots, a handful of American mechanics and some maintenance equipment, searching for advanced German aircraft designs that were not too badly damaged to prevent them from being made airworthy after just a few days' work. Meals were typically

Army C-rations; the men slept wherever they could find shelter. Woolams said the team flew about 40 aircraft of many types to Cherbourg that summer. The men took a German test pilot who knew some English along, and also canvassed prisoner-of-war camps along the way to find skilled German mechanics and pilots to help with the aircraft recoveries. Because some German warplanes had been booby-trapped with explosives, Woolams said his team always had German mechanics work on them first to ensure nothing untoward would happen, followed by a first flight by a German pilot. The Americans sustained no mishaps due to known sabotage, and some figured their caution paid dividends.[46]

In 1946, Woolams recounted how many German aircraft he was checked out in. He not only flew them in Continental Europe, but again at Farnborough in England and then back in the United States, helping to relocate the precious cargo to Freeman Field in Indiana from HMS *Reaper* once it reached Newark, New Jersey. Woolams' list of German aircraft checkouts included: Ar 234, Do 335, Fw 190, He 162, He 219, Ju 88, Ju 188, Bf 109G, Bf 110, Me 262, and Ta 152. His opinion was that the Germans had an advanced grasp of jet propulsion and their planes showed superior aerodynamics, but American aircraft enjoyed superior build quality, were more rugged, and more versatile. He surmised some of the perceived workmanship deficiencies in German aircraft stemmed from the use of slave labor.[47]

Diminutive Heinkel He 162 jet fighters, their wings spanning a mere 23ft 7½ in., were collected for American inspection. With a distinctive dorsal pod mounting a single BMW 003-E-series turbojet engine that exhausted between twin canted rudders, the He 162 was said to achieve a short-duration burst speed of 553 mph at just under 19,690ft; or, at that same altitude, the Heinkel jet could sustain a respectable 521 mph. However, its handling qualities left something to be desired. Although hundreds were built by war's end, combat encounters appear to be very few. Nonetheless, it was a jet and therefore a candidate for inspection back in the United States. Several examples located near Halle were dismantled and trucked to Cherbourg; probably more than were needed, to enable the best ones to be selected for overseas shipment.

The Americans were aware final partitioning of postwar Germany would put cities like Merseberg in the Soviet occupation zone. Quick work by American teams culled as much as could be removed quickly from that area before May 30, 1945. Relocating near Munich, the USAAF appropriators found short-nose Fw 190s and some Bf 109s at Neubiberg, about five miles south of Munich. The Americans opted to ferry the wide-stanced Fw 190s, but chose to truck the sometimes tricky Bf 109s to Cherbourg.

More long-nose Fw 190s were secured at Flensburg. As two of Watson's pilots began readying one for towing to another part of the airfield, they quickly learned the hazards of randomly flipping switches in a German fighter cockpit when one lever activated an explosive canopy separation device that sent the Focke-Wulf's plastic enclosure lofting about 30 feet into the air before crashing back to earth near the tail of the fighter. Fortunately a surfeit of Focke-Wulfs let the Americans pick a different one to take.

Logistical needs did not escape the attention of the Americans, who did their best to stockpile supplies of spare parts, even engines, intended to permit sustained flight operations of as many aircraft as possible once the booty arrived in the United States.

The Americans occasionally made use of German test pilots to ferry war-prize aircraft to France for shipment to the United States. It seems a combination of cajoling, camaraderie, and confinement was employed to get the Germans to do the will of the Americans. The Germans were typically escorted by American fighters or at least Americans in other captured aircraft, although in the case of the speedy Do 335 fighters ferried to Cherbourg, the Germans handily outran their American escorts en route. When one German pilot was to accompany Americans in delivering Ar 234 jets, the American flight lead deliberately did not equip the German pilot with maps of the route. Over foreign territory in a thirsty jet, it would behoove the German to stay in sight of the American pilot who knew the way to go. Some of the German pilots chafed at what they considered confinement when they were at bases held by the Americans. Some were evidently hopeful that their cooperation would be rewarded with a trip to the United States. Some developed friendships with their American counterparts.[48]

A May 24, 1945 draft USAAF memo about the foreign aircraft program said the ultimate test fleet of German aircraft could reach 91 examples of several types, added to 75 anticipated Japanese warplanes and 20 British and 20 other types. This argued for using "a facility near Wright Field, so that Engineering Division personnel can closely observe and control the work ... to handle approximately 203 foreign aircraft." When testing was finished, the 1945 draft memo suggested "the aircraft can be disassembled and stored – later to be made a part of the desired museum."[49]

Clearly some foresight existed that saw to the preservation of some of the captured German warplanes, but in the 1940s who could forecast the phenomenal swell of interest in World War II that would remain unabated decades later?

At war's end, British and American technology-gathering teams occasionally arranged to enter the other country's designated sector on Continental Europe for the purpose of retrieving aircraft or other items. This enabled the British to inspect and obtain examples of the tandem-engined Do 335 fighter at the manufacturer's factory in Oberpfaffenhofen, which is where American examples were secured as well. Similarly, some of Watson's men flew into northern Germany, Denmark, and Norway – all under British control in the summer of 1945 – to inspect discoveries of the British teams there. Occasionally, the Americans reported determined resistance from French forces who guarded some German aircraft and refused to give the Americans access. But the Americans would not be outdone when it came to securing German aero technologies, as other Allied nations soon came to understand.

A typed memorandum contained in the air disarmament files at the Air Force Historical Research Agency (AFHRA) in Alabama listed where a number of conventional piston-engined aircraft were found by air disarmament teams, citing the reason for making the list was "it revealed the tactical disposition of the German Air Force in the latter days of the war." Mainstay Bf 109 and Fw 190 fighters "were found throughout Germany and the occupied countries." Radial-engine Fw 190s that were secured by the Americans for later use were found "at Nurenburg Airdrome where they were surrendered by Luftwaffe pilots. The so-called long nose 190s equipped with a liquid cooled, inline engine were secured from Flensburg, Germany, five miles from the Danish border." A late-war Ta 152 variant of the Fw 190 "was one of two known flyable aircraft, both of which were found at Aalborg Airdrome, Denmark." The captured Bf 109s "were all found at Ainring, in south Germany. This Airdrome located ten miles northwest of Salzburg, in the Bavarian Alps was used both as Hitler's private Airdrome and a highly secret experimental laboratory."[50]

German bombers, "including those used as nightfighters were found mainly in the areas of maximum night air activities," the air disarmament memorandum noted. The Ju 388 high-altitude reconnaissance bomber appropriated by American forces was in excellent condition, and was found on the airfield at Merseburg, Germany, "where apparently the retreat had been so rapid that the Germans were unable to destroy the many aircraft found on this field." A late-war Ju 88G-6 nightfighter was taken by the Americans from Grove airdrome in Denmark. It was noted in the aircraft memo that several airfields in this area "were largely equipped with aircraft for shipping strikes by day and nightfighters by night." Hence Denmark's Grove airdrome also surrendered three Heinkel He 219 nightfighters. The Heinkels and the Ju 388 were "completely equipped with the latest German radar, ground search IFF equipment." The memorandum noted with interest that these particular warplanes "had not been flown operationally for nearly six months due solely to the lack of gasoline and oil."[51]

The radical tandem twin-engined Do 335 fighter that survives in the United States at the time of writing was appropriated at the Dornier factory on Oberpfaffenhofen airdrome a dozen miles north of Munich. Even though the Dornier factory had been heavily bombed and strafed by the Allies, several flyable Do 335s were gleaned. The key American example was captured along with a Dornier test pilot familiar with the type. Reconstruction of Do 335 aircraft was accomplished by a repair team using a C-47 to ferry a dozen specialists as well as tools, gasoline, and lubricants for the job. To make the Do 335s ready for flight, the memo noted, "both German and American parts and supplies were used." The memo said the collecting and ferrying of these aircraft for American use was met with "complete cooperation in every phase ... by both the French and British Air Forces."[52]

Col Donald L. Putt, survivor of the Boeing 299 Fortress prototype crash in October 1935, was assigned to the USAAF's Air Technical Service Command (ATSC) in Europe when the war was winding down. The American team sent to obtain German aeronautical technologies labored under the contrived acronym of Project LUSTY (LUftwaffe Secret TechnologY). Col Putt gave overall guidance for Project LUSTY and the collection of German aircraft, equipment, and technical documents in the ETO. Col Putt did much more than guide the effort; he was a hands-on participant. He later recalled:

> since I had nearly all of the technical people in the theater assigned ... our technical people went out to examine shot-down aircraft and whatnot ... The ground armies traveling east uncovered this secret research and development base outside of Brunswick [Braunschweig], Germany, in a place called Völkenrode. And this was the Hermann Göring Aeronautical Research Establishment, a great place. It had been started in 1935, and until the ground armies went through it in [March] 1945 nobody ever knew it was there, including British intelligence. It was well camouflaged. [53]

Col (later Lt Gen) Putt said he was tasked to go to Völkenrode "and take over that place." He described the situation in a 1974 oral-history program interview:

> I got [Theodore] von Kármán and the [American] Scientific Advisory Group to come over and interview the scientists that we had rounded up. They had buried a lot of things in the forests and metal-lined the wooden boxes which we dug up. It was kind of a cloak-and-dagger operation. Lots of fun.

The lucrative German technology at Völkenrode, however, was in a part of Germany that had been earmarked for British control whenever the war ended.[54]

Some of the German scientists at Völkenrode had quietly blended into the Braunschweig community once the war front had advanced beyond them. Putt's group heard of one man who had buried something of interest on his property. The German was persuaded to reveal his cache and took the Americans to a garden shed in the backyard of his home. Beneath the brick floor, which he removed piece by piece, the scientist dug into the earth and retrieved a number of sealed metal cans. One contained a rocket fuel formula, Putt recalled. This was a recurring event in Germany, as the scientists and engineers who had developed these remarkable technologies were loath to see them squandered or destroyed.[55]

Putt said one of the finds at Völkenrode was research that helped Boeing confirm the benefits of swept wings for its nascent XB-47 bomber. The documentation, viewed in Germany by Boeing engineer George S. Schairer on a fact-finding trip in May 1945, would agree with developing NACA findings (see Chapter 5). Quickly executed wind-tunnel tests back in the United States confirmed the German data, and helped Vic Ganzer, a Boeing engineer, in his efforts to define the optimum sweep for the B-47; it was 35 degrees. The XB-47 proceeded to become a graceful embodiment of wing sweep that continues to characterize large and fast subsonic aircraft designs.[56]

Putt recalled a bounty of "very good laboratory equipment, wind tunnel models and all kinds of things." With the knowledge of the USAAF's Air Technical Service Command's leader in Europe, Maj Gen Hugh J. Knerr, Putt ran an aerial operation between Braunschweig and Wright Field, shipping items home. "I don't know how many B-24 loads we sent back. We had a B-17 and a B-24, alternating." After enjoying the run of the place, Putt said a British scientific group arrived. "When the British moved in, we realized that we would probably have to stop shipping stuff out. But we didn't stop right away. We'd wait until they were asleep at night, and then we had a gang of men move into the laboratories to pick up stuff, haul it across town where this little field was." Col Putt said by the time the British scientists awakened in the morning, the pieces appropriated by his team the night before were already winging their way toward American researchers.[57]

For as long as he was in the area, Col Putt worked the local German sites for items of use to the USAAF. He recalled, "I remember one night we picked up a new type of internal combustion engine. It was a single-cylinder affair that was in the propulsion plant. We'd take these things down to a central place where they were boxed and packed. And the British had seen that thing during the day." The following day the British wanted to look at the engine, but it had vanished. After they queried Putt about the missing motor, he asked for some time to locate it. He put it back where the British could inspect it. This time, the British tried to quietly appropriate the motor when Putt's team did not ship it off immediately. Col Putt learned the motor now resided in the automobile of one of the British team members. Demonstrating what some might call that American brashness, Putt complained soundly about the missing motor, and the British returned it. "Then we packed it up and sent it off," he said.[58]

Col Putt and the other Americans explored a tunnel where they discovered instrumentation with highly polished mirrors that enabled visualization of airflow over an airfoil. Putt was impressed; the USAAF, he recalled, had not done extensive work in this area of measurement. He enlisted the aid of a handful of German scientists or engineers who were familiar with this interferometer device to dismantle it properly and help the Americans move it across town so it could be shipped off to Wright Field. The Germans dismantled most of the device one night, but Col Putt learned the British had heard of its existence and wanted to inspect it. Putt had his German accomplices reassemble the device, allowing the British to see it in operation. The next night, it disappeared into the one-way pipeline of commandeered German materiel headed for Wright Field.[59]

Apparently Col Putt and his team, by virtue of their early arrival at Braunschweig and the military base organization they quickly established there, managed to retain status as hosts for visiting inspection teams even after it became known this region would fall under British supervision with victory. The Americans helped visitors during the day, Putt said. "But as soon as everybody was in bed and the lights were out, we'd spring into action."

"Finally, the British became aware of our operation," Putt recalled years later. "Shortly before the Potsdam Conference [in July 1945], the British threw this up to Gen Arnold. Very shortly after that ... Gen Knerr flew in one day and said: 'I think we ought to get you out of here.'" But it is likely the other American officers who knew of these operations were at least secretly happy for Putt's successes in skimming German technologies in a supposed British portion of Germany.[60]

As a participant in the American efforts to exploit German technologies and the people who devised those technologies, Putt had some involvement with Operation *Paperclip*, the drive to identify and encourage specific German technical experts to come to the United States to share their expertise. Col Putt and Gen Knerr appeared to agree on the need to use German scientists as well as their technologies in the postwar era. A June 1, 1945 memorandum from Knerr to the commander of USSTAF suggested the American plans to exploit German technologies should also embrace transporting key German scientists and engineers associated with the desired technologies. "Due to the political and economic factors involved in uprooting these scientists," Knerr opined, "it is considered essential that their immediate dependent families accompany them. Such a realistic arrangement will guarantee willing cooperation and maximum contribution to the program of aeronautical development that we must expedite if we are to come abreast of an attempt to surpass those of other countries."[61]

Knerr believed a group of German scientists should be relocated to Wright Field, where their appropriated tools and instruments could be used for American benefit. Knerr's comments were not punitive; he espoused paying the Germans a decent salary and ensuring they were not treated as prisoners of war or forced labor. Knerr said he believed that the minds of scientists do not function when they are under duress. As if to allay any fears others might have expressed about importing such recent enemies into the United States, Knerr suggested a simple understanding with the Germans that any breaches or violations could be dealt with by deporting the offender back to his original area in Germany. This must have been an especially onerous threat for those Germans who deliberately moved out of Soviet-held areas to avoid the Russians, or any other Allied nation they felt less comfortable with.[62]

Gen Knerr, not shy about speaking his mind, reported that the American inspection of German technology sites made it apparent to him that the United States had been "alarmingly backward in many fields of research." Knerr wrote: "If we do not take this opportunity to seize the apparatus and the brains that developed it, and put the combination back to work promptly, we will remain several years behind while we attempt to cover a field already exploited."[63]

The apparatus established for gleaning German scientists and technicians, Operation *Paperclip*, was administered by the Joint Intelligence Objectives Agency (JIOA). The agency functioned until 1962.

On March 19, 1945 as the Allies moved across Germany, with the fighting not yet over, Lt Gen Spaatz wrote to "Hap" Arnold, espousing the evacuation to the United States, and permanent employment, of significant German scientific leaders. Spaatz saw this move as beneficial to the future of the USAAF, and possibly helpful in the ongoing prosecution of the Pacific War against Japan. Spaatz, evidently concerned about Germany's potential for rebuilding its military in peacetime once more, suggested another reason for relocating German scientists would be to diminish the talent remaining in Germany.[64]

Some American scientific advisors cautioned against trying to bring too large a contingent of German engineers and scientists to the United States. Their concern was a perception that wholesale raiding of German technical academia would cripple a needed revival of education in postwar Germany, and might cause resentment and backlash against the Allies as had happened because of some of the harsher measures imposed on Germany after World War I.[65]

The enticing of German scientists to aid the postwar efforts of the various Allies occasionally took on an edginess seemingly born of the nationalistic priorities of the Allies. Research by historian Murray Green indicates Gen Knerr bluntly opposed a September 24, 1945 Combined Chiefs of Staff paper in which the British chiefs advocated allocations between the United States and Britain to yield equal exploitation of captured German technology and science. The British expressed some of their concerns over appearances if they paid ex-enemy scientists. Robert A. Lovett, the US Assistant Secretary of War for Air, told Gen Knerr that the British suggested German experts should be pooled between the United States and Great Britain, with their output shared between the two countries, according to Green's research notes. Lovett said other British worries included the potential for German scientists to obtain British secrets and take them back to Germany. All of this seemed to be causing inertia in the plans to recruit German scientists and bring them to the United States, and Gen Knerr was unimpressed. In his response to Lovett, Knerr indicated he believed this was a move by the British to control scientists who might otherwise benefit the United States. Knerr opined that the British, during and after the war, treated the United States as a colony only entitled to cooperation that suited the interests of the British. Knerr indicated disdain for British concerns over losing control of German scientists in regard to military secrets. He said the United States had come so far in the defeat of Germany, that if this country was unable to control a small contingent of intelligent Germans within the United States, "it is high time that we faced that fact and did something about it." Knerr argued against overly restricting Germans brought to the US because this would stifle their productive capacity. "I am certain I can control them within my jurisdiction," Knerr said, possibly including annoyance for the expressed British security concerns.[66]

The mirrored interferometer that Putt's team spirited out of Braunschweig was followed to Wright Field by an engineer named Zobel who was credited with pioneering the device. That piece of equipment later operated at Wright Field; Zobel remained at Wright for a number of years before joining General Electric. Another German specialist ultimately went to the Airesearch company; another went to Bell Aircraft. Two others became USAF chief scientists, one at Holloman AFB in New Mexico and another in the former Air Force Systems Command. Others went to academia in the United States. Col Putt, upon his return to Wright Field from Germany in 1945, was put in charge of the large detachment of about 163 German specialists retained there.[67]

Putt said he found the Germans to be cooperative and interested in contributing to the USAAF's efforts. He recalled:

> It was somewhat amazing and embarrassing, too, because all they wanted was an opportunity to work … We had them in a barbed wire compound which was required and included their barracks, their housing. They asked for drafting machines and drawing boards to put into their living quarters so they could work at night. They were just glad to have something to do.

To assist in his administration of the *Paperclip* engineers at Wright Field, Col Putt obtained the services of Capt Walter Boesch, a German-born US citizen. Boesch became a valuable go-between bridging Col Putt's office and the Germans; his native familiarity with Germans enabled Boesch to interpret what the engineers were going through, and to communicate with them. His prior credentials as an Army intelligence officer included his role in the interrogation of Hermann Göring and other high-level German officials in Germany.[68]

Less than a week after the traditional American holiday of Thanksgiving, on November 28, 1945 Col Putt reported to Gen Knerr that Army G-2 Intelligence policies were restricting the utility of the knowledge being gained from German scientists then at Wright Field in Ohio. At that time, Army policy effectively prohibited government contractors from coming into contact with the Germans or seeing any reports they had written at Wright Field. The ability to leverage the Germans' knowledge for the benefit of the American defense establishment was hampered. It was a time when the status and treatment of the Germans was not universally embraced in the same way by all Americans. As a result, at Wright Field as well as at other locations administered by the Army, the Germans sometimes felt underutilized and frustrated. This would change in time, but it was a problem in late 1945. Putt indicated some of the Germans expressed frustration at having their contact with American industry and universities stifled. The Germans also were concerned about their peculiar status in the United States at the time that did not appear to offer a path to US citizenship. Without hope of achieving citizenship, Col Putt said the Germans would likely opt to return to Germany.

Changes would come, and eventually many of the German scientists and their families became US citizens; many eventually worked for US defense contractors.[69]

CUTTING UP THE LUFTWAFFE

By July 1945, the historian for the 1st Air Disarmament Wing (Provisional) reported the task of collecting Luftwaffe specimens was virtually complete. During that month, the wing and its subordinate units learned they would be responsible, the historian said, "for carrying out the second phase, that of scrap disposal." During that month Wing headquarters moved from Oberursel to Fulda, Germany. A few choice Luftwaffe caches were discovered that month, including, "a railroad station at Staffelbach, containing six tail assemblies believed to be for ME 263s ... three barns at Elsfield containing 2970 airplane tires and 1410 tubes ... garage at Schetten, containing 2000 aircraft instruments and 1000 assorted radio tubes ... Arnold Kiekert and Son plant at Guntershausen, containing 10,000 bomb releases for 50kg bombs and 2000 releases for 70kg bombs ... assembly plant at Wolfshofen, with enough material to complete 20 ME 262s."[70]

The German aviation material not earmarked for research was to be scrapped quickly. The American forces agreed that ground units, not USAAF organizations, would dispose of the scrap. It was important for the USAAF air disarmament teams to work closely with the ground Army teams to ensure the correct German aircraft and materiel were identified for salvage. The Air Disarmament Division had acquired about 55,000 captured Luftwaffe personnel; these were transferred to the custody of ground forces as well.

The quantity and quality of aircraft and hardware appropriated by the Allies in Germany at war's end pointed up a salient difference, especially between the disposition of German assets and American materiel. If Germany had so-called "wonder weapons," the German armed forces were constantly hounded by Allied attacks that destroyed and dispersed these mechanical marvels and reduced the remaining pilots to ill-trained shadows of their early-war predecessors. Meanwhile American losses, both in men and machines, seemed to be replaced by an unstoppable and inviolate flow of new P-51s, new B-17s, new B-24s, and the trained crews to operate them, fresh from a continent unmarred by bombing campaigns. USAAF chief Gen Henry "Hap" Arnold rightly called World War II a war of logistics. He could just as well have called it a war of attrition, in which America was positioned to emerge on top due to its immense and unthreatened industrial base.

V2s FOR AMERICA

The aggregation of German aerospace technology by the United States in 1945 was not always accomplished in complete harmony with its allies Great Britain and the Soviet Union. A NASA history of the Soviet space program chronicled the arrival of American forces in advance of the Soviets at the V2 (A-4) construction facility at Nordhausen in April 1945. A somber scene of many murdered Nordhausen slave-labor workers plus unfinished V2 rockets confronted the Americans. The Americans, aware of the potential of the rockets they surveyed, quickly loaded enough pieces to create at least 100 V2s and shipped the booty into the US zone of occupation. The rocket acquisitions filled 16 Liberty ships at Antwerp. Much of what remained at Nordhausen after the Americans picked it over was damaged, lessening its value to the Russians, to Stalin's dismay.[71]

The unilateral arrival by the Americans at Nordhausen in 1945 was a modified outcome from the one a USAAF representative espoused during a May 11, 1944 meeting with the Soviet foreign minister Molotov. During a session to coordinate aspects of impending USAAF shuttle-bombing missions that were to land in the Soviet Union after hitting targets deep in Germany, Maj Gen Fred Anderson, deputy commander for operations of USSTAF, sought information about German progress on long-range guided missiles. Maj Gen Anderson listed Peenemünde as a site of particular USAAF interest. He told Molotov the United States wanted to inspect the German experimental facilities (like Peenemünde) as soon as Germany surrendered, moving in swiftly to preclude destruction of papers and equipment by the Germans. The USSTAF representative said the required haste might dictate flying inspectors to various sites in Germany in bombers or transports protected by long-range escorts, airdropping the inspectors on the same day Germany capitulated. Maj Gen Anderson acknowledged this might be a dangerous prospect since word of the German surrender might not have reached all locations by that time. He told Molotov the preservation of this German technological wealth was in the interest of both the Soviets and the Americans. Anderson left the meeting with the impression that the Soviets would cooperate in such a venture, although Molotov's reception of Anderson's suggestion was called noncommittal. Ultimately, the United States moved to the V2 complex independently while the Soviets appeared to dither about the issue in 1945.[72]

A then-secret American "Outline Plan for Disarmament of the German Air Force," undated but almost certainly produced in 1944, spelled out the assertive behavior expected: "USSR Sphere. Pending establishment of firm policies relative to areas of ultimate USSR responsibility which may be initially occupied by United States, United Kingdom or French Forces, you will, within your respective spheres of operation, institute primary air disarmament operations as though such area was an ultimate United States responsibility." If some stiffness was to be expected between the US and the Soviets, the American plan left no doubt about what was expected in British sections of Germany: "In the areas initially occupied by the Sixth or Twelfth Army Groups, which ultimately will be United Kingdom areas of responsibility and jurisdiction, you will proceed with primary air disarmament as though such areas were to be ultimately United States areas of responsibility and jurisdiction." At least in the British zone the USAAF, subject to the approval of the Army group commander, could allow RAF air disarmament teams to attach to the American units. The document later instructed: "No arrangements have been made for attachment of USSR disarmament detachments for operations in areas in which will be ultimate responsibility zones of the USSR." A thorough American effort wherever US forces found themselves in Germany was anticipated and encouraged, evidently.[73]

Another undated, and apparently early, discussion of Luftwaffe disarmament offered this on the United Kingdom and the Soviet Union:

The United Kingdom will have an important role in the disarmament and ultimate occupation of Germany. National aims will differ from those of other Nations on some major issues. The most outstanding difference currently expected is one on final disposal policies of captured war material and installations. The US Forces will initially occupy major German areas which are to be ultimately the responsibility of the United Kingdom. This procedure will necessitate close harmonization of disarmament and occupation plans. Firm decisions and close relationships must be established and announced at an early date ... The Union of Socialist Soviet Russia [sic] has been generally non-committal on all disarmament plans and postwar aims. The USSR Armed Forces are exerting continual ground pressure against the German East Front and may reach the heart of Germany prior to other Allied Forces. Russia has been allotted the N.E. third of Germany as an occupational area but may initially occupy portions of Southern Germany which are presently designated as ultimately US areas of responsibility. The disarmament procedure planned by Russia is unknown but will most likely be thorough and complete. Presumably Russia will plan to re-establish devastated Russian industries and areas by exploiting German resources controlled. Recent and projected conferences with Russian representatives should serve to clarify the Russian view.[74]

Different goals and interests between Soviet air and artillery forces initially may have diluted and delayed efforts by the Soviets to gather German technology in the volatile period surrounding VE Day. Some evidence suggests the Russians' earnest rocket scientists pursued a mutually beneficial alliance with powerful artillery officers in an effort to gain some priority for researching German rockets in the face of perceived air force indifference. But when Soviet specialists arrived at Peenemünde and Nordhausen at the end of May, they found mostly debris through which they rummaged for usable items. Also disappointing to the Soviets was the lack of high-level German scientists remaining on site; some technicians with production experience were found.

If the lack of hardware and high-level scientists was bitter medicine for the arriving Soviet inspectors, there was also a tonic for the Russians. The documentation they uncovered corroborated Soviet rocket theory from the 1930s. Had internal Soviet issues not hampered the rocketry program before the war, it might have paralleled or even exceeded the work of the Germans. While poring over Peenemünde, the Soviets found a copy of a Russian rocketry and spaceflight book in which Wernher von Braun had written copious notes. The Russians placed a priority on trying to persuade scientists like von Braun to leave American-held sanctuary and come to the Soviet Union, but to no avail.[75]

When the Russians entered the Mittelwerk factory at Nordhausen in July 1945, they marveled at a huge plant carved into a mountainside deep enough to closet entire railroad trains. If the Americans had skimmed off the best V2s extant, the Soviet occupiers of the region now contemplated reopening the Mittelwerk assembly line to make new examples of the V2. Soviet aspirations were elevated by subsequent uncovering of caches of V2 combustion chambers and other parts in their occupied territory. Germans amenable to the Soviet cause even traveled into territory occupied by the Western Allies, and obtained additional V2 components through bartering with commodities including tobacco and alcohol – universal, if unofficial, exchange currency. Ongoing efforts by the Soviets to recruit German scientists seemed to fare best if the scientists' desires to remain in Germany overrode the presumed emigration of Germans to the United States. While key players like von Braun were unmoved to join the Soviet team, some others did cross back into Russian-held Germany in 1945.[76]

A gathering of the Western Allies at Cuxhaven on Germany's North Sea coast in October 1945 witnessed several firings of captured V2 rockets. The British wanted to assemble and launch the missiles, and German scientists worked with British rocketry experts to make this happen.[77] For the third V2 demonstration, launching on October 15, Soviet representatives were invited by the other Allies, although American Maj Gen Alexander M. Cameron exerted authority to keep one prominent Soviet engineer at bay, outside the immediate launch area. It was during this event that the Soviets let it be known that they were aware American V2 treasures were destined for White Sands, in the New Mexico desert, even though this information was considered classified at the time. A proposal by the Russians to trade visits by Soviets to White Sands with visits by Americans to Nordhausen went unfulfilled. The process of exploring and exploiting V2 technology would not be shared by the Americans and the Soviets.[78]

The early advantage enjoyed by the quick-acting Americans in May 1945 began to dissipate slowly over the next year as the Soviets gathered what parts and technicians they could, and began assembling V2s of their own. But the Americans' estimated 100 V2s overshadowed the Russians' ability to piece together perhaps 18 of the missiles from scavenged German parts.

This treasure boosted American efforts to comprehend and elaborate upon German rocket technology in the early postwar years. Those efforts were aided by the large-scale migration of Germany's rocket scientists, including seminal leaders like Wernher von Braun, toward the American lines in the waning days of the war. This was a deliberate effort on the part of the Germans to avoid capture by the Soviets. It was undertaken at personal risk, but the enmity between Germans and Russians was deep, and some Germans presumed a better postwar future awaited them under American auspices than with any of the other Allied nations. The scientists, numbering more than 500 individuals, brought with them the secret locations of hidden documentation on German rocket efforts spanning well over a decade. They were led by the charismatic Wernher von Braun, and exhibited a team ethos many of them had forged in the 1930s based on a belief in the future of space travel.[79]

The German scientists' movement toward American forces to the south was partly their own invention, later facilitated by the SS who, some have speculated, may have wanted to use this German brain trust as a bartering chip at war's end. Or worse, the SS may have contemplated killing them all to prevent the scientists' capture and the transfer of their knowledge outside Germany. The rocket men traveled the roads only at night to avoid marauding bombers and fighters. They stopped at Oberammergau in the Bavarian Alps, where they were closely guarded by the SS. After Hitler's suicide on April 30, 1945, the SS guards began to melt away into Germany and the scientists felt emboldened to approach the American lines on May 2. They dispatched Wernher von Braun's younger brother Magnus, whose command of the

English language was considered a plus. After bicycling a couple of miles, Magnus encountered an American patrol; the following day, Wernher and other leaders of the team convoyed their way to the Americans.[80]

American interrogation of von Braun and the others soon convinced the victors that these really were rocket scientists. Involved in the German interview process was a General Electric scientist, Richard W. Porter, who later would work with von Braun and the others on US V2 operations. The Germans were told to write their own biographical accounts, from which the Americans began investigating their new wards. Now began a potentially awkward, sometimes artful, evaluation of the German scientists' backgrounds. Substantial rancor and restrictions existed in the United States against coddling bona fide Nazis. Discussions included whether a person had been an ardent Nazi, or merely a Nazi of convenience – a distasteful position some of the rocket scientists said they had been forced to accept. However, America quickly obtained both hardware and intellectual talent in Germany that would yield benefits back in the States.

CHAPTER 5

EVALUATING THE TECHNOLOGIES

American assessments of captured German aircraft, rockets, and documentation began quickly in Germany with visits by members of the Scientific Advisory Board. The delivery of hardware, documents, and eventually German nationals to the United States later in 1945 and 1946 made the process more detailed and thorough.

One of the most celebrated examples of technology flow to the United States was the relay of German swept-wing research back to Boeing in Seattle by that company's aerodynamicist George S. Schairer on May 10, 1945. Schairer conducted a quick study with the German materials he found while on a Scientific Advisory Board exploratory trip into Germany right at war's end. His sometimes chatty, handwritten pages, airmailed to the home address of his Boeing colleague Benedict Cohn, encapsulated the rationale and benefit of a swept wing – either forward or backward – for high subsonic speeds. Construction methods and materials of the day argued for the practicality of aft-swept wings at the time.[1]

Even as he shared pleasantries about life in Germany at that pivotal point in history, Schairer got to the point on page two of his letter:

The Germans have been doing extensive work on high speed aerodynamics. This has led to one very important discovery. Sweepback or sweepforward has a very large effect on critical Mach No. This is quite reasonable on second thought. The flow parallel to the wing can not effect the critical Mach No and the component normal to the airfoil is the one of importance. Thus the critical M is determined by the airfoil section normal to the wing and by the sweepback ... This is not complicated by adding a body at the center but is badly affected by most nacelles.[2]

Schairer's opportunity to preview advanced German swept-wing research even before it was eventually shipped back to the United States was not only a boon for Boeing, but for other American aeronautical concerns as well. His letter urging Boeing to expedite swept-wing research also contained a most collegial request from Schairer: "I don't know how soon this info will get around to other manufacturers so will you write letters of [sic] Ozzie, C.L. Johnson, R. Bayless, E. Horky, E. Sheafer, and Darby quoting pages 2–5 for their information."[3] Ozzie referred to W.B. Oswald of the competing Douglas Aircraft Company; Johnson was famed designer Kelly Johnson of rival Lockheed Aircraft; Ralph Bayless worked for Convair; Ed Horky presumably used such information to advocate sweeping the wings of North American's F-86 Sabre jet fighter; Sheafer was at Martin Aircraft and Bob Darby at Curtiss.[4] The genie first let out of the bottle by Schairer's 1945 trip to Germany set the tone for many jet aircraft designs for decades to follow.

If German investigations into the high-speed benefits of swept wings ultimately helped the Allies in early postwar jet designs, aerodynamicist Schairer qualified that value in a report he submitted to Dr. Theodore von Kármán, the esteemed director of the Americans' Scientific Advisory Group, on July 20, 1945. Schairer concluded an analysis of swept-wing developments in Germany by opining: "without question sweepback would have become known as an important variable in the United States during the year 1945, even if no information concerning this had arrived from Germany."[5]

Schairer participated in interviews with a number of German aviation specialists while he was in Germany in the summer of 1945. His access to such interviews prompted him to offer a scenario about the evolving comprehension of swept-wing benefits:

The relationship between industry and research organizations [in Germany] was very similar to that in other countries. There was no assurance that research advancements would become known and used by those directly concerned with the design of the actual production articles. The sweepback problem was quite typical of this. The value of sweepback at high speeds became known to research people throughout the world as far back as 1935. This information, however, was not transmitted to airplane designers until very recently. Apparently in Germany, as well as in all other countries throughout the world, the men designing the airplanes were not sufficiently advanced in aerodynamic training to have followed closely the finer points being studied in the research laboratories. They were not even familiar with the publications which contained this information. At the time that high Mach number problems became serious in Germany various industrial aerodynamicists searched actively for a solution to their problems, and only after considerable discussions with Busseman [sic] and Betz [German designers Adolf Busemann and A. Betz] did they learn from these two men that "possibly sweepback might help a little bit." It was then that active experimental work to prove the value of sweepback was undertaken. Apparently German industry was as greatly disconcerted over their lack of knowledge of sweepback two years ago as American and English people are at this time. It would appear that the practical utilization of sweepback resulted from the "need" and not from the "knowledge."[6]

The dawn of swept-wing technology, and George Schairer's observation that it would have occurred in the United States even if Germany had not made initial advances in that field, may have been scant comfort for prescient NACA engineer Robert T. Jones at the agency's Langley Aeronautical Laboratory. Jones was known for his ability to comprehend solutions to arcane and important aeronautical issues. He was also an unstoppable worker who once operated an elevator in a government building to pay for night classes in aeronautics during the Great Depression. In 1934, Jones obtained a temporary position at Langley as an assistant scientific aide in the 7ft x 10ft wind tunnel. Jones's uncanny aeronautical knowledge was not recognized by a college degree, and for a number of years the NACA used varied means to keep him employed, recognizing his acumen as being worth far more than a diploma. In the productive professional give-and-take that characterizes some aspects of the aeronautical enterprise in the United States, in August 1944 Jones learned about promising delta-wing design tenets from a contractor who learned from designer Michael Gluhareff of Vought-Sikorsky. Jones began theorizing about possible high-speed benefits, but set his conjecture aside when he could not reconcile some of the flow dynamics involved using mathematical tools of the day.[7]

Early in 1945, Jones realized some mathematical models for airflows at supersonic speed did accommodate his earlier theorizing, and he soon conceptualized a high-speed benefit to be derived from sweptback wings. Robert Jones comprehended a swept-wing design that effectively eliminated the wave drag and compressibility phenomena from aircraft at or near supersonic speeds. At this point, Jones was unknowingly independently confirming some of Adolf Busemann's 1935 assertions about the high-speed benefits of wing sweep. It has been said Busemann's 1935 pronouncements about swept-wing benefits at high speeds were so far ahead of practical aircraft speed considerations of the era that they probably were not embraced as useful by the attendees at the world conference where the German designer shared his concepts. In fact, two Americans in attendance who later did not recall Busemann's forward-leaning treatise on wing sweep were no less than Dr. Theodore von Kármán and the capable Hugh Dryden, who went on to become the NACA Director after World War II.[8]

In the middle of February 1945, Jones explained his concept to Ezra Kotcher, with whom Jones was working on the Americanized JB-2 variant of the V1 buzz bomb. Kotcher was also the steward of the project that would bear fruit with the Bell X-1, the first supersonic aircraft. On March 5, Jones told NACA Langley's chief of research that he had "recently made a theoretical analysis which indicates that a V-shaped wing traveling point foremost would be less affected by compressibility than other planforms." Jones asked the research chief to approve testing of experimental wing shapes to minimize the effects of compressibility. Compressibility was a phenomenon that made transonic and supersonic flight problematical. By late April, Jones had finished a report advocating his theory, but that report was resisted by at least one influential member on Langley's editorial committee who reportedly wanted to see less "hocus-pocus" and more "mathematics." Jones's early work at that time was further savaged by terms like "delusion." The upshot was a delay by the NACA in publishing Jones's paper until experiments could validate the wing sweep theory. And such tests had already been underway even before the paper was presented by Jones for review; by the end of May 1945, the benefits of wing sweep were confirmed in tests. It was not until June 21, 1945 that Robert Jones's report was published as a Confidential Memorandum Report (CMR L5F21), and then in July 1945 as an Advance Confidential Report (ACR L5G07) that would be received by certain representatives of the military as well as the aeronautical industry. Professional recognition for Robert T. Jones' independent research into high-speed flight benefits of wing sweep came more than a month after Boeing's George Schairer had already got the jump on such technology by sending preliminary German swept-wing concepts back to the United States. Nonetheless, Jones of NACA had fulfilled the highest aspirations of that organization by conceptualizing and validating the benefits of wing sweep; had no German research been available, the seminal turning point for wing sweep would no doubt be credited to Jones and NACA within a month or two of Schairer's trip to Germany.[9]

It was during Schairer's explorations in Germany that he, von Kármán, and others were present with Busemann as the German designer reminded them of his public 1935 theoretical presentation on the supersonic benefits of a swept-wing design. But in 1935, supersonic flight was so far out of reach that the German's conceptualization of swept-wing benefits evidently failed to make a lasting and pragmatic impression until the need arose during World War II.[10]

Busemann subsequently accepted the Americans' invitation to come to the United States in 1947, where his considerable comprehension of advanced aeronautics enabled him to make contributions to the body of knowledge nurtured by NACA and later NASA. In 1963, Adolf Busemann accepted a professorship at the University of Colorado in Boulder. Over the next two decades, Busemann conducted research that led to further contributions in space vehicle design, trajectory optimization, and re-entry methods. His research at the University of Colorado led him to propose using ceramic tiles on the space shuttle, which NASA adopted. Adolf Busemann died in 1986. The university named its Busemann Advanced Concepts Laboratory in his honor.[11]

Schairer's July 1945 report characterized German military aircraft as more tactical than strategic, and fundamentally "a device to be used with the ground forces as in the early Panzer Divisions with Stuka dive-bomber cover and attack." No doubt Schairer, whose Boeing company was heavily invested in the strategic thinking that drove the wartime USAAF, was interested in figuring out why Germany did not similarly develop strategic bombardment assets. He posited: "The [German] policy, with respect to use of airplanes, undoubtedly derives from several important factors. Germany does not have any adequate fuel supply for maintaining a large active air force and therefore it has been necessary for them to concentrate only on a few types which they consider most important and even on these production is liable to be limited by fuel availability." Schairer also cited the German General Staff's apparent preponderance of officers schooled in traditional land and sea warfare that had not previously relied on aviation. "This was undoubtedly one of the greatest handicaps that German aviation had to put up with," Schairer opined. "A number of comments made by German airplane designers indicated a belief among them that the Battle of Britain was lost entirely as a result of misunderstandings and clashes between the German Air Force and the German General Staff. The German Air Force was not prepared for such a battle either in aircraft types or crew training and had expected to use the concentration of aircraft at that time to assist in an invasion of England by water and not as a strategic bombing attempt. The failure of this battle and the subsequent success of Allied aircraft flying unchecked over Germany produced a rift in government circles which resulted in a great reduction of expectations from aircraft." Schairer said this situation in Germany, which had both political and military ramifications, led that country's aircraft design and procurement agents to design bomber interceptors.[12]

The vehicle of choice would have turbojet or rocket power, these devices having been researched and honed in Germany for a number of years. Schairer observed: "It is evident that much progressive thinking had been occurring in Germany during the peacetime years. To what extent this was general is not known, but in some manner or other sufficient interest was aroused in the more capable engineers to develop ideas and devices such as the V1 engine, the rocket projectile such as [the] V2, the turbojet engine, [rocket] engines such as that used in the [Me] 163 airplane, and many other similar developments." Even though such devices were incubating in Germany, Schairer said they often were unable to be fielded operationally until the last year of the war. "This was partially due to prejudice against the new devices, although mostly to lack of sufficient development."[13]

Schairer further described his impressions of a German industrial rush to fill the interceptor void: "Contracts were given to all parties interested to develop any conceivable means of intercepting bombers. All types of devices were in the process of being tried in the hope that someone would be successful." He suspected that some of the proposed interceptors "had been sold on the basis of pretty pictures and fast talk." He believed "very few of the efforts were being sufficiently well coordinated to give much chance of success. Great reliance was being placed on invention and practically none upon sound engineering treatment of the problem at hand. This was to a great extent caused by the lack of understanding of engineering development processes by Hitler and his immediate advisors." Interestingly, Schairer noted: "It does not appear, however, that the projects most likely to succeed were greatly hampered by the many projects of lesser probable importance. A very free hand was given with respect to manpower and materials and money was readily available to the various [scientific] investigators."[14]

Schairer contemplated the relationships between different players in the development of German aircraft: "As in the case of sweepback, there is every reason to believe that the relationships between German industry and German research, the Air Ministry, etc. were essentially identical to the same relationships in this country and the same problems were being encountered."

Schairer's July 1945 report to von Kármán characterized the German aeronautical specialists: "The majority of these personnel were interested in aviation as such without reference to military uses or the future of Germany, although these same people were quite willing to utilize their efforts in such directions when war became imminent even though originating among their own political leaders." Schairer observed: "The majority of these aviation leaders appeared to be former glider manufacturers and pilots who had then graduated into small civil airplanes and only in recent years had turned towards either large airplanes or high performance military airplanes."[15] Restrictions placed on German aviation in the Versailles Treaty ending World War I gave German aeronautics specialists and enthusiasts little recourse but to exploit seemingly harmless glider flight.

Schairer analyzed German aircraft development out of the glider movement: "Herein lay its start, but also its greatest weaknesses. Some of the concerns, such as Junkers, date back to the last war and are quite substantial industries, but in most cases the companies were relatively new and inexperienced. This was as intended by the Versailles Treaty. Without doubt the many years the Germans lived under the terms of the Versailles Treaty paid great dividends to the Allies in this war. The Germans did not have as well established an industry and as large a background of experience and backlog of trained men as was available in the United States and England." Though prodigious numbers of warplanes, some of which were on the leading edge of aeronautics, were manufactured by Germany during World War II, Schairer characterized the whole of German wartime aviation in general as "a small-scale operation even up to the end of the war." Schairer noted difficulties in expanding German aviation that he attributed to a lack of proper personnel. "Nearly every successful aircraft device seen by the undersigned in Germany stemmed directly from the abilities and knowledge of men who had been active in German aviation for ten or more years," he observed.[16]

Schairer's conclusions from these observations in the summer of 1945 suggested to him the possibility of a new round of restrictions on post-World War II aviation activity in Germany: "It is believed that further investigation of this phase of the German problem can lead to certain very definite recommendations as to the future limitations to be placed on Germany with respect to aviation matters. If the training of these men had not been permitted and their experience with aircraft matters even in the form of small gliders had not been permitted, they would have been unable to catch up with aviation in sufficient time to have used the airplane successfully in this war."[17]

As has been seen earlier in this volume, not all American advisors were as confident that limitations comparable to those imposed at Versailles after World War I would ensure a peaceful postwar Germany. For example, these men cautioned against removing too great a component of the German intellectual engineering cadre, lest postwar Germany should suffer from a dearth of scientific educators, leading to a resentment of Allied actions in this area. Some observers opined that the dictates of the Treaty of Versailles had been seen as so harsh within Germany that this led to a backlash that actually empowered the rise of groups like the Nazis.

Schairer's May 1945 illuminations on the value of wing sweep were buttressed by subsequent interviews with other German engineers. On June 11, 1945, Schairer, along with Hugh Dryden, H. S. Tsien, F. Wattendorf, and A. M. O. Smith from Douglas Aircraft, interrogated Junkers designers Otto Frenzl and Phillip von Doepp. Available at the time were exhaustive Junkers wind-tunnel data files. One can imagine the heady, if professionally restrained, excitement that must have accompanied the Americans as they probed the newest research of their erstwhile enemies so quickly after the end of hostilities.[18]

The discussions (which are preserved in their entirety as an Appendix to this narrative) ranged from wind-tunnel designs that could supposedly sustain Mach .98 airflow to the merits and demerits of various placements for jet engine nacelles on wings and fuselages. One part of the interrogation centered on the forward swept-wing Ju 287 and the problems thought to be inherent in high-speed forward swept wings – problems that would not be fully tamed for three decades with the development of computer flight controls and tailored composite wing construction methods that made the radical Grumman X-29 possible.[19]

As George Schairer and other American specialists were interrogating German aeronautics pioneers and evaluating technologies *in situ*, other Americans were tasked with finding and removing technologies for further study in the United States. Technical reports were shipped to the US and translated; other pieces of German hardware were treated in American-generated evaluation reports, and portions of this paper trail exist in various American archives. Ultimately, the Luftwaffe gave up its secrets.

FASCINATED BY THE NATTER

Natter – German for viper or adder – was a curious, small, manned rocket envisioned as a bomber destroyer. Though it did not see service, the Natter's radical propulsion, vertical launch, diminutive size, and general rationale made this captured weapon an object of curiosity bordering on fascination. Built by Bachem, the BP 20 Natter began giving up its secrets to Americans who encountered files – some scorched by fire – and Germans familiar with the program who were interrogated. From these sources, USAAF and RAF disarmament investigators pieced together a summary report. About 30 Natters were built. Eighteen of these were consumed in unmanned takeoff launches, and one was allowed to crash following a glide test. A manned launch went awry, claiming the life of the pilot along with that Natter. Four Natters were burned at Waldsee (to prevent their capture by the Allies), two more were consumed by fire at Otztal, and the surviving four Natter airframes wound up at St. Leonard, where the Allies found them along with parts. Additionally, one Natter was said to have been completed by Wolf Hirth Flugzeubau at Naber unter Teck as the only one of ten on order that was finished. The Germans interviewed said they had been ordered to furnish details of the Natter to the Japanese, but transportation difficulties prevented detailed information from getting to Japan. Nonetheless, the Japanese were said to be interested in the Natter concept.[20]

A manned launch of a Natter, made against the advice of its designer, killed volunteer Luftwaffe pilot Lothar Siebert on February 28, 1945. The sequence of crash events included loss of the canopy, which may have caused the hapless pilot to strike his head, losing consciousness.

The summary report listed the Natter materials that were isolated for retention, and gives a glimpse into the air disarmament teams' workings in immediate postwar Germany in 1945:

1. Two-drawer cabinet containing detail drawings, parts lists and alteration sheets for the BP-20.
2. Drawing of Walter liquid rocket unit 109.509.
3. Two slightly burnt drawings of jet rudders for BP 20.
4. Descriptive report of Natter (BP 20) project.
5. Report on the examination of vertical takeoff, by Dr. K. Petrikat.
6. Bundle of drawings of Walter rocket unit 109-509.
7. Envelope of letters from Bachem personnel at St. Leonard.[21]

Along with this documentation, airframes and hardware were prepared for shipment to the ATI (Air Technical Intelligence) collection point at Stuttgart, including two of the repairable Natters made by Bachem at Waldsee, four Natter wings, two serviceable liquid-fueled Walter 109-509 A-2 engines, four serviceable SR-34 assisted takeoff powder rockets, two boxes of 7.3cm rocket ammunition, a parachute for the BP 20, and miscellaneous Natter instruments and fittings.[22]

Despite its lack of operational success, the sense of desperate urgency telegraphed by the radical Natter made this portable captured item a popular display at postwar events in the United States. Two Natters (operational designation was Ba 349) were said to be in the booty shipped to the United States. The fate of one of these is unknown; the other was saved for the

National Air Museum (later the National Air and Space Museum) of the Smithsonian Institution. It was assigned the US identification numbers FE-1 and T2-1.

As the sole known surviving Natter, this airframe proved popular as a portable display in the United States as early as 1945. When a number of captured aircraft were transferred to the Chicago Orchard Place Airport in Park Ridge, Illinois, in the late 1940s, the Natter was among them. One of its outings was for Army Day on April 10, 1948, when the Natter joined other diminutive war prizes, including a Japanese Baka bomb and a V1, on the backs of Army flatbeds for use in a Chicago parade.[23]

Technical reports on the Natter abound. In one, a description of a Natter wind-tunnel model reveals the design ironically used an American airfoil – NACA 0012. This report also suggested some problems with the Natter's horizontal tail effectiveness in some conditions of high-speed flight.[24]

DOCUMENT DELUGE

In London, Col Howard M. McCoy led the USAAF's Air Documents Research Center (ADRC). ADRC was involved with translating, cataloguing, indexing, and microfilming captured German technical documents. In 1946, ADRC relocated to Wright Field, becoming the Air Documents Division of T-2, the Technical Intelligence arm of the Air Materiel Command. The magnitude of the task is reflected in the assignment of 300 people who ultimately processed more than 1,500 tons of documents. It is said their translations and comprehension of the documents led to the addition of 100,000 new technical terms to the English language. The amalgamation and dissemination of this translated technical data to American industry gave benefits beyond aerospace advancements. Advanced designs in vacuum tubes for communications, magnetic recording tapes, night vision gear, improvements in fuels, and even advancements in things as disparate as food preservation, drugs, and textiles all have been credited to ADRC's pioneering postwar efforts. ADRC eventually evolved into the ongoing postwar Defense Technical Information Center (DTIC).[25]

GERMAN DELTA – MORE NOVELTY THAN NECESSITY

The American team sent to obtain German aeronautical technologies pondered a starkly simple delta-wing glider that looked much like the result of a folded paper airplane. What they beheld in May 1945 was the yet-unfinished wooden DM 1 glider intended to verify low-speed handling characteristics of the delta as intended for a supersonic ramjet interceptor, the un-built P13a. Radical technologies such as this had been the passion of German aerodynamicist Alexander Lippisch since the 1920s. His knowledge and aeronautical acumen had been put to use in the development of the semi-tailless Me 163 Komet rocket fighter. After his stint at Messerschmitt on the Me 163 program, Lippisch moved to the Aviation Research Institute in Vienna, Austria, where he was director of research from 1943 to 1945. Up to the war's end, Lippisch embraced his longstanding advocacy of delta wings with the proposed P 13a fighter and its slow-speed testbed glider, the DM 1. The unfinished DM 1was completed in Germany and shipped to the United States.

The USAAF and US Navy had a longstanding working relationship with NACA, which operated a series of national aeronautical laboratories that explored promising new technologies, and made research results available to the US aviation industry and the military. Unlike NACA's successor, NASA, the older NACA was less involved in operations and concentrated on being a research agent for the betterment of American aeronautical state-of-the-art technology. NACA's Langley Research Center in Virginia received the full-size DM 1and began testing it in a huge full-scale wind tunnel in February 1946.[26] Ironically, records exist in Lippisch's papers showing he corresponded with NACA on aeronautical design issues in the last half of the 1930s.

Lippisch's DM 1 had a blunt wing leading edge which may have been at least partially a vestige of one of his earlier pre-war notional delta-wing designs, with thick wings providing more room for internal storage on a projected transatlantic aircraft.

Results initially differed substantially from wind-tunnel tests of smaller theoretical delta-wing designs, giving the DM 1 a lower than expected maximum lift coefficient and a lower stalling angle of 18 degrees compared with as high as 40 degrees for some models. The acquired German DM 1 proved to be a catalyst for NACA researchers who performed a number of changes on it and on smaller scale delta-wing models, thinning the leading edge and generally cleaning up the design in the manner for which the Langley laboratories had earned great respect over decades. The leading edge modification by NACA at Langley led to a breakthrough in delta-wing design rationale that paid dividends in ensuing years. The smaller wind-tunnel models had thin leading edges, and also exhibited vortex airflow patterns over the wing upper surfaces at high angles of attack in the region of maximum lift. NACA engineers rightly presumed this was the reason for the wide variance in performance from the blunt DM 1 wing. The DM 1's original blunt leading edge inhibited vortex flow formation; the thin leading edge applied at Langley across half the wingspan of the German delta elevated the maximum lift coefficient at the steeper angle of 31 degrees.[27]

Convair, already pioneering delta-wing concepts independently, consulted Lippisch, but the indigenous Convair development probably was far enough along that little was gained from Lippisch's work.[28]

Alexander Lippisch's research and rationale into swept and delta wings in wartime Germany was significant, but it would be incorrect to characterize him as the reason American delta jets happened. The American aeronautical enterprise did not toil in ignorance until Lippisch's delta-wing glider disembarked from a ship in the United States. As early as 1939, Vought-Sikorsky engineer Michael Gluhareff conceptualized a delta wing as a way to delay the onset of compressibility effects in the transonic region. Some of his work was reviewed by NACA in 1944. Convair's Adolph Burstein may have had his own independent epiphany on the benefits of delta-wing designs when the XF-92 needed something different than its original swept wing that fared poorly in wind-tunnel tests in 1946.[29]

That Lippisch predated other delta-wing vehicles with his admittedly flawed thick-wing triangular glider may have fostered stories that have circulated for decades crediting him with boosting American postwar delta-wing designs. But a review of the events leading up to successful delta-wing evolution in the United States argues for more independent indigenous design breakthroughs, and less copying of Lippisch's ideas.[30]

Nonetheless, perhaps Lippisch believed some of his work was impacting American postwar delta wings. In an essay published in the February 1951 issue of *Aero Digest* magazine, he observed that some perceived difficulties in delta-wing designs might be explained by saying: "(w)hen somebody is cooking with someone else's recipes, he might not get too good a meal the first time."[31]

WAR BOOTY ON AMERICAN SHORES

Imagine an aircraft carrier loaded with exotic German high-performance aircraft, docked on the Atlantic coast in Newark, New Jersey, with great aeronautical promise waiting to be exploited in the United States. By the late summer of 1945, this exotic menagerie was being cleaned of protective coatings from the transatlantic sea voyage, and groomed for delivery to the USAAF and US Navy flight test establishments. Some aircraft, especially the rocket-powered Me 163s, were freighted to their final destinations from Newark Army Airfield. Others, considered more robust and reliable for cross-country flight, were readied for aerial delivery. It was evident that Wright Field at Dayton, Ohio could not support such a large influx of aircraft, so a large number of them were sent to the quiet Freeman Army Airfield in rural Seymour, Indiana. It was not far from Wright Field by air, and it afforded one location to consolidate foreign aircraft holdings.

While the aircraft were being readied at Newark, Bell's enthusiastic test pilot Jack Woolams made the first flight of a Do 335 by an American; it nearly proved to be his last. The Do 335 featured one tractor and one pusher V-12 Daimler-Benz model DB 603-E1 engine in tandem, ahead of and behind the pilot's cockpit. Each engine could deliver 1,800 hp for takeoff, and the unusual fighter topped out at 474 mph according to some sources. The Do 335 reflected late German crew-protection rationale, including an ejection seat and explosive bolts that would automatically detach the fighter's upper vertical fin and aft propeller to protect the pilot during an ejection sequence.

Woolams taxied the tricycle-gear Do 335 to the end of the Newark runway and pushed throttles forward to take off. Immediately after getting airborne, the Bell pilot noticed cooling issues with the rear engine. The temperature of that powerplant climbed until the cockpit gauge could no longer register it, and Woolams was less than 100ft high. With an inoperative hydraulic system, Woolams could not retract the landing gear to reduce drag on the big airframe. Trying to be a good steward of the Daimler-Benz engines, Woolams recalled being told that the Do 335 could remain aloft on the power of only one of its V-12s, so he shut down the hot aft engine as a precaution, feathering its propeller. But single-engine flight was not sustainable that day, possibly due to the extra drag of extended landing gear, Woolams conjectured later. Even with full power applied to the engine up front, the Dornier was descending. The pilot saw a swampy area looming ever larger, and determined that was no place to park an airplane with him in it. Woolams scrambled to restart the aft engine, finally coaxing enough power from it to enable the plucky test pilot to roar between two buildings on the airfield as he made an emergency crosswind landing. The liquid-cooled Dornier spewed oil, steam, and smoke, but it and its pilot were basically intact. Woolams was amused to report that although his aborted hop in the Do 335 probably lasted only two minutes, he was nonetheless held aloft as the US authority on flying the type.[32] It is possible the two Do 335s sent to the United States were never flown again.

The Me 163B Komet rocket-powered fighter was a fascinating operational Luftwaffe aircraft that cried out for postwar evaluation. Its incredible top speed of 596 mph nearly reached 600; untouchable by any contemporary. Its swept-wing semi-tailless design promised simplicity and streamlining. In addition, its choice of rocket propulsion, although risky, was very cutting edge in the mid-1940s. In the United States, Bell Aircraft expressed special interest in evaluating the Me 163 since the Bell company was America's leader in rocket-propelled aircraft designs at the time. Only two years after the end of the war, an independent Bell design, the rocket-powered X-1, became the first aircraft to fly at supersonic speeds.

But the choice of fuel for the Me 163B involved mixing hydrogen peroxide-based T-stoff with a 30 percent hydrazine hydrate solution in methanol, known as C-stoff. Rollover mishaps could cause the volatile fuels to mix and explode; T-stoff was very caustic and Me 163B pilots wore special protective coveralls in an effort to resist chemical burns.

With this background, the American testers initially planned powered tests of the Me 163B at Muroc Army Airfield (later Edwards AFB) in California's Mojave Desert. In addition to paved runways, Muroc embraced the 44-square-mile Rogers dry lakebed that was suitable for omnidirectional takeoffs and landings with ample overrun room. Me 163B Komet number FE-500 remained stored at Freeman from the late summer of 1945 while the Me 163B flight-test project received consideration, and then a go-ahead in October of that year. By March 21, 1946, Me 163B FE-500 was pronounced refurbished. It was pickled – preserved and protected – for shipment to Muroc. The plan originally called for using a B-17 Flying Fortress as the tow aircraft for the Komet in its initial unpowered evaluations. This subsequently changed to become a B-29 Superfortress. Komet FE-500 made the journey from Freeman Field to Muroc in the belly of a Fairchild C-82 Packet twin-boom transport on April 12, 1946. As this was transpiring, the USAAF obtained 3,000 pounds of hydrazine hydrate from the US Navy as part of the fuel mixture intended for later powered Me 163B tests.[33]

The USAAF testing of the Me 163B was beset with problems. In the austere postwar drawdown of military resources, the Air Materiel Command faced a daunting workload as new technologies were explored in research and production aircraft. The Flight Test Division, led by Col Albert Boyd, requested to be notified once the Me 163B was ready for flight, with sufficient support spare parts at hand at Muroc. Only then would flight test crew resources be dispatched from Wright Field to conduct the evaluation. Col Boyd was a respected, capable, and sometimes stern leader who was not to be trifled with. The Me 163B adventure tested his patience.[34]

Late in April, after the Me 163B had been shipped to Muroc, the Flight Test Division was informed transportation of spare parts to Muroc was not available, and this could likely delay testing. A decision was made to divert the intended B-29 tow plane from Wright Field to Freeman Field on its way to Muroc on April 30, to pick up the parts. Tow-plane pilot for the Me 163B tests was Maj Robert Cardenas, an experienced bomber and tow-plane pilot who would gain fame in the following year as pilot of the B-29 mother ship that carried the Bell X-1 aloft for its epic first supersonic flight. Col Boyd subsequently relayed what the B-29 crew said they found at Freeman: "Upon arrival at Freeman Field only a few parts were found ready for delivery; however, the B-29 crew were told that it would be a week before most of these parts would be ready and then they would be shipped to Muroc by railway express." This imperiled the scheduled completion of the Me 163B flights, set for May 7, 1946. The B-29 departed Freeman that afternoon, bound ultimately for Moffett Field near San Francisco to pick up a stick-force recorder as test instrumentation. (Moffett was home to NACA's Ames Research Center, likely the source of this instrumentation.)[35]

The flight-test crew arrived at Muroc on May 1. The group included Dr. Alexander Lippisch, designer of the Me 163, and also a German Komet test pilot, L. Vogel. Lippisch and Vogel inspected the Me 163B at Muroc, and determined that it was not ready for flight after all. They identified slack in the controls, and expressed concerns about the durability of glue joints in the structure. (Wings of the Me 163B were of built-up wooden construction.) The jettisonable takeoff dolly and extendable landing skid functionality were found unsatisfactory too, according to a USAAF memo. The controls were corrected, but the glue joints prompted a decision to limit flights to relatively low Mach numbers (even subsonic flights can be characterized as a decimal equivalent of Mach). To Col Boyd's evident chagrin, the Komet landing gear functionality appeared to perplex those working on it at Muroc.[36]

Finally on May 3 (some accounts say May 4), the Me 163B, with USAAF test pilot Maj Gus Lundquist in the egg-shaped craft, began its towed takeoff behind the giant B-29. But the tow latch released prematurely at about 90 mph – just about takeoff speed. Maj Lundquist had his hands full with the Me 163 rolling along the runway on its dolly, no braking capability available since this was not its intended use.[37] Lundquist deftly kept the narrow-tracked Me 163B dolly rolling forward in a safe course as speed gradually diminished while team members watched the agonizingly long drama play out.

Continuing issues with the dolly and skid system postponed flights the next day; ultimately, some tow-and-release unpowered flights were completed over Muroc. The tiny Komet buffeted in the turbulent wake behind the huge B-29 tow plane, and this may have exacerbated glue delamination problems. The glue joint issues contributed to the decision to cancel rocket-powered flights of Me 163B FE-500.

Powered flights had long been considered an option, not a foregone conclusion. An Air Materiel Command news release dated May 7, 1946 said: "Tests of this plane require extreme care and meticulous planning. The test program includes three possible phases; glider, powered flight, and powered take-off tests. However, if first-phase tests fail to indicate additional valuable information is to be had, the remainder of the program will be abandoned."[38]

Following the early problems experienced with the Me 163B at Muroc, on May 8, 1946 Col Boyd made a number of succinct recommendations for any future conduct of this project:

> Do not permit any officer who is not a licensed aircraft mechanic to meddle with any part of this airplane – an example of this is that one of the Project Officers from T-2 stripped the threads of an 1800-lb. pressure fitting by improper use of a wrench thereby cancelling the 5 May flight and necessitating cancellation of further flights … No German spare parts of this type were available and American fittings could not be substituted without changing all fittings in the entire system … Tests should not be attempted without having many spare parts such as skids, complete hydraulic systems, etc … It is believed that this airplane was not nearly ready for flight when test crew arrived and that if this airplane is to be made ready for flight it will require at least three weeks for the airplane to be put in flying condition. In order to save time of testing all maintenance should be done at night so tests can be conducted at the break of dawn.[39]

The flight testing of Me 163B FE-500 at Muroc in 1946 may ultimately have been overcome by the transitory nature of the German technology phenomenon. American production fighter aircraft relied on jet engines, not rockets, and American research rockets had their own indigenous powerplants. Perhaps the most telling is the 1948 introduction of Northrop's semi-tailless X-4 research aircraft. Intended to explore whether the lack of a horizontal tail would improve transonic controllability, the X-4 indicated that it would not. Although the X-4 was an all-new jet-powered design, its rationale and dimensions were not that far off those of the Me 163B. The Me 163, phenomenal in 1944 over Germany, was a risky relic not long after.

FREEMAN FIELD, INDIANA

Freeman Field, at the time of writing, is a civilian airport serving the town of Seymour, Indiana, in the sometimes-humid, bucolic, friendly heartland of the midwestern United States. It bears evidence of its military past in the shape of some of its hangars and buildings. Home to a museum dedicated to preserving its history, this airfield has become legendary in the literature of captured German aircraft. Photos in the museum show a surfeit of German airplanes and rockets at Freeman Field in 1945 and 1946. Six decades later, only some arcane aluminum remnants of German wreckage remain, in the museum's holdings.

As enigmatic as Freeman Field's story is, a letter sent to the director of the Air Force Museum back in 1968 is intriguing for the Freeman information it contains, even though the sender's identity has been lost in the loops of the cursive-only signature at the bottom. The excerpted text of that letter is presented here:

Dear Mr. Frey …

I occupied the job you indicated for about six months, at Seymour, Indiana, the latter part of 1945. The original purpose of reconstructing some of these airplanes was to check their flight performance. Although one Me-262 was flight checked, it was not one of the Seymour, Indiana, airplanes. A rocket powered Me-163 which we had under reconstruction at Seymour was eventually completed at Edwards and some flight testing was done … The work at Seymour was under the Technical Intelligence Division at Wright Field, headed by then-Col. Don Putt. A Col. Hal Watson headed up the Collection Subdivision to which Seymour was assigned.

The organization at Seymour was never built up to the technical capability that was needed to accomplish the original objective. We lacked completely a flight test instrumentation capability, for example. Because of these shortcomings we concentrated on putting some of the airplanes in the best mechanical shape possible. Primarily the Air Force used Seymour to get as much publicity value as possible out of the possession of these foreign airplanes, and for this purpose some were kept on flight status (Me-262, long-nose Fw-190) while the others were dressed up for static display. There were some bomber flights but these were rare …

There was little in the way of Technical Literature with these airplanes, and no combat record at all, to my knowledge. At Seymour we depended on an engineering test pilot, Karl Bauer [Baur] … and a Messerschmidt [sic] inspector, who went back to Germany, to keep us straightened out on various details, and the German way of doing things. Their information was excellent, by the way, and freely given.

I have perhaps a dozen photos of the airplanes given to me by these two former Messerschmidt employees and some photos taken at Seymour which I would [be] glad to make available to you for copying.[40]

Freeman Field's moment in the spotlight as a repository for foreign aircraft happened quickly. An April 4, 1945 letter from Maj Gen Oliver P. Echols, who was Gen Arnold's Assistant Chief of Air Staff for Materiel and Services, conveyed Arnold's interests to the Director of the Air Technical Service Command (ATSC) at Wright Field: "The Commanding General has recently expressed the desire that immediate action be taken to preserve in the United States all important items of enemy aeronautical equipment. Air Technical Service Command is designated as the organization responsible for the procurement, reconditioning and preservation of enemy aeronautical equipment and the placing of such equipment in storage for postwar historical and scientific purposes, at least one (1) each of every type of item used by the Enemy Air Forces."[41] Such a broad mandate was not ultimately practical, unless it is interpreted to mean one bomber could represent all types of bombers; one transport could represent all types of transports, and so on. But in actuality, a number of captured German and Japanese aircraft were retained and placed in storage and museums for years.

The expected bounty of foreign aeronautical equipment would be boosted by Japanese holdings from Gen George Kenney, Far East Air Forces (FEAF) commander. Accordingly, Maj Gen Echols, acting on behalf of Gen Arnold, directed ATSC that "an immediate study be undertaken ... and this office furnished a plan for the collection, cataloging, and storing of equipment for postwar historical and scientific purposes. Studies will not include plans for the museum at this time."[42]

Shortly after this letter, "Hap" Arnold sent a teletype message to the ATSC director indicating more examples of captured aircraft might be desirable in order to furnish copies of the technologies to American aeronautical contractors for study. Arnold now emphasized the letter from Maj Gen Echols: "Reference letter directive is amplified hereby to include preservation for making complete aircraft and all other types of captured material available at one or two centrally located points in sufficient quantities to permit detailed examination by contractors." He suggested that "suitable closed down war plant may be available to house this project." Arnold instructed the ATSC director that "requisitions for captured equipment should be increased by amount considered necessary. Provide for circular letter to contractors at intervals to advise receipt of new articles of particular interest."[43] The reference to a closed war plant may be the Chicago, Illinois Douglas C-54 assembly plant at Orchard Place, where some historic and foreign aircraft were later stored after their use at Freeman Field. Orchard Place/Douglas gave the letters ORD to the airport identifier that became Chicago's O'Hare International Airport.

The emphasis placed on collection and preservation of foreign aeronautical technologies by Gen Arnold was a clear mandate. The rapidly concluding European war made hasty action necessary. The Engineering Division scrambled, requesting on April 28 that portable hangars and buildings be erected at Clinton County Army Airfield in Wilmington, Ohio to protect the influx of foreign materiel, because all other hangars and buildings in the greater Wright Field area were unavailable. The situation was presented in the request for portable hangars:

> Increasing quantities of foreign aeronautical equipment including flyable enemy aircraft and aircraft of our allies is being received by the Air Technical Service Command for study, engineering evaluation and flight testing. The importance of this work is being increasingly stressed by higher headquarters. The Air Technical Service Command may be subject to criticism unless this work is expedited and suitable facilities are provided for maintenance and storage ... Because of the value of this equipment, enhanced by the fact that usually only one aircraft of any one type is sent to the Air Technical Service Command, it is extremely important that hangar facilities be made available ... Due to lack of buildings or hangars, large quantities of foreign engines and other aeronautical equipment must now be left unprotected in open lots.[44]

The one available hangar at nearby Vandalia, Ohio was coveted by other ATSC users, the letter explained, "and is not nearly adequate for the 16 active and 11 inactive foreign aircraft now on hand. Additional foreign aircraft are known to be enroute from the European and Pacific Theaters." Clearly, existing and inbound inventories of high priority foreign aeronautical items demanded facilities.

As discussions continued about the number and type of aircraft that would be preserved by ATSC, at one point estimates approached 300. American military aircraft earmarked for museum preservation became part of the mix. No longer could temporary hangars at crowded airfields in the greater Dayton, Ohio area handle the forecast magnitude of the task levied by Gen Arnold. ATSC launched a search to find an air base that met the physical plant requirements, including good railroad access. By May 24, 1945, Freeman Field was identified as a good candidate, near enough in flying miles to Wright Field, yet not part of the bustling, crowded ATSC network of fields in the Dayton vicinity. A letter on that date officially requested the transfer of Freeman Field from First Air Force to ATSC.[45]

The quickly unfolding and changing plan for Freeman Field as a center for foreign aircraft technology presumed that: "In connection with the project for enemy aircraft, it is planned to conduct exhaustive tests for purposes of evaluation and experimentation while these aircraft are still in flyable condition and while replacement parts may be available." Planners knew the clock was ticking on the airworthy enemy aircraft. Coming from a vanquished foe whose logistics were in disarray across the ocean, these high-performance aircraft would be difficult to keep airworthy indefinitely. In the letter requesting Freeman Field for ATSC, it was noted: "At the present time the estimated workload is about 200 enemy aircraft in addition to innumerable items of foreign equipment and accessories and about 95 US aircraft for collection and preservation." Actual tallies of aircraft delivered to Freeman Field indicate far fewer were placed there ultimately. The request for Freeman Field's transfer to ATSC concluded with a reminder of the urgency required to make it happen: "Inasmuch as captured enemy equipment is now being held in the theaters awaiting shipping instructions, and some captured enemy equipment is now at US ports of debarkation also awaiting shipping instructions, immediate action is required to transfer this facility to ATSC and provide required personnel authorizations for its operation." [46]

The transfer was accomplished in the phenomenally short span of three weeks – in an era that predated many of the bureaucratic steps that could be expected to make such an action much slower today. Commanding Freeman Field for ATSC was Col Harvey C. Dorney. With the mid-June transfer of the field to ATSC, foreign material stored at Wright Field began migrating to Freeman Field.

Living quarters for the ATSC military complement at Freeman Field consumed fewer housing units than when this had been a larger First Air Force training base. As a result, the former enlisted barracks buildings, which were closest to the flightline, were repurposed as warehouses, the official ATSC base history for the period noted, for "the large quantities of both foreign and early American equipment shipped in for storage." [47]

Engineering Services was the largest of the new Freeman Field organizations in 1945. Included were the Foreign Aircraft and Equipment Section as well as the US Aircraft and Equipment Section. The foreign aircraft activity included liaison with teams in the various war and occupation theaters. The Liaison and Translation Branch was responsible for working with numerous manufacturers' representatives who came to Freeman Field to glean information about foreign equipment. This branch also translated documents received from the theaters, and kept a file said to be "complete accurate information on all foreign equipment, on the field," according to the official ATSC base history written at the time.

In parallel, the same history noted that the "US Aircraft and Equipment Section, obtaining aircraft for storage for a future museum of the AAF, was charged with the responsibility for both procurement of the aircraft and the maintenance of complete and accurate files on the history and data of each of the types received." Though not all of the aircraft initially procured were ultimately preserved, the work at Freeman Field did secure a number of German and American aircraft that are icons of the National Museum of the United States Air Force (NMUSAF) and the National Air and Space Museum (NASM) of the Smithsonian Institution.

The mission of Freeman Field, as written in the ATSC base history, was initially conceived as "receiving, reconditioning, evaluating, and storing at least one each of every item of enemy aircraft and aircraft materiel. This was to include the obtaining of personnel items such as clothing and parachutes as well as the aircraft themselves. Also to be included were such items as anti-aircraft guns, radar, and similar devices. The field will also assemble and catalogue US equipment for display at the present and for the future AAF museum, the site to be determined at a later date."

If Freeman Field provided a large enough physical plant for the gathering and retention of foreign aircraft and equipment, it was not a full-fledged flight test and evaluation facility. The 1945 ATSC base history explains: "Evaluation at Freeman Field is, of a necessity, of a broad nature dealing more or less in generalities. Items to be subjected to further evaluation are selected and sent to Wright Field and other laboratories for such detailed breakdowns. In addition, foreign aircraft placed in flyable condition for test purposes are also sent to Wright Field, as adequate facilities for such work do not exist at Freeman Field."

For a while, Freeman Field was designated broadly as a repository for American aircraft kept for historic purposes: "As a result of an early decision, the base is also a collection point for US aircraft which are preserved and placed in permanent storage for post war historical and scientific purposes. These will include one each of production models used by the AAF during the war as well as earlier types dating back to the World War I and experimental types that never reached the production stage." During the few months between VE and VJ days, Freeman Field's mission included trying to determine what, if any, German aircraft and equipment might be in service with the Japanese, given the cooperation that was known to have taken place between the two nations during the war.[48]

With victory over Japan later that summer, evaluation of foreign technologies at Freeman Field received less emphasis, while the use of war trophies in displays was brisk business. The official Freeman Field base history covering the last half of 1945 detailed it:

Victory celebrations, plus the Victory Loan Drive and the recruiting program of the AAF drew numerous requests from both civilian agencies and Army groups all over the United States for displays of materiel stored at the field.

These ranged from small shipments of smaller equipment and instruments to two and three complete aircraft at one time and called for the dispatching of truck convoys of from one to five large flat trailers to locations as far from Freeman Field as Tinker Field, Oklahoma and Kelly Field, Texas ... Inasmuch as the Freeman Field mission is the only one of its type within the whole of the AAF, the field was called upon to furnish equipment for every type of exhibit, display, and show for which Wright Field received requests.[49]

When foreign materials that had been in outdoor storage at Wright Field were sent to Freeman for consolidation with other foreign shipments, deterioration was evident: "This materiel has been stored at Wright Field for some time in open air storage lots, and was received at Freeman Field in weather-beaten condition. It was, therefore, an almost impossible job to obtain any materiel that could be used for museum purposes from this group of equipment."[50]

The arrival of the German war booty from the aircraft carrier HMS *Reaper* at Newark, New Jersey by the end of July 1945 brought a team from Freeman Field to make the potentially flyable aircraft airworthy for the ferry flight inland to Indiana. The American maintainers reported numerous problems with hydraulic leaks in the German aircraft. Engine condition was another issue, with unfamiliar American maintainers initially facing difficulties getting maximum power out of the German motors. German brakes also came under scrutiny: "Braking systems on all of the planes were in very poor condition, and much work was needed before they could be passed by technical inspectors. This was a common fault caused, not by deterioration of the systems, but by the very nature of the systems themselves. German designers had never placed the stress on brakes that American engineers had done, and the fault was common in all German aircraft inspected." (In retrospect, German braking systems may have been adequately designed for vast German sod landing fields, but less so for the expectations placed on high-performance aircraft working from typical paved American runways.) Subsequent ferrying of these aircraft to Freeman Field took place in clear conditions, since the German radios could not be used for navigation purposes in the United States.[51]

The arrival of the war booty from Col Watson's efforts in August 1945 launched Freeman Field's efforts to share information about the equipment with manufacturers' representatives and military personnel. Observers from the Institute of Aeronautical Sciences (one of the predecessor groups to the current American Institute of Aeronautics and Astronautics) were accommodated in two groups of about 75 guests each on successive Saturdays on September 15 and 22, 1945. "During their visit they were shown captured equipment, and qualified guides were on duty to answer technical questions. Several German aircraft were also flown to demonstrate to the visitors the flight characteristics of the planes. Planes flown included the FW-190, ME-262, JU-88, JU-388, and the HS-129," the Freeman Field history recorded.[52]

Yet "all mention of the collection of foreign aircraft at Freeman Field was withheld from the press until the end of September," the official history stated, "when a National Press Conference, attended by the news services, photo services, news reels, and leading aviation magazines was held at the field. During the two-day meeting the complete history of the field, its mission, and all of its equipment and planes were explained to the assembled group."

Freeman Field's foreign aircraft mission suffered from staffing issues that were only made worse by the rapid demobilization that accompanied VJ Day. The nature of the work – repairing and maintaining sometimes exotic foreign aircraft on flight status – demanded technical skills often found only in USAAF mechanics with long years of service. These men were likely to have earned enough points to achieve demobilization sooner than some men with less experience. The base history noted the problem: "With the speeding up of demobilization ... the field found itself in a constant state of flux, with enlisted personnel leaving the base at [a] rate greatly exceeding replacements." Overall, the base support functions experienced a drawdown in experienced staff, meaning an ever-increasing workload was placed on an increasingly inexperienced staff. The vital Engineering Services group went from an assigned enlisted strength of 55 men to a low of only 25 late in November 1945. Those technicians remaining had to prioritize their work, "forcing the virtual abandonment of several projects because of the shortage of manpower," the history noted. An effort was made to replace some of the departed military members with civilian specialists hired to do the job, but a sense of the transitory nature of the foreign aircraft program at Freeman Field made it difficult to keep civilians, as they looked for more permanent employment. "Field officials ... could offer no more encouragement than that the field would, in a probability remain open for at least another six months." This was accompanied by a cut in the civilian personnel budget, "which made it nearly impossible to secure highly trained personnel in the upper pay brackets."[53]

An accelerating emphasis on making foreign aircraft available for exhibits coincided with the loss of manning, the base history reported. "Thus, with a rise in exhibits there was decrease in manpower available to prepare them, and more personnel had to be transferred from the task of preparing aircraft for flight." To assist the Americans with installation and operation of German jet engines, two German civilians (alluded to earlier in the letter reproduced

43

44

46

47

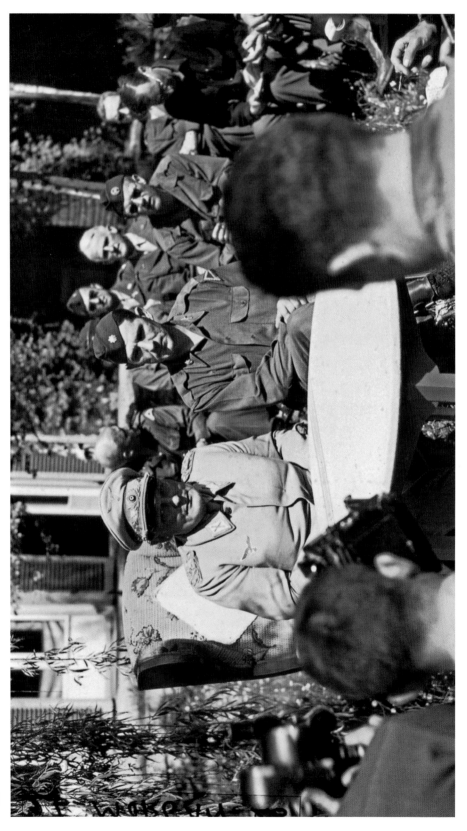

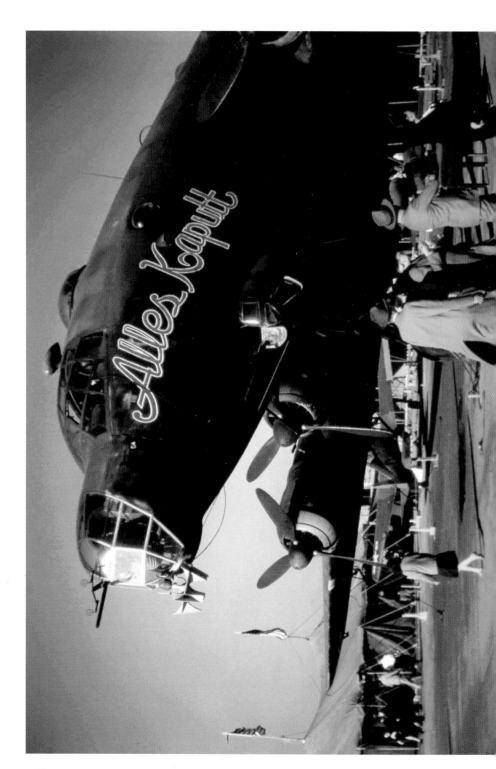

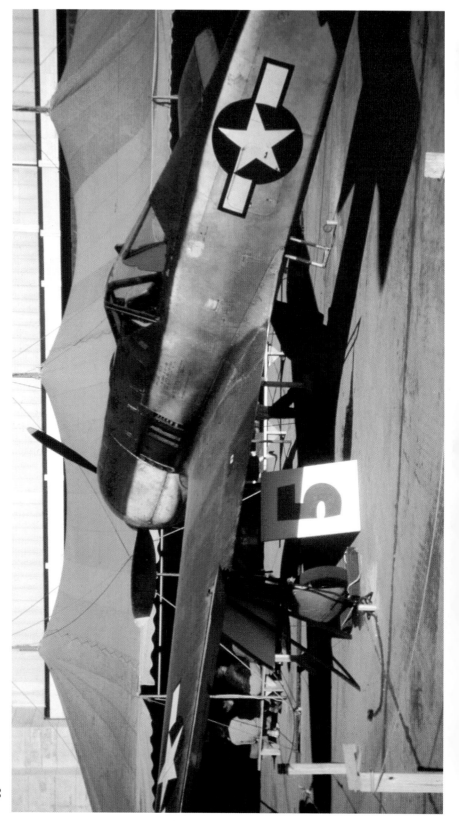

HE-162 Fighter

60

61

62

above) worked under a two-month contract with the US government at Freeman Field.[54]

The initially urgent sense to create a foreign aircraft center at Freeman Field was rapidly overcome by events as VE Day and VJ Day changed the manpower picture dramatically. It is also possible the real, and more lasting, benefit of German technology transfer was realized in the amalgamation of German scientists, engineers, and technicians who came to the United States after the war, where they continued to innovate as they had done in Germany previously. Less useful as the months moved on, though undeniably intriguing, were the artifacts of the last war. Flight activity at Freeman Field for the last six months of 1945 involved a mix of foreign and US aircraft in about 1,800 flights, both local and cross-country. One accident occurred, involving an Fw 190 that did not pull out of a dive during a demonstration flight.[55]

By early January 1946, Japanese equipment and materiel were to be located at the Middletown Air Depot in Pennsylvania instead of at Freeman Field. This diminished the influx of items to Freeman Field, allowing more of the German aircraft to be reconditioned, with no new projects inbound, according to the field history for the period. This placed ever more emphasis on Freeman Field's role in displays, "with a gradually decreasing emphasis on the evaluation portion of the mission of the base."[56]

The decision to place inbound Japanese aircraft and equipment at Middletown was made because of the backlog of German aircraft requiring attention at Freeman Field. There was no more hangar storage space at Freeman to protect the Japanese aircraft until they could be refurbished, and it was anticipated at least four to six months of work remained on the German acquisitions at Freeman Field. "Furthermore," the Freeman Field history recorded, "the condition of much of the Japanese equipment was such that it necessitated the work of a large overhaul depot with facilities which Freeman Field did not possess, if it were to be done as rapidly as was desired."[57]

The lingering dearth of experienced military personnel still hampered completion of some German aircraft in 1946, the base history recorded. "In an attempt to alleviate the situation, eighty-three (83) civilian technicians from Wright Field were assigned to Freeman Field for an approximately ninety (90) day period to assist in the reconstruction and restoration of several German aircraft on which a high priority had been set, as the planes were needed for test purposes." Efforts continued to bring civilian workers to Freeman on a permanent basis to replace departing military members, but issues of wage levels and a lack of civilian housing in the area hampered this process.[58]

In the early summer of 1946, up to July, Freeman Field's Technical Operations staff made good headway on refurbishing a number of German aircraft that were needed for flight testing. These included two of the Me 262s, some "Focke-Wulfs" as identified in the history (almost certainly Fw 190s), an Me 163 and one He 162. American testing of the rocket-powered Me 163 would not extend beyond some glider test flights at Muroc in California's Mojave Desert. The history report singled out one of the Me 262 projects: "The outstanding project was, perhaps, the reconditioning of an ME-262 with a smooth finish similar to that used on the P-80. Principal use to which this aircraft was put was to be that of comparison with the P-80, both in flight characteristics and top speed." Once refurbished, the German aircraft required for test and evaluation flying by the USAAF were relocated to either Wright Field or Muroc Army Air Base, since Freeman Field lacked the flight-test capabilities of the other two fields. Beyond the flying of German war prizes, a number of the former enemy aircraft were refurbished for static display only, including another Me 163, He 162, Bachem BP 20, V1, and V2. The static display aircraft were chosen for their unusual traits; the more prosaic German aircraft were typically not included in this effort. The history explained: "All of the aircraft prepared for display purposes were chosen primarily for their spectacular appearance and unusual features. It was felt that materiel of this type would be the most receptive [sic] to the general public, which would not be able to distinguish the characteristics of conventional foreign fighters as compared to those of US aircraft." By mid-1946, the team at Freeman Field had prepared about 35 aircraft, including those for static displays only, as well as others for flight status.[59]

By early June 1946, display items were being relocated to sites including Wright Field. That month, ten large items including aircraft were transferred to the Collection Division at Wright Field. Folded in with Freeman Field's German technology mission was its role as a collection point for US aircraft intended for the USAAF museum. About 71 USAAF museum-bound aircraft had been moved to Freeman and were stored on the ramp by mid-1946. The American aircraft parked outdoors in the Indiana climate suffered more deterioration due to weather than if they were stored indoors or in a drier locale. To protect these historic assets, USAAF T-2 officers decided on two sites for historic aircraft storage. Those that could be moved indoors at the former Douglas C-54 plant at Orchard Place, Illinois would be sent there. Others, especially those that were large and could be ferried, would go to the dry desert storage location at Davis-Monthan AAB near Tucson, Arizona. The US aircraft were taken out of stored status at Freeman Field, removed from their wheel jacks, and prepared for movement. This activity spelled the end of Freeman Field's Preservation Section, which was deactivated in early June as all aircraft earmarked for the museum departed Freeman Field. The Foreign

Aircraft Section deactivated the Evaluation, Liaison and Translation Branch around that same time. Freeman Field's role in the collection, interpretation and preservation of German aeronautical technologies was on the wane.[60]

A letter from the Freeman Field Engineering Services director on May 9, 1946 identified the first 15 German and American historic aircraft to be flown to Orchard Place, Illinois, one state away from Seymour, Indiana. The German warplanes were listed with their American-assigned T-numbers; the USAAF aircraft were listed with their serials:

1. JU-88 T-2 1598
2. FW-190 T-2 125
3. FW-190 T-2 116
4. P-40N 44-7084
5. BT-13A 41-22124
6. O-47A 37-279
7. C-45A 41-11864
8. C-82 45-25437
9. PT-26 42-14299
10. B-17G 44-83504
11. P-51D 44-74939
12. P-47D 44-32691
13. P-61B 42-39608
14. A-20H 44-306
15. XP-47H [42]-23298

Pilots at Freeman Field would be given first preference to deliver the aircraft.[61]

On June 7, 1946, Air Materiel Command at Wright Field sent the Freeman Field commander a letter requesting the ferrying of a number of aircraft specified for Orchard Place and Davis-Monthan, refining the earlier list in the process:

Orchard Place Airport, Park Ridge, Illinois
P-59A-1   44-22627
P-51D   44-74939
XP-51   41-38
P-38J   42-67762

Davis-Monthan Field, Tucson, Arizona
A-20H   44-306
C-45A   41-11864

AT-7	41-1144
XA-38	43-14406
C-82N	45-25437
B-17G	44-83504
P-61B	42-39608
B-25J	45-8813
TB-26C	41-35784
C-54A	41-37295
C-60A	42-55995
XB-26H	44-68221
A-26C	44-35933
YP-61	41-18878
RB-17E	41-2407
XC-53A	42-6480
C-47	41-38734
B-24D	42-72843
C-87	41-11608
TB-29-15	42-6364
TB-29-90	45-21728
B-32	42-108474

The list included three US gliders that were to be towed by air to Orchard Place:

XCG-15	43-37082
XPG-2A	42-77062
XCG-16	44-76193

Comparison of this list with known surviving aircraft indicates not all of the aircraft set aside for the museum were ultimately retained. Yet from these identified aircraft, a number of American and German display icons can be recognized. The entire concept of air museums hosting vast collections of full-size aircraft was in its infancy at the end of World War II. To be sure, some famous aircraft like the Wright Flyer and the Spirit of St. Louis had been preserved by the Smithsonian Institution, but the large-scale air museums that have gained momentum in the decades following World War II were hardly in vogue in 1946. That makes it all the more remarkable that some of these aircraft were saved for preservation at that time.[62]

Additional extensive lists were drawn up in this same period identifying American and foreign aircraft and how they were to move to their new storage sites. It is possible some of these aircraft were not at Freeman Field at the time of their movement. (See Appendix 12 in this volume.)

Keeping a small gaggle of German aircraft airworthy had to be a logistics and maintenance nightmare. Lack of parts and lack of familiarity with the German aircraft rationale could be taxing. In an era when aircraft crashes of all kinds were more common than they are today, it is not surprising some German war prizes succumbed in the United States.

One of the coveted Me 262s never made it from debarkation in New Jersey to Freeman Field in Indiana. On August 19, 1945, Lt James K. Holt took off in Me 262 500098 (possibly FE-4011) in the company of Col Harold Watson, piloting another Me 262. Their en route stop was to be the Greater Pittsburgh (Pennsylvania) airport. Col Watson landed first; the round-profile nosewheel tire of his Messerschmitt jet blew out on landing. Watson quickly taxied off the runway so his lame Me 262 would not impede Lt Holt's landing. The lieutenant's landing may have been a bit fast, and touchdown was about halfway down the runway. With no usable radio in the German jets, only tower light signals could communicate with the pilots, and Holt was given a red light to signal a go-around. But the Me 262 was not a familiar aircraft to the tower controllers, and the jet was committed to land. Holt applied brakes, but later said they appeared ineffectual. The mishap report said the Messerschmitt veered off the runway, crunching to a halt upright. It burst into flames, and although the fire was extinguished in about five minutes, the Me 262 was a loss. Lt Holt sustained minor injuries. The literature of American flight operations in German aircraft contains more than one reference to issues with brakes and landing gear, possibly indicative of design differences in each country based on operational use and philosophy.[63]

On September 12, 1945, Fw 190 FE-113, with large number 10 on fuselage, suffered a left brake failure during an emergency landing at Hollidaysburg, Pennsylvania. Pilot Lt Robert Anspach elected to ground-loop the wayward fighter in an effort to avoid hitting trees and a ditch. The German fighter's propeller wrenched free of the aircraft; damage occurred to the engine, propeller, landing gear and wings. The damaged aircraft, considered beyond repair at the time, was moved to the Middletown Air Depot. Curiously, the mishap report for this event lists the Fw 190 as "FE 113 #1."[64]

A second mishap report involving Lt Anspach and an Fw 190 identified as FE-113 is dated September 28, 1945. This incident occurred at Allegheny-Coraopolis Airport. The report said that after a normal touchdown close to the approach end of the runway, "at first application of brakes about a third of the way down runway, left brake locked. Pilot checked veering to left with right brake and rudder. Right brake held him straight for approximately 100 yards, then right brake burned up and broke loose allowing plane to swerve to left and causing right gear to collapse as plane left runway. Plane traveled 75' on belly in the sod on the left side of runway." Images taken of the accident indicate the propeller remained attached on this Fw 190.[65]

A jarring, fatal crash of an Fw 190D (FE-119) at Freeman Field on September 22, 1945 happened during a demonstration flight for members of the Institute of Aeronautical Sciences. Apparently a low-altitude wingover maneuver led to a steep dive as the pilot attempted a pullout. The USAAF mishap report stated:

> Contrails appeared at the tips of the wings as the aircraft approached the horizontal, but the airplane pancaked into the ground at a speed estimated between 250 and 350 mph. The impact tore off both wings in a shower of gasoline, while the fuselage bounded into the air, across a road, and onto the flying field … The aircraft was completely wrecked as were all its major components and most of the individual parts. The only instrument found to be intact was the horizontal stabilizer trim indicator.

Accident investigators said the tail struck the ground first; marks made by the tail and then wings "indicate the aircraft was actually in a tail low altitude [attitude?] and 'mushing' against the pull-out."[66]

On July 24, 1946, the ferry flight of a scarce Henschel Hs 129 (FE-4600) ended with a deadstick landing in an open field near Gallatin, Tennessee. At least one tire failed in the uneven field and its wheel broke away from the stricken aircraft. The airframe, not badly damaged, was trucked to Orchard Place for storage instead of Davis-Monthan. During the Korean War, Orchard Place was needed for other purposes, and the museum aircraft stored there needed to find new homes. At that time, the Hs 129 was sold for scrap. Its nose section survived in private ownership, and is said to be in Australia after spending many years in the United States.[67]

Fw 190D-9 number T2-121 suffered a partial landing gear collapse at Freeman Field while being taxied by an authorized civilian. The cause was possibly due to some unknown previous strain on the landing gear. All three propeller blades snapped off at about mid-span and the left wing was said to be damaged beyond repair. The mishap was on August 2, 1946; this Focke-Wulf was soon recommended for salvage.[68]

Me 262A number 111711 (T2-711) was lost to an inflight fire near Xenia, Ohio on August 20, 1946 (see Chapter 4).

CHAPTER 6

JET AGE AND SPACE AGE REFINEMENTS

In July 1947, just two months before the birth of an independent United States Air Force, the T-2 Technical Intelligence office produced a study that mapped a cogent, considered future for the USAF's future gathering and use of technical intelligence. Twice in the past, in both world wars, the US Army's aviation branch found itself playing catch-up as it strived to comprehend and leverage foreign aviation state-of-the-art technology. One result of the LUSTY and *Paperclip* efforts in Germany was to acknowledge the need to keep abreast of foreign aeronautical developments in a postwar world dominated by the United States and the Soviet Union, at opposite ends of political and philosophical spectra. The perceived postwar need was for a planned integration of intelligence and engineering. A key goal was to prevent strategic, tactical, or technological surprises from any source. Counter-intelligence was considered vital, as was the need to provide intelligence on foreign developments to allow leadership to make informed command decisions.[1]

Between 1945 and 1950, the USAAF/USAF's technical intelligence emphasis metamorphosed to meet Cold War needs. The assimilation of German technology, while vital at war's end, became increasingly perishable as it was digested and then surpassed by newer technologies in the United States and abroad. What took its place was the perceived need to continually comprehend technological developments made by other nations, particularly the Soviet Union. While an office had been set up as early as 1943 to monitor wartime Soviet weapons developments, it understandably resided in the shadow of more pressing efforts to comprehend and counter German and Japanese technologies for the duration of the war. In the postwar era, a proactive technical intelligence function would do its best to avoid the surprises visited on the United States defense establishment in the past two wars.[2]

COMPONENTS

Technology transfer took place with components, and not just complete aerospace vehicle concepts. American 20mm cannon used during World War II were effective weapons, yet considered too large for widescale employment in single-engined fighter aircraft. German successes with cannon-armed fighters were noted. One war prize that paid dividends in the United States was the German MG 213/20 20mm cannon. It remained unfielded by war's end, but German expectations were a rate of fire of 1,200 rounds per minute with a 3,900 ft/sec velocity at the muzzle. A 1949 USAF armaments document described the original captured Mauser cannon undergoing rebuilding to repair damage. It acquired the US nomenclature T74 at that time. A redesign led to the T110 variant, with Springfield Armory and the Naval Gun Factory involved in its evolution.[3]

Ford Motor Company further refined the design, leading to the T-160 20mm cannon that received a combat trial in modified GunVal F-86 Sabres over Korea in January 1953, and was said to have a rate of fire of 1,400 rounds per minute. Though results were mixed in the early F-86F installation, development of the T-160 led to its successful employment as the weapon of choice for the substantially different F-86H, the F-100 Super Sabre, the F-101 Voodoo, and the F-5 Freedom Fighter. Still later, an expression of the T-160 as the M39 cannon saw service in later F-5 models. M39 specifications indicate a rate of fire of 1,500 rounds per minute. The American use of the captured Mauser revolver-style MG 213/20 weapon as the basis for a successful Cold War design represents a clear benefit from German war booty, and one that is at least referenced in some USAF documentation.

In the late 1940s, tests of German ribbon parachutes were made with a jumper from Wright Field, at Eglin Field in Florida. In the 1930s in Germany, Theodor Knacke and Georg Madelung validated the concept of using ribbons of material forming a parachute canopy to slow the speed of fast objects while still allowing spillage of air. Knacke did his research at FIST (Flugtechnisches Institute Stuttgart, or Flight Institute of the Technical University/Stuttgart), where he worked for Madelung. The initial quest was to develop suitable parachutes for braking the speed of diving and landing aircraft. The first parachute deployed behind an actual aircraft, a Klemm Kl 25 light sport airplane, was a solid parachute that oscillated, making the aircraft uncontrollable. Opening shock was also noted as excessive. From this unsatisfactory start, Madelung, Knacke and the team investigated a variety of ways to tame oscillation and opening shock from the parachute as it deployed. The ideas they tested included parachutes with holes in the canopy, vertical and horizontal slots, and high-porosity canopy fabric. To ensure structural integrity of these special canopies, some of them were reinforced with ribbon webbing. Next, a reinforced parachute was tried with material cut out between the ribbons to enhance airflow porosity. The ultimate expression of this experimenting was a parachute made only of ribbons. The FIST ribbon parachute was the outcome. In June 1937, a ribbon parachute measuring nearly 30ft in diameter was demonstrated as a landing brake for a Junkers W 34 single-engined transport weighing more than a ton-and-a-half empty.[4]

The German FIST ribbon parachute of the 1930s set the pace for ongoing German research and development. Engineer Knacke said a further breakthrough was the invention by Walter Kosteletzky, a supplier of ribbon material for FIST parachutes, who created the WAKO ribbon parachute. Its stability and uniform, smooth-opening characteristics initially suited it for the slowing of mines and torpedoes. A high-speed WAKO ribbon parachute was developed for pilots of the fast, jet-propelled Me 262 and Ar 234. Even as American engineers were evaluating German ribbon parachutes after the war, it is said the Soviets adapted the WAKO-type ribbon design for MiG-15 pilots.[5]

As ribbon parachutes proved their worth in wartime Germany, the need for mechanical ejection seats became urgent as increasing aircraft speeds made manual bailouts difficult or impossible in some circumstances. Credit for the first test ejection with a human subject goes to German test parachutist Wilhelm Buss, who tested a Heinkel-designed ejection seat in an He 219 in June 1944. The seat was boosted clear of the airframe by a compressed-air charge, and then stabilized by a small, square ribbon parachute. Presaging later seat designs, the Heinkel device automatically separated the pilot from the seat, but then it was left up to the pilot to manually deploy his parachute. By the end of 1944, He 219 nightfighters were being equipped with this ejection seat. Postwar American seat developments included the use of automatic parachute deployment.[6]

Knacke emigrated to the United States in 1946, bringing his German parachute development expertise to Wright Field where his acumen led to the improved ringslot parachute by 1951. With colleague and fellow expatriate Alfons Hegele at Wright-Patterson AFB in 1951, Knacke was instrumental in developing the ringslot parachute as a low-cost replacement for the ribbon parachute. This postwar collaboration in the United States yielded a parachute design useful as an aircraft drag, or deceleration, parachute as well as for extracting heavy load pallets from military transport aircraft in flight.[7]

Exemplifying the building-block nature of the acquired German technologies, the ringslot led to the development of the ringsail parachute by Edgar Ewing of the Radioplane Company in southern California. The ringsail, with lineage traceable to the original ribbon 'chutes of Germany, provided safe recovery of American Mercury, Gemini, and Apollo spacecraft.[8] In a full-circle twist, Radioplane was acquired by Northrop in 1952; Theodor Knacke worked for Northrop, where the Mercury, Gemini, and Apollo ringsail parachutes were developed by the company's Ventura Division at Newbury Park, California. Knacke was Northrop's chief of technical staff for these and other recovery systems from 1962 through 1976.

High-speed German wind-tunnel technology that would benefit the United States was embraced by NACA at its Langley research complex in 1945. An 11in. hypersonic tunnel designed for NACA Langley to explore high-Mach flight was informed by Allied discoveries related to the V2 program at Peenemünde. At a cost of about $200,000, this blow-down wind tunnel used a high-pressure tank upstream and a low-pressure tank downstream from the 11in. test section. The release of the air produced useful high-speed and desired pressure characteristics for a time period of about 100 seconds, until the two tanks' pressure variables stabilized. Operational by 1947, the 11in. hypersonic tunnel was cost-effective compared to high-speed tunnels that sustained their test speeds but at far greater equipment cost, since much useful high-speed data could be acquired in the limited time window of the 11in. tunnel. This German-inspired device was in use by NACA's successor, NASA, until 1973 when it was dismantled and presented to the Virginia Polytechnic Institute.[9]

The 11in. blow-down tunnel served as a pilot model for NACA's larger continuous-flow hypersonic tunnel, which opened in 1957; the German dividend was embellished by this device, also known as the Mach 10 tunnel. Among the accomplishments of the continuous-flow hypersonic tunnel was the characterization of what happens to spacecraft as they leave or enter the earth's atmosphere at extremely high speed. Programs including Apollo and the space shuttle benefited from this knowledge.

SWEEP AND SLATS FOR THE SABRE

If Boeing's George Schairer gets credit for illuminating salient fundamentals of German swept-wing research and sharing it with multiple American manufacturers in 1945, Larry Green at North American Aviation deserves notice for his perseverance in digesting German documents shipped back to the United States. Green, head of design aerodynamics at North American, took nightschool classes in German to enable him to decipher the war-prize documents made available by Wright Field evaluators. The German answer to some swept-wing instability issues that American designers found vexing was the use of movable leading-edge slats on the wing, as seen on the Me 262. The XP-86 (later F-86) metamorphosed from a straight-wing jet fighter design to a swept-wing world-beater in fairly short order.[10]

As North American designers began to embrace swept-wing tenets, such a radical redesign of the original P-86 planform could benefit from any viable shortcuts. To comprehend the German use of slats, a complete wing from a Me 262 was airlifted to North American, where engineers dissected the slats' mechanism, modifying the slat tracks to fit the XP-86 wing. The German slat control switch and lock were appropriated for initial use in the XP-86 as well. This overt use of German hardware validated the slat concept on the XP-86, paving the way for slat designs on Sabres to come. While both the United States and the Soviet Union would soon field masterful swept-wing jet fighters that would duel over Korea, both nations also benefited from shortcuts made possible by captured German research.[11]

FROM MESSERSCHMITT TO BELL

The discovery by a US Army unit of the unfinished Messerschmitt P 1101 single-engine experimental jet aircraft at Oberammergau on April 29, 1945 was exciting and perplexing for the Americans, for this aircraft and its experimental plant was not on the list of known German test sites. The P 1101 used a sharply swept wing at 40 degrees, but its designers intended to set the sweep at different angles on the ground for more comprehensive exploration of the values and vices associated with swept-wing technologies. The advanced P 1101 was appreciated by American designer Robert J. Woods from Bell Aircraft, who was part of the corps of American aeronautical specialists invited to inspect and help harvest German technologies in Europe in 1945. Woods worked to secure members of the Messerschmitt team along with the P 1101 airframe. But before the Germans could retrieve a treasure trove of P 1101 technical documentation that had been cached to protect it from destruction, French forces found the materials, which were not reunited with the actual aircraft. The P 1101 airframe subsequently became a technical curiosity at Wright Field before Woods and Bell Aircraft received permission to ship it to the Bell factory in New York for further evaluation.[12]

Woods envisioned a modification to the P 1101 that would permit changing the wing sweep angle in flight. Ultimately, Bell built two new adapted lookalikes under the research aircraft designation X-5. Some changes from the Messerschmitt design are evident in photos of the X-5s, but the resemblance remains striking. The original P 1101 was used for some structural testing before succumbing to the scrapper, never flown in Germany or America.[13]

The X-5s performed a research program at Edwards AFB, California, where one example crashed in 1953, killing pilot Maj Raymond Popson. The other finished its work by 1955. These pioneers of inflight wing sweeping were beneficial to subsequent designs that used variable sweep to accommodate low and high speeds.[14]

FROM PEENEMÜNDE TO EL PASO

The amalgamation of German rocket scientists into the American space program yielded benefits for the US, while giving the Germans a safe haven. Wernher von Braun became the spokesman for imaginative space-travel stories on American television in the 1950s, his previous association with the Nazi regime largely forgotten and forgiven.

Beginning in the fall of 1945, the arrival of more than 100 German scientists in El Paso, Texas, as invitees of the US Army, at Fort Bliss happened with little fanfare – a deliberate US Army action. Fort Bliss' huge open range area abutted the White Sands Proving Ground (to become the White Sands Missile Range) in adjacent New Mexico, giving vast isolation in which to conduct missile launches with little fear of collateral damage or prying eyes. Some of the Germans were amazed at the expansiveness of the American west – easily capable of swallowing up all of Germany's area many times over. Also curious to them was the ease with which they, with their US Army escorts, traveled thousands of miles across many state lines with no policed border crossings.

The Germans were guests of the US Army who arrived without the normal processing of foreign visitors to the United States. They had one-year contracts. Initially they were closely watched and escorted by their US Army hosts any time they wanted to go off Fort Bliss. Over time, the restrictions relaxed. Von Braun, in particular, urged his German associates to learn English, which many of them accomplished with the colorful inflections of the American southwest. Some of the men initially felt their talents were underutilized at Fort Bliss. Von Braun did what he could to keep them focused and motivated, discussing their unifying vision of space travel.

During their first Christmas in America in 1945, some of the Germans, including Wernher von Braun's younger brother Magnus, devised a skit foretelling the first launch of man into space from White Sands in the year 2000. Little did they know then how the American-Soviet space race would buoy many of these same German émigrés on an aggressive adventure to put men on the moon by 1969.[15]

The first year for the Germans in El Paso saw some of them assist the US Army in early V2 launches. For the Germans, the future was in new missiles and new goals in space, while for the Americans, self-sufficiency with the V2s was a worthy milestone. Before the first year-long contracts were up, it was evident the Germans possessed knowledge and skill levels not yet attained by their American counterparts. In an effort to retain the services of the Germans, five-year contracts tied to civil service wage rates were offered. In addition, the scientists and engineers could bring their families from Germany. The rocket men did what they could in those first few postwar years in El Paso, caught in a limbo where some American decision-makers did not want to fund extensive new missiles as a military venture, and the notion of non-military manned spaceflight was too far-fetched to gain traction. But in 1949, Soviet testing of their first atom bomb, coming on the heels of the contentious Berlin blockade and airlift the year before, prompted a change in thinking. The Germans would be employed initially in the creation of a new ballistic missile with a 200-mile range and nuclear capability. Longer-range missiles were expected to follow this initial effort. Col Holger N. Toftoy, the US Army ordnance officer entrusted with leading this effort, needed a better physical plant than the makeshift operation he had at Fort Bliss. When his request to build proper rocket research facilities was turned down for other operational requirements at the Texas site, he inspected, and then requested, two mothballed US Army arsenals in Huntsville, Alabama. His plans for the US Army missile facility survived some challenges to become funded at Huntsville.[16]

In 1949, with multi-year work agreements and a planned move in the following year to the green hills of northern Alabama, the German scientists encountered a new dilemma. Their status as invitees of the US Army had circumvented normal immigration processes. They could not apply for US citizenship because they were technically illegal aliens. In a bit of old west choreographing that met the letter of the law, the Germans in El Paso simply stepped into neighboring Mexico and returned to Texas, this time as recognized aliens seeking American citizenship.

If a summation of the German rocket scientists' experiences can be made, it must include recognition of the team spirit they managed to hold on to, in spite of their upheaval in Germany, and perceptions of underutilization early in their U.S. sojourn. Their integration into US Army ballistic missile programs of the 1950s gained for them the next new missile program, the Redstone, followed by the Jupiter. But much more fortuitously, it kept them available to form a cadre at NASA for developing the space exploration vehicles and rationale they had dreamed of since the 1930s. In 1960, with President John F. Kennedy's stirring challenge to the United States to put a man on the moon within the decade, much of the US Army's missile development team at Huntsville transferred over to the National Aeronautics and Space Administration (NASA) who created the Marshall Space Flight Center in Huntsville to enable creation of the Apollo Saturn V multi-stage moon rocket. Naturalized US citizen Wernher von Braun was selected to become the first director of the new Hunstville NASA center.

If the spectacular acceleration of America's space program outstripped the efforts of early V2 launches in the New Mexico desert under the overarching moniker Project *Hermes*, those flights nonetheless set the stage for what followed. After a number of basically stock V2s (albeit usually with some American-made components) reached various altitudes and achieved differing levels of upper atmospheric research over New Mexico, scientific and engineering entities in the United States began modifying the German war booty in an effort to make the V2s more effective research vehicles.

The US Navy's Naval Research Laboratory (NRL) accepted the US Army's invitation in January 1946 to become involved with V2 research in the New Mexico desert. The NRL held a key position in the US V2 program, conducting upper atmospheric science and developing the technology to enable this research. The NRL logged 80 experiments between 1946 and 1951. Major accomplishments included the first photos of Earth from altitudes of 40, 70, and 101 miles; the first detection and measurement of solar X-rays; the first direct measurement of atmospheric pressure higher than 18 miles; the first photography of the ultraviolet solar spectrum below 285 angstroms; the first detection of solar Lyman-alpha radiation; and the first direct measurement of the profile of ionospheric electron density versus height.[17]

The NRL's Richard Tousey took advantage of the V2's altitude capability to design special spectroscopes to measure solar ultraviolet radiation from above the filtering blanket of Earth's atmosphere. His first instrumentation package was destroyed in a shattering desert crash, but in October 1946, the device survived and provided the first solar spectrum in the far ultraviolet range.

The military V2 s had warhead nose cones that were ill suited to housing scientific payloads. The Naval Gun Factory in the District of Columbia manufactured new lookalike nose sections that had appropriate access panels and the ability to better accommodate research packages. The 7½ft-long science noses initially answered the need. As science flights continued, instrumentation packages in the extreme nose of a V2 were sometimes irretrievably damaged on impact with the ground. Researchers noted the lower sections of the rocket body tended to survive the return to Earth better than did the nose cone. Some effort was made to use explosives to separate the rocket nose from the rest of the body, and to mount instrumentation in the lower body areas for an increased chance of data survival. Launches of anesthetized monkeys provided data on weightlessness and other phenomena that increased the scientific confidence level that humans could survive the rigors of spaceflight.[18]

Navalized V2s included a trio of the missiles trucked from New Mexico to Norfolk, Virginia in 1947. The three V2s were loaded aboard the aircraft carrier USS *Midway* (CVA-41) for Operation *Sandy*, the shipboard launch of a V2. A US Army team familiar with the German rockets assembled the V2s for the US Navy and trained a US Navy launch crew. While *Midway* cruised in calm waters a couple of hundred miles off the east coast of the United States, Operation *Sandy* launched one of the V2s on September 6, 1947. The launch succeeded, but the missile destroyed itself at about 12,000ft. With little delay, *Midway* began aircraft launch operations once the V2 was gone. The test was called successful because it showed the possibility of handling a large rocket like the V2 aboard a ship at sea, then launching it without impeding the ship's normal operations. The US Navy's missile aspirations were whetted by the Operation *Sandy* flight. But what if rough seas caused a calamity in which a V2-type missile tipped over on deck after being fueled? Operation *Pushover* used a replicated section of steel aircraft-carrier deck installed at White Sands, plus two V2s that were deliberately toppled at different times in the pre-launch sequence to gain an appreciation for the inferno a fully fueled missile could cause. Ultimately, the US Navy's unique leg of the strategic triad in American nuclear deterrence would come in the form of specialized submarine-launched Polaris missiles.

The USAAF's (later USAF's) Cambridge Research Laboratories in Massachusetts participated in upper-atmosphere measurements made aboard V2s launched over New Mexico. Instrumented balloons of the day typically only reached about 19 miles high; the V2s promised altitudes of 100 miles or more. It was in the service's interests to quantify as much as possible the characteristics of the upper atmosphere and near exoatmosphere, to aid in the development of viable high-altitude aircraft and even higher-flying missiles.[19]

Records show seven V2s were assigned to the Cambridge labs, under the name *Blossom*. They were modified by lengthening them about 5ft 5in.

in the midsection, as well as extending the nose cone and developing parachutes for instrument and experiment recovery purposes. Their modifications were designed to cause the *Blossom* V2s to break up in flight, separating research sections for, hopefully, survivable landings in the desert. Four of the seven *Blossom* V2s were considered to have successful missions.

The American testers of V2s in the desert gained valuable experience with large-rocket staging when they mounted an American product, the WAC Corporal rocket, to the nose of a V2. The staging and separation enabled the WAC Corporal to ride aloft, boosted by the massive liquid-fueled V2, and then accelerate ahead to achieve research altitudes unattainable by other means of the day. Suggested in mid-1946 by Col Toftoy, the ensuing lash-up of the American and German rockets constituted the first multi-stage liquid-fueled rocket tested in the United States. The modified missiles were operated under the project name *Bumper*. The existing WAC Corporal was modified with the addition of another fin and the enlargement of all fins to help stabilize it in the extremely rare atmosphere in which it would begin its solo boosted flight after separation from the V2. As the WAC Corporal eased out of the V2 nose cone on rails, two small rocket motors imparted a gyro-stabilizing spin to the smaller missile to enhance the accuracy of its flight into space. The first *Bumper* launch was on May 13, 1948. It was a test of the system. The *Bumper* team made several launches of varying degrees of success leading up to *Bumper 5* on February 24, 1949. The full-up V2 and WAC Corporal combination delivered as designed, and after leaving its V2 booster behind, the slim Corporal reached the then-astounding altitude of 244 miles above the stark desert, and a speed of 5,150 mph. It was the highest a man-made object had soared at that time.[20]

Two *Bumpers* were earmarked to explore flight dynamics around Mach 7. This required a flatter trajectory and not maximum altitude, which translated into a long 250-mile downrange profile. Even the vast reaches of White Sands could not contain a run that long, so *Bumpers 7* and *8* were launched from the USAF's newly designated overwater range at Cocoa Beach, Florida, on Cape Canaveral. They inaugurated the Florida facility. One of the Florida *Bumpers* boosted its WAC Corporal in a trajectory that enabled the smaller rocket to reach nine times the speed of sound – a record.

Seventy-two Americanized V2s are counted in the launch statistics between April 16, 1946 and September 19, 1952. Of these, only 68 percent were called successful launches, although some of the failed missions still yielded useful information and experience. If the scientific research was sparse over this large batch of V2s, the experience gained in missile operations and how to conduct missile research was very valuable, and is generally credited with saving the US years of delay in maturing its missile development program.[21]

One can only imagine the excitement of US Army, US Navy, and industry rocket testers as they pondered the availability of as many as 100 supersonic German V2 missiles in 1946. These early American rocketeers were fresh from victory in the most technologically complex war the world had known. Yet by their very use of appropriated German technology, they had to be cognizant that even as they were pioneering new experiments, they were doing so with a design made by their erstwhile mortal foe. Subsequent space developments would show just how important the sometimes-controversial decision to bring German rockets and rocket scientists into the United States would be.

If Wernher von Braun's enthusiastic, upbeat, yet authoritative persona made him the natural leader of the transplanted German rocketeers in America, he wisely kept his wartime deputy, Dr. Eberhard Rees, close at hand and in pivotal positions in the nascent postwar American rocketry discipline. Rees, a mechanical engineer by training in Germany in the 1930s, was summoned to join the rocketry team at Peenemünde in February 1940. It would be his introduction to rocketry, and to Wernher von Braun. Years later Rees recalled how he and von Braun discussed the spaceflight potential of rockets – the kind of talk that once got von Braun incarcerated for a brief time. Both men agreed that their peacetime vocations would involve development of rockets for spaceflight.[22]

When Wernher von Braun was chosen to be the first director of NASA's Marshall Space Flight Center in Huntsville, Alabama, he tapped his old colleague Eberhard Rees to be deputy director to handle technical and scientific issues. At Marshall in the 1960s, Rees and von Braun were seminal to the success of the evolutionary Saturn I, I-B, and Saturn V that were required to boost manned Apollo vehicles to the moon. Rees would later say the Saturn development was the most interesting work in his career. When von Braun departed Marshall, Rees assumed duties as director until his retirement in 1973.[23]

Nor did the early American rocket breakthroughs end with the last captured V2 launch in 1952. General Electric built upon another German rocket, the unfielded surface-to-air *Wasserfall*. Smaller than a V2, but with similar aerodynamic shaping, the *Wasserfall* silhouette had German research to back up its reasoning; General Electric capitalized on this research, but improvised with a different internal motor system in their variant known as the Hermes A-1. The wealth of experience General Electric gained in its White Sands V2 and Hermes efforts can be traced through several iterations, each more original than the previous, leading to the US Army's successful Redstone surface-to-surface missile.

The Consolidated Vultee Aircraft Company – Convair – was, like all American aircraft manufacturers after war's end, in search of new business. Convair diversified its aviation portfolio with contracts for the giant B-36 strategic bomber, forays into twin-engine airliners, and exploratory military work. (See XF-92, above.) When the USAAF solicited proposals for projects as part of a decade-long study of guided missiles, Convair received approval to explore a theoretical 5,000-mile-range ballistic missile projected to deliver a nuclear warhead with an accuracy of just under one mile. The first step in this ambitious plan was creating a smaller liquid-fueled missile to validate the use of swiveling rocket nozzles instead of movable vanes for control. The use of telemetry, and improvements in guidance systems also were to accrue from this demonstration missile, given the USAAF project designator MX-774.

Convair's Vultee division undertook the challenge. Vultee lead engineer Karel Bossart began with a known quantity – the V2 – and his resulting MX-774 bore a strong resemblance to the German wartime product. But Bossart and his team made a salient change that saved substantial weight. Where the V2 had a steel shell housing separate fuel and oxidizer tanks, the Convair engineers reasoned that the external skin of the rocket body could be the outer wall of integral tankage for the two fuel components. The pressure of the liquids in the tanks lent rigidity to the missile while on the ground; in ascent, the loss of fluids due to fuel burn was offset by gas pressure to maintain rigidity. This clever mating of German silhouette as a design shortcut, plus revolutionary integral tanking and swiveling nozzles, permitted the MX-774 to be built in less than two years. After static engine tests, the first launch of an MX-774 took place at White Sands on July 13, 1948. It and two other copies suffered problems in their flights, but they validated two key concepts – swiveling nozzles and thin-wall integral fuel tank/rocket body construction.

The Germanic connection does not stop there; photos of MX-774 launch recovery operations show what appear to be German-inspired ribbon parachutes intended to slow the fall of the instrument-laden missiles.

The innovative design of the MX-774 gave Convair and the USAF sufficient confidence to proceed with an operational intercontinental ballistic missile (ICBM) derivative – the much larger, and finless, Atlas. Late variants are still in use as satellite boost vehicles at the time of writing. Visitors to the Atlas assembly plant are surprised at the hollow, vibrating drum-like sensation that comes from thumping the skin of a cradled and unpressurized Atlas. The original Atlas missiles deployed by the Air Force as ICBMs in October 1959 no longer looked like V2s, but they owed their successful development time to the use of V2 aerodynamics in the MX-774 more than a decade earlier. Withdrawn from USAF service as an ICBM in the middle of the 1960s, the Atlas will forever be associated with its decades-long service as a boost rocket, including the mission that put John Glenn, America's first orbital astronaut, aloft in 1962.

CHAPTER 7

DUSTY JEWELS REDISCOVERED

While many captured German aircraft in the United States were unceremoniously scrapped in the 1940s after their value as technical oddities was gone, a core of the Luftwaffe war prizes passed over to the stewardship of the National Air Museum (now the National Air and Space Museum) of the Smithsonian Institution. A few more resided with the Air Force Museum (now the National Museum of the United States Air Force) in Ohio, while in southern California a visionary named Ed Maloney made efforts to keep a Bf 108 (T2-4610), Bf 109G (T2-122), He 162 (T2-489), and an Me 262 (T2-4012) intact for his dream museum years before such efforts were generally appreciated by the public. As this is written, Maloney's Planes of Fame Museum still retains all but the sharklike Me 262, now part of Paul Allen's Flying Heritage Collection at Washington's Paine Field Airport, Everett (and reported to be in England undergoing restoration at the time of writing).

Visitors to Goleta Airport near Santa Barbara, California in the late 1960s could see a partially complete Fw 190D-13, parked silently on the ramp in an era when the comings and goings of warbirds were less well documented than they would be in subsequent years. This was FE-118, later bought by Doug Champlin for his museum collection in Mesa, Arizona, where it went on display after meticulous restoration in Germany in the 1970s. Later, FE-118 also became part of the spotless Paul Allen collection in Everett, Washington. Flying Heritage also breathed life into pieces of original V2s from Germany, displaying a restored V2 in May of 2013. Other Flying Heritage German icons include a flyable Fw 190A, a Fieseler Storch, Me 163 Komet, and an early Bf 109E. Only the long-nose Fw 190D and the Me 262 are part of

American war booty; the others include rare European crash finds that have been meticulously restored. The Me 163 was once part of the British postwar German collection. The Allen collection also hosts a Fieseler V1 and an Fi 103R piloted V1 variant.

The National Museum of the United States Air Force (NMUSAF) has kept some examples of captured German warplanes for decades, adding others along the way at its extensive campus on Wright-Patterson AFB near Dayton, Ohio. At the obscure, yet fascinating, end of the spectrum is a Focke-Achgelis Fa 330 Sandpiper autogiro kite-like device. The Sandpiper's three-blade rotor would turn when the small device was towed by a surfaced submarine, giving the tethered Sandpiper's pilot an elevated observation post. The museum's Fa 330 (FE-4617, later T2-4617) was part of the postwar booty brought back to the United States. The USAAF briefly tested an Fa 330 at Wright Field, towed behind a truck running the length of the runway. Other tests were begun at MacDill Field in Florida to determine whether the Fa 330 had merit as an observation position to be towed by a fast rescue boat in the Gulf of Mexico, but a mishap that dunked the pilot and sank the Fa 330 put a quick end to that thought.[1]

NMUSAF's Ju 88D entered the United States in October 1943 on a transatlantic ferry flight for which it was emblazoned with huge painted American flags to help aircraft spotters see it as friend, not foe. A defecting Romanian Air Force pilot landed the Ju 88 in Cyprus, where the RAF took it, eventually ferrying it to Cairo's Heliopolis airfield where the Junkers was transferred to the USAAF. Its transatlantic delivery flight included stops at Ascension Island; Natal, Brazil; British Guiana; Puerto Rico; Morrison Field, Florida; Memphis, Tennessee; and finally Wright Field. With several coastal stops before entering the mainland of the United States, it is understandable why this Ju 88 carried extra US national star insignia on both wings and huge red, white, and blue American flags on its vertical tail. The Ju 88 flew a number of evaluation hours at both Wright and Eglin Fields during the war before joining the aggregate of captured German aircraft at Freeman Field by September of 1945. If the permanent retention of examples of German warplanes looks sporadic by today's standards, at least some of the war booty including this Ju 88 made it into safe storage when no longer required for other USAAF service. The Ju 88 was an unlikely member of the storage fleet of aircraft at Davis-Monthan AFB near Tucson, Arizona for many years, before being shipped back to Wright-Patterson AFB and the Air Force Museum in 1960, where it was parked outdoors for a number of years, wearing paint not representative of its past. In the 1980s, the museum refurbished it extensively and reverted the bomber to its colorful Romanian markings.

The Fw 190D-9 at NMUSAF is on loan from the extensive National Air and Space Museum collection, and is one of the postwar captures (FE-120). The single-seat Me 262 at Dayton is one of the flightworthy 1945 deliveries to the US aboard the British aircraft carrier HMS *Reaper*. Instead of being a USAAF asset, it went to the US Navy at Patuxent River, Maryland, where test pilots including Marion Carl flew it on test sorties intended to evaluate the ability of jet-powered aircraft of that era to execute missed approaches, or wave-offs, to aircraft-carrier landings.[2]

NMUSAF also displays some German armaments and bombs. Another major American aerospace museum, the National Air and Space Museum of the Smithsonian Institution, had a number of German bombs in storage for many years, and this is consistent with reports of German bombs being marked, crated, and shipped to the United States in 1945.

Legendary for some of its long-closeted German aircraft, the National Air and Space Museum (NASM) was the beneficiary of much of the USAAF's war booty. Known simply as the National Air Museum in 1946, before the addition of "Space" to its title in 1966, NASM kept the bulk of its German technology collection disassembled and stored in several metal buildings in the Washington, D.C. suburb of Silver Hill, Maryland for decades. In recent years, especially with the museum's grand expansion facility adjacent to Dulles International Airport, increasing numbers of these rare German relics are coming to light. Following their retention first at places like Freeman Field, Indiana and then Orchard Place, Illinois, the NASM German relics were valued for what they were in a time when the museum did not have the opportunity to restore and display them all. Museums, even large and seemingly prosperous repositories like the National Air and Space Museum, still must prioritize the acquisition, retention, restoration, and ultimate display of items. It has long been estimated that a typical major museum may have only ten percent of its collection on display at any given time. With so much competition for limited display floor space and funding, it is a credit to the foresight of NASM (and the National Air Museum before 1966) that so many German war prizes were kept at all.

Some images in this volume depict stored German aircraft at Silver Hill in early August, 1979. Washington, D.C. in August can be oppressively humid and hot. Aircraft stored in metal buildings at Silver Hill escaped the punishment of direct sun and rain while they were on hold for future display. Some still bore vestiges of German wartime markings and camouflage, others had been overpainted with USAAF evaluation numbers, and sometimes bogus German markings and camouflage to dress them for long-ago air base displays and temporary events. Shoehorned into close proximity with aircraft of other nations, with wings and propellers removed to keep everything compact, the warplanes in the sleepy sheds of Silver Hill were an aeronautical archaeologist's playground.

Once a German trophy aircraft is selected for restoration, NASM specialists typically follow protocols to ensure its authenticity. Layers of postwar paint are carefully sanded with delicate movements to preclude damaging the underlying structure as well as to gently reveal original German markings wherever they may still be present. Some portions of an aircraft must be considered consumable – hence replaceable – and this typically includes fabric on control surfaces and soft goods like rubber and upholstery. When the Silver Hill crew tackled their Me 262, they soaked the age-flattened tires in a rubber treatment that eventually allowed the old tires to revive. The Me 262's plastic cockpit canopy glazing was dulled from the decades, but ginger polishing brought it into presentable shape again. The ability of restoration shops to fabricate brand-new replacement parts keeps expanding, often with the aid of computer-driven machinery that can replicate one special part or fitting where this would have been impossibly costly decades ago. When NASM refurbished the Me 262 in the 1970s, it faced a mountainous task of treating metal corrosion in much of the airframe. Years of storage in humid climates probably did little to help this situation, and author Walter Boyne points out that the German aircraft industry spent little time on corrosion preventive measures late in the war, with the Luftwaffe clamoring for more aircraft quickly – aircraft that often were lost with few hours of flight time. The Me 262's curious mix of aluminum and steel, each of which can corrode by itself, only exacerbated the problem where the two dissimilar metals came in contact. Electrolytic corrosion can occur where two different metals touch, and while some aircraft construction methods use barriers in an effort to halt this problem, NASM's Me 262 team found evidence of dissimilar metal corrosive effects.[3]

The marching order that came from NASM curator Robert Mikesh called for restoring the Me 262 to a like-new appearance. The result was a finished airframe that used carefully added metal skin patches of original gauge plus the occasional use of bonding filler to return a once-weary old German airframe to pristine condition. The team replicated Messerschmitt's use of cloth tape to streamline seams in the structure, painting and sanding repeatedly to fair the cloth in smoothly.[4] The finished product, when viewed with NASM's assembled yet unrestored Me 163B Komet, gives rise to philosophical discussions about the role of restoration in museum work. The Me 262 is a startling presence, a completely overhauled piece of machinery that looks ready to do battle for the first time. The unrestored Me 163, with its scuffs and minor dents ill-concealed by various paint-scheme changes, is also evocative for its timeworn appearance seems to hold stories of German reach and American grasp.

NASM's Arado Ar 234 (FE-1010; German serial 140312) is a stunning restoration of this fast twinjet bomber. It is the last of its type extant. Visitors have remarked how small the Ar 234 appears in person, compared with its apparent size in photos, but as a single-seat aircraft, it was designed to optimize the speeds offered by its jet powerplants. Acquired by the RAF at Stavanger, Norway, the Ar 234 was assigned to Col Watson's recovery team, and made the voyage on the HMS *Reaper*. This Ar 234 counted more than 20 hours of flight time at Wright Field before being flown to Park Ridge, Illinois for museum storage.

Another piece of war booty in the NASM collection is the slow and diametrically opposite Arado Ar 196 radial-engine floatplane, one of two in the United States. It was part of the complement aboard the German battlecruiser *Prinz Eugen* when that warship surrendered in Copenhagen. The US Navy briefly flew the two Ar 196s from the *Prinz Eugen* in tests of the ship's catapult system at the Philadelphia Naval Air Materiel Center. NASM's Ar 196 carries German *Werk Nummer* (W.Nr.) 623167; the other Ar 196 from the German battlecruiser, W.Nr. 623183, was displayed for many years outside at the Willow Grove Naval Air Station in Pennsylvania. It is said to be in the holdings of the National Naval Aviation Museum in Pensacola, Florida.

One of only two Bachem Natters known to exist is the former USAAF test piece T2-1, transferred to Smithsonian custody on May 1, 1949. It carried evaluation number FE-1 (later T2-1). With German wind-tunnel test data available to characterize the Natter, this radical, vertical-launch interceptor was never flown in the US, but it was a favorite display piece, probably for its radical concept as well as its diminutive size which made it readily transportable.

The last Blohm und Voss aircraft of any kind is the Bv 155 V2 high-altitude interceptor that received USAAF test number FE-505 when the British made it available for shipment to the US sometime after November 1945. The first Bv 155 V1 made some test flights; the V2 article was never flown. This developmental fighter promised altitudes in excess of 50,000ft.

NASM's Bücker Bu 181B Bestmann light trainer and transport was transferred from the USAF. After a brief stint as an impressed light transport in France for Col Watson's team of aircraft gatherers, this Bestmann (FE-4611) was given a ride to the United States aboard HMS *Reaper*, winding up at Freeman Field. One of two of the light trainer utility aircraft that were shipped to the US, FE-4611 survived; its stablemate FE-4612 was earmarked for salvage in the summer of 1946.[5]

The Do 335 in the NASM collection boasts a restoration by Dornier decades after this aircraft was part of the fleet shipped to the United States onboard HMS *Reaper*. The US Navy evaluated this Dornier.

Some confusion exists over the test number assigned to NASM's Focke-Achgelis Fa 330 unpowered rotorcraft. It is either T2-4616 or T2-4618, evaluated by the USAAF at Freeman Field and possibly MacDill AFB, Florida, and later finding its way into the National Air Museum collection.

The Fw 190D-9 that has been displayed on loan at NMUSAF in Ohio since the 1970s is the former foreign evaluation aircraft FE-120, which the USAF transferred to the Smithsonian in 1960. NASM's Fw 190F-8 (FE-117) was part of a fleet of 12 Fw 190s moved to Freeman Field by late summer 1945. It went into storage soon after and never flew in the US after that. By 1949, this Fw 190 was assigned to the Smithsonian and stored at Orchard Place, Illinois, along with a number of other former Freeman Field warplanes. When the Orchard Place facility was needed during the Korean War, some of the former enemy aircraft like this Focke-Wulf fighter were moved to other safe storage, but some less fortunate were scrapped. NASM also has a Ta 152 fighter. Looking like an elongated Fw 190, which it is in effect, this is the last Ta 152 known to exist. Appropriated by the British in Denmark, it was given to US disarmament specialists and ferried to France for loading on the aircraft carrier that brought so many German aircraft to the United States in 1945. Given Foreign Equipment number FE-112 (later T2-112), the Ta 152 was flown to Freeman Field, then to Wright Field. When no longer used, this Ta 152 was stored by the US Army until it was turned over to the Smithsonian in 1960. NASM restoration specialists gently sanded through layers of post-German paint and markings to reveal as much of its original late-war paint as could be discerned. They also learned that the aircraft's wooden aft fuselage and empennage were modified and structurally reinforced at some point – work which they carefully reversed to return the airframe to original specifications.[6]

The single-engined He 162 in the NASM holdings was given Foreign Evaluation number FE-504 (later T2-504), and spent time at Wright Field and Freeman Field, although it served as a static display, its wings sawed and hinged for easy overland transport. This Heinkel was transferred to the Smithsonian in 1949, and relocated to the museum's storage facility six years later.

Though called the owl, there's an almost serpentine look to the Heinkel He 219A-2 "Uhu" nightfighter in NASM's collection of German aircraft. Records indicate it was tested at Freeman Field, as FE-614 (later T2-614) following its journey from Denmark to France where it was loaded aboard the aircraft carrier bringing German materiel to the United States.

Germany's prescient Horten brothers built a number of streamlined, aesthetic flying wing gliders and some powered aircraft that were picked up by US military teams in Germany in 1945. NASM lays claim to five Horten wings: H II L, H III f, H III h, H IX V3, and H VI V2. Perhaps most intriguing is the H IX, a twinjet military flying wing design the center section of which was captured, apparently, a number of miles from where a set of outer wing panels was found.

The only known Ju 388 twin in existence is NASM's example, Foreign Evaluation number FE-4010 (changed later to T2-4010). Carried to the US onboard HMS *Reaper* in 1945, the Ju 388 logged at least ten hours of USAAF evaluation flight time at Wright Field before being relocated to Orchard Place in 1946.

The Lippisch DM 1 delta-wing research glider was unfinished when appropriated by US forces in southern Germany in early May 1945. So intriguing was the design of the DM 1 that the United States had German technicians continue its construction to completion, upon which it was shipped by sea to the NACA research facility at Langley, Virginia for wind-tunnel evaluations, explored elsewhere in this volume.

NASM's Bf 109G FE-496 was a combat acquisition by the USAAF when its pilot defected to Italy in July 1944. This wartime treasure was evaluated in the US, finally being transferred to the Smithsonian in 1948.

The Me 262A-1a in NASM's collection was amongst the jets obtained at Lechfeld, Germany by Col Watson's team. Assigned number FE-111, this Messerschmitt flew in the US after arriving via aircraft carrier in the summer of 1945.

NASM's Me 410 (FE-499) was acquired from the USAF. Found intact on Sicily in August 1943, this Messerschmitt twin-engined fighter was logged at Wright Field by early October 1944.

The Smithsonian's Me 163B Komet carries evidence of USAAF evaluation number FE-500. It is one of five Me 163s brought to the United States at war's end. After arrival at Freeman Field in 1945, the following spring it was airlifted to Muroc Army Air Base (later Edwards AFB) in California. At Muroc, this Komet performed limited glider flights after being towed aloft by a B-29. The test program was ended early, and before any powered flights could be contemplated, due in part to the discovery of delamination in the wooden wings. For many years, NASM has displayed the Komet as received, unrefurbished and evoking the essence of a war prize, more than a prized restoration.

At least one and possibly two Schneider-Hofmann-Rehberg SG 38 primary training gliders were low-tech war prizes the USAF later passed to the Smithsonian. They carried numbers FE-5004 and FE-5005.

Other FE-numbered German aircraft faded away; some, like Me 262B FE-610, were earmarked for colleges and technical schools after the government was through with them. FE-610 was last reported to be at Cornell University in New York state in about 1950, but some accounts suggest the German jet was scrapped instead. Another Me 262B became an outside exhibit at Naval Air Station Willow Grove, Pennsylvania for decades before being used as a master pattern for replicating several Me 262s. The Willow Grove original has since been refurbished and returned to the US Navy for display. Its restoration was its second rebuild, if one counts the nose-over and engine fire it sustained at Cherbourg on July 6, 1945.

The Museum of Science and Industry in Chicago, Illinois boasts a Ju 87B Stuka, a rare find that had spent some display time with the Experimental Aircraft Association (EAA) at its former museum site in Hales Corners, Wisconsin. A North Africa wartime capture, it is said this Stuka was never flown in the United States due to engine problems.[7]

Visitors to Travel Town in Griffith Park, Los Angeles, California could inspect German diesel aircraft engines for years after the war. The venerable Parks Air College in St. Louis has, for many years, displayed a V2 rocket motor system in its powerplant area.

There was an era in postwar America when V1s – almost certainly US-made JB-2 Loon variants – decorated aviation vocational schools and the occasional war-surplus store, with a casual carnival air to them as they competed for attention with other more staid signs on adjacent businesses. No longer cutting-edge technology, German-related hardware that owed its existence to the USAAF's intelligence-gathering efforts began to find secondary and tertiary jobs as curiosities.

Original German aircraft instruments and parts fetch ever-higher prices as collectors' items, and post-Cold War eastern Europe has opened up enough to allow other Luftwaffe aircraft restoration projects to be sold on the market.

TRANSITORY IMPORTANCE

The dazzling reach of late-war German technologies deserves some context. The growing presence of jet and rocket fighters over Germany rightly concerned the leadership of the all-piston-engined USAAF. The menace of unpiloted V1s and V2s dropping from the sky over England and the Low Countries, exploding with blind and sometimes pointless fury, elicited responses from the RAF as well as the USAAF. Allied bombing of the V-weapons took resources away from prosecuting other aspects of the war at a time when the invasion of Western Europe was imminent and filled with its own demands for air power. Meanwhile, German aerodynamicists and rocket scientists used complex facilities to validate theories that put Germany on the cusp of several world-class breakthroughs.

Still, Germany lost the war. Good technology in abundance trumped great technology in small numbers. Germany was unable to leverage its technological edge as an effective force multiplier. Once the air and sea supply routes to England were relatively secure, the United States enjoyed salient advantages over Germany. American production capacity was never touched by bombers. American natural resources, though husbanded for maximum efficacy, remained relatively abundant. American flight training produced sufficient numbers of confident aircrews to match the output of the aircraft factories. American air power remained on the offensive; Germany was forced to cast its air force in a defensive role. With the offensive position, the USAAF was able to initiate tactical and strategic changes that kept the air war moving in its favor, like a boxer landing repeated and varied blows on an opponent who can only hope to shield himself.

In the end, the USAAF wrung the last measure of utility out of its aging four-engined B-17s and B-24s over Germany. As the Korean War showed just a few years later, heavy bomber formations, even with newer B-29s, could no longer stand up to the postwar breed of jet fighters. The age of classic mass-bombardment formations came and went over Europe and the Pacific in three short years.

While this drama was inexorably moving toward its conclusion, senior American military planners embraced the advice of scientists who foresaw technology as an ingredient of growing importance in shaping the usefulness of the postwar American defense establishment. That is where the availability of German technology played a critical yet transitory role. Examples of German prescience incorporated into American designs validate the effort expended by the United States to obtain technology from the recently vanquished foe; George Schairer's 1945 epiphany on swept wings immediately comes to mind.

But the aerospace establishments of the Allied powers were not ignorant, nor incapable of independent discovery. The value of the German technologies lay in their ability to shortcut progress for the victors. Yet within two or three years, both the United States and the Soviet Union were well on their way with their own F-86 and MiG-15 jet fighters that rewrote the effectiveness and reliability of this class of weapons. It was the mutual belief that other nations would employ modern technologies in practical military applications that made rapid assimilation of German technology valuable, and time-limited.

By 1946 – the first year of peace – a number of the once-prized German aircraft were in storage or identified for disposition by the USAAF. It would be decades before cultures and governments would embrace large-scale collecting and display of full-size aircraft on the scale now seen in the world's foremost aerospace museums. The German aircraft phenomenon, though important at war's end, was short-lived as indigenous postwar aircraft designs pushed the envelope out farther than the German relics could reach. It is fortunate that some of these German machines were saved; the rest were easily sidelined in that era.

If German hardware and German test reports accelerated or at least informed American designs for a brief period after the war, a far greater benefit to the United States occurred with the successful engagement of hundreds of German scientists and aeronautical specialists. Specifically, the cohesive band of rocket scientists shepherded by Wernher von Braun gave America a resilient, growing intellectual body of space specialists that continued to create for their adopted country long after the static articles of World War II had lost scientific relevance.

EPILOGUE

GERMAN TECHNOLOGY IN RETROSPECT

As Fred Johnsen has amply shown in this remarkable book, German aviation technology greatly influenced the postwar progression of aerospace technology in the Cold War. Britain, France, the Soviet Union, and the United States all benefited from the evaluation and exploitation of German technology – America, arguably, most of all.

This was not without precedent. In the years after World War I, those same nations had greatly benefited from the exploitation of German technology of the "Great War," specifically the technology of the all-metal monoplane, thick-wing aerodynamics, and refined structural theory. Then, too, the greatest beneficiary had been the United States. The transfer of leading aeronautical personages – most notably Max Munk and Theodore von Kármán – led to the migration of the so-called "Prandtl school" of aerodynamic research and theory, with dramatic consequences upon the conduct of American aeronautical research. Munk, for example, developed the world's first variable-density wind tunnel for the National Advisory Committee for Aeronautics. This pressurized tunnel, which still exists at the now-NASA Langley Research Center, enabled much greater accuracy in predicting the flight behavior of new aircraft by more accurately accounting for scale effects in going from model tests to full-size flight.

Throughout the interwar years, a variety of aeronautical observers maintained contact with Germany through industrial visits, diplomatic missions, trade meetings, personal research and contacts, and from observing military/technological developments. While many signals were missed and some (such as German pre-war air strength) greatly exaggerated, in general there was a growing recognition that German aeronautical development was advancing at a remarkable, even alarming rate. Indeed, the story of the interaction of American and German technology prior to World War II is a study of intrigue and idiosyncrasy; sleuthing and strategizing. Most remarkable is the rapid way in which these former arch enemies pooled their resources after the war, with a veritable A-list of what might be termed a "German brain trust" invited to come to the United States in the uncertain, yet heady early postwar years.

American engineers and planners who evaluated the halted German war machine in the summer of 1945 were generally staggered by the widespread and pervasive excellence of high-speed aerodynamic and propulsion research, though, at the same time, they equally marveled at how fractured, fragmented, and disorganized it had been at the higher levels of the German government. Truly, the Nazis were their own worst enemies, whether in their detestable racial and anti-Semitic policies that removed many of the brightest and most creative people from their midst – just one example being Theodore von Kármán – or their aggressive foreign policy that turned the world against them, or their petty feuds and bickering which set the stage for organizational chaos. Thus native talent within Germany was often stifled by constricted resources and sometimes contradictory directives. America, on the other hand, enjoyed unrivaled manufacturing capacity and access to resources. Moreover, the American scientific and engineering community, having reformed and reshaped itself in the years between 1915 and 1933, was certainly not second-rate, as evidenced by such high-quality aircraft systems as the Douglas family of transports, the Boeing family of strategic bombers, and Lockheed P-38, Republic P-47, and North American P-51 fighters, and individuals such as John Stack and Robert Jones (NACA), Clark Millikan (Caltech), and Ezra Kotcher (USAAF).

Closer study of these erstwhile antagonists in this volume adds necessary nuance to understanding various aspects of World War II. Yes, wartime Germany (and Britain, too) stole the march on early operational jet fighter developments. But the United States was not that far behind, and while the capture and appropriation of German jet technologies in 1945 accelerated and validated American efforts, the simple fact is that by the end of 1947, just two years after the war, American jet aircraft developments were far beyond the frontier created by German advancements. Three examples suffice: the North American XP-86 Sabre, the Bell XS-1, and the Douglas D-558-2 Skyrocket. All three – a swept-wing jet fighter, a supersonic research airplane, and a supersonic swept-wing research airplane – were more sophisticated and advanced than their comparable German projects, the Focke-Wulf Ta 183, and the Deutsche Forschungsanstalt für Segelflug DFS 346. A fourth, the Convair XP-92A Dart, was still on the drawing board, but likewise more advanced than the thick-wing deltas advocated by Alexander Lippisch.

During the war itself, while the appearance of German jets was alarming, the United States (and Britain) took a calculated risk in its plan to defeat Germany with vast quantities of proven aircraft versus the Luftwaffe's reliance on limited (albeit growing) quantities of superior jet aircraft. History shows which strategy won, but, on the whole, it is still not the way to live one's life. The shock of the jet transformed America's approach to national security, and, afterwards, Gen Henry H. "Hap" Arnold established both a Chief Scientist position (the first being the polymath von Kármán) and a Scientific Advisory Board within the USAAF. This continues today, in the modern USAF.

The media and the public were awed by postwar displays of advanced German aeronautical devices. But it is too facile to say that hardware constituted the important prize America and the other Allied powers acquired. As one example, the German rocket scientists who followed their own V2s to the American southwest knew this. They were finished with the V2 by the time they arrived in the US, and were already making preliminary calculations for moon launches in the 1940s. They hungered to evolve spacecraft – though, as Michael Neufeld and others have clearly shown, this was not their sole interest in rocketry – and over time the German expatriates got their chance to infuse the nascent US space and missile program with their expertise. Again American engineers were behind in the development of large-rocket technology, but not dramatically so, as the work of the Jet Propulsion Team at Caltech and the US Navy and USAAF after the war swiftly confirmed. Today, it is the figure of Gen Bernard Schriever, far more than that of Wernher von Braun, that is associated with giving America the routine space lift and national security space capabilities that America now possesses.

Before vanquished Germans came over to help the Americans, World War II demanded concerted effort to comprehend how the German military and the German economy functioned, and where the potential pinch points were that could be exploited by the Allies. Target selection for the flagship Eighth Air Force was far more than a relentless charge against the enemy. It was an intellectual exercise that deciphered meaning out of serial numbers, inspection stamps and data plates on all manner of captured German equipment, coupled with underground observations from within the German sphere and aerial reconnaissance to allow Allied planners to predict with a degree of accuracy the downstream effects of particular bombing campaigns. It was indeed, as Britain's R. V. Jones, a noted practitioner, observed, "The Wizard War." The adage "know your enemy" took on strategic importance as the USAAF, in concert with the RAF and other Allied commands, prosecuted the war based on ever-increasing knowledge about the German economy. In the US, this knowledge included an ever-growing menagerie of captured airworthy German military aircraft, enabling the US to gauge the Luftwaffe's sophistication and to plan ways to counter its effectiveness. Far from simply a dry and academic exercise, as Fred Johnsen has amply shown, it involved stories of adventurous discoveries and sometimes heroic and brazen actions by Americans who seized what they wanted, snatching some technologies from under the noses of their erstwhile Allied partners in the drive across Germany in 1945.

As the melding of German theory and practice, joined to American financial power, organizational and planning excellence, and industrial might, had transformed aviation in the interwar era (leading to aircraft such as the transformative Douglas DC-3), so too did that same melding and mingling come together again in the years after World War II, to create the aircraft and missile systems that deterred the Soviet Union and its alliance partners, leading to the West winning the Cold War in 1989.

Today, the United States faces continued challenges maintaining its aerospace science, technology, and industrial edge. The story here is a useful one, both for tracing the "near run thing" that World War II was, but also as a cautionary tale that in an era of growing acquisition times and rapidly evolving technology, the kind of "catch up" that America played after the Great War and the greater war that followed is no longer permissible.

Richard P. Hallion

LIST OF
ILLUSTRATIONS

1: In the 1930s, Charles Lindbergh, left, enjoyed an international reputation that gained him access to the emerging Luftwaffe in Germany. In the photo, Lindbergh stands near a Curtiss P-36 pursuit at Wright Field. Ever in demand as an aviation consultant, Lindbergh may have flown this P-36, as evidenced by the goggles in his hand. (*AAF via AFTC/HO*)

2: Promotional photographs touted the growing Luftwaffe, as seen in this line-up of prewar Heinkel He 111 bombers, early models with stepped windscreens. (*Via Karl Bartsch collection*)

3: The He 111's emergence as a bomber was a deliberate choice by Germany to simultaneously develop the airframe, both as a transport and as a bomber. The transport variant was publicly revealed first; bombers like this example followed. (*Via Karl Bartsch collection*)

4: Americans trudged through Icelandic snow to learn the secrets carried by a reconnaissance Ju 88 downed on October 18, 1942. Intelligence information gathered from this wreck ranged from aircraft equipment to personal effects found on the German aircrew who perished with their aircraft. (*AFHRA*)

5: The severed tail of a Ju 88 downed in Iceland on October 18, 1942. The wreckage carries mission marks and a map outlined on the vertical fin. (*AFHRA*)

6: The main landing gear of the crashed Ju 88 in Iceland was photographed for later study. (*AFHRA*)

7: The USAAF evaluation report on a captured Bf 109F included this drawing depicting the location of armor protection for the pilot, something that could be of interest to US fighter pilots and bomber gunners. (*AFHRA*)

8 Ninth Air Force personnel loaded this dismantled V1 into a C-47 on November 8, 1944 to airlift it for further study. (*USAFA*)

9: A section of V1 fuselage is winched into the cargo doorway of a Ninth Air Force C-47 on November 8, 1944 to be shipped away from the fighting where it could be evaluated further. (*Ninth Air Force photo by Private Harker, via AFHRA*)
10: German V1 parts are inspected by Americans including Maj Ezra Kotcher at Wright AAF. The men are identified as "Halpern, Pierce, EK [Kotcher], Weldon Worth." They were discussing plans for wind-tunnel testing. (*USAAF via Ezra Kotcher Collection*)
11: Mangled but manageable, dented V1 parts were arranged in their approximate positions as American engineers began the reverse-engineering process in 1944. (*USAAF via Ezra Kotcher Collection*)
12: The throb of a pulse jet motor in the summer of 1944 signaled progress in the rapid reverse-engineering of the V1 by the USAAF and industry. (*USAAF via Ezra Kotcher Collection*)
13: A JB-2 American copy of the V1 was photographed on the launch ramp at Eglin Proving Ground in Florida on March 5, 1945. The rapidity with which the German flying bomb was reverse-engineered in the United States was remarkable. (*USAAF via Ezra Kotcher Collection*)
14: A Bf 109E-3 in British markings, with RAF serial AE479, came to Wright AAF for study in May 1942. A forced landing at Cambridge, Ohio that November ended its career. It had carried W.Nr. 1304. As part of *Jagdgeschwader* 76, it made a forced landing in France on November 22, 1939. (*USAAF*)
15: "Satan" is the nickname given to this captured German 1,000kg bomb employed as an instructional device in a bomb reconnaissance school in Overcourt Manor, Almondsbury, England in February 1944. (*US Army Signal Corps via NARA*)
16: Allied comprehension of the Luftwaffe during the war included this rendering of a Ju 88. It depicts fields of fire for the guns onboard as well as armor locations and placement of fuel, oil, and oxygen. Spellings and word usage suggest this file was shared by the British with the USAAF. (*AFHRA*)
17: This 1943 USAAF evaluation of the Bf 109F fighter used artwork to clearly telegraph the origin of this warplane under review. Because the fighting in North Africa resulted in the Allies overrunning German-held territory, the prospects for obtaining German aircraft there in 1942-43 were greater than in some battle areas where the aircraft returned to bases unreached by the Allies until much later. (*AFHRA*)
18: Far more than souvenirs, data plates like these from downed German aircraft were photographed and shared for the intelligence value they could impart to the teams making target selections for USAAF bombing campaigns. (*AFHRA*)
19: A scavenged desert Stuka was out of the fight forever, and evidently serving as a laundry rack for G.I.s from the 12th Bombardment Group in

North Africa. The coveted tail swastika had been cut from this side of the vertical fin. (*Marv Hawkins Collection*)

20: Carrying a 1942-43-style star in a blue disc under its wing, this Bf 109 is probably the F-model given the Evaluation Branch number EB-1, which may later have become EB-100. EB-100 was a gift of the Soviet Union in November 1942. This may be the Messerschmitt which lost its canopy in flight over Ohio. (*USAAF*)

21: Details of Fw 190 W.Nr. 210194's engine mount are evident with cowling removed. A scribbled sign warns curiosity seekers and especially souvenir hunters: "Keep Away. Violators will be fired upon by gun crew." (*USAFA/ Esmiol Collection*)

22: Scavenged Fw 190 number W.Nr. 210194's instrument panel may indicate the work of souvenir hunters, or possibly intelligence gatherers; the former were the bane of the latter. (*USAFA/Esmiol Collection*)

23: A sign on the other side of Fw 190 number W.Nr. 210194's fuselage warned passers-by to stay away from the bellied-in fighter in the snow. The missing swastika from the vertical fin suggests souvenir hunters had already visited the wreck. (*USAFA/Esmiol Collection*)

24: For a period, the USAAF's Ju 88D carried a US-style tail number, 30650, based on its original German W.Nr. 430650. This did not conflict with any assigned serials of USAAF aircraft. The Junkers later was known as FE-1598, and it became a survivor in the Air Force Museum, subsequently restored in Romanian Air Force markings representing the way it looked when the Allies obtained it in July 1943. In this wartime photo, it carries US insignia on the top and bottom of both the left and right wings. (*USAAF via Peter M. Bowers*)

25: Looking pugnacious with its wide-tracked stance and large propeller, Fw 190G DN+FP became the USAAF's EB-104 at Wright AAF, first flying there in February 1944. A new paint scheme was applied later; the newer designation number for this captured aircraft was T2-125. (*USAAF photo via Peter M. Bowers*)

26: Ninth Air Force hurled the war back at the Germans with abandoned Luftwaffe drop tanks fitted as napalm bombs for fighter-bombers. One Ninth Air Force unit history said the detonator for these improvised bombs was an externally attached hand grenade. The resulting swath of fire could engulf an area 40 yards wide and 100 yards long. (*AFHRA*)

27: Capt John Higgins of the 266th Engineer Combat Battalion, 66th Infantry Division, loosened packing folds in a captured German barrage balloon during inflation to test it for structure and leaks near Chateaubriant, France on February 21, 1945. (*US Army Signal Corps*)

28: A line of foreign aircraft under USAAF evaluation. From left to right: Mitsubishi Zeke or Hamp, possibly number EB-201; Fw 190, which may be

EB-101 or 104; Hawker Typhoon, which may be FE-491 (RAF MN235); Me 410 number FE-499; and Ju 88, probably FE-1599 known as "The Comanche." (*USAAF photo 159725 via Kenneth Chilstrom via AFTC/HO*)

29: German salvage operations included reclamation of damaged German aircraft like these Bf 110s. This train was photographed on March 9, 1945 at Uerdingen, Germany, where it was overtaken at the station by the US Army before it could reach the scrapyard. (*US Army Signal Corps*)

30: The USAAF's 10th Air Disarmament Group (Provisional) undertook its share of the rapid dismantling of the Luftwaffe. The wing of a long-nose Fw 190 rested at an unnatural angle as workers dismembered the potent fighter, circa July 1945. (*AFHRA*)

31: This photo of a German military funeral, replete with swastika emblem and German flag, was taken at the PoW center at Camp Claiborne, Louisiana, on June 15, 1944. American comprehension of the German military during the war included the honoring of international norms for such ceremonies even in wartime. (*US Army Signal Corps*)

32: A 42nd Infantry Division soldier peers into the shattered fuselage of a spray-dappled He 111 bomber at Kitzingen, Germany on April 15, 1945, less than three weeks before the end of the European war. (*US Army Signal Corps*)

33: The unfinished Me 262A number 711 was the first of these jets to come to the USAAF intact when Messerschmitt test pilot Hans Fay made a dash toward the American lines on March 31, 1945. The location is Frankfurt's Rhein-Main airfield. This photo was taken two days later; 711 subsequently shipped for the United States on a fast freighter. (*US Army Signal Corps*)

34: Later to become part of the National Air and Space Museum, this Me 410 shipped from Sicily arrived at Wright AAF in 1944. It carried US identification number FE-499. (*USAAF via Peter M. Bowers*)

35: Bf 109F EB-100; W.Nr. 7640 was posed for walkaround photos at Wright AAF like any other aircraft in USAAF markings. Aileron mass balance suspended beneath the control surface is visible. (*USAAF*)

36: American mechanics worked on a reasonably intact Me 262A at Lechfeld, Germany. Some Me 262s were encountered with damaged nose gear struts. This may have been due to a combination of German efforts to render the jets useless as the Allies approached, as well as initially improper towing by the captors before USAAF recovery teams arrived. (*USAAF via Gary Boyd*)

37: Desolation in the form of broken and incomplete Me 262 airframes greeted the Americans as they advanced into Lechfeld, Germany in 1945. Jet number 26 in the photo has nose bulges associated with the photo-reconnaissance variant. Ultimately, a number of airworthy Me 262s were gleaned for testing in the United States. (*USAAF via Gary Boyd*)

38: The moment of surrender is recorded in a snapshot as this Fw 200C Condor bomber drew a crowd of curious Americans who inspected its dorsal open-air gun emplacement, its German occupant still at his station. The Luftwaffe crew left their base in Norway, flying to Braunschweig (Brunswick), Germany to surrender since some of the crewmembers were from there. (*Allen E. Troup Collection*)

39 and 40: Spotted and scratched though they may be, these historic G.I. snapshots were taken right after a German pilot belly-landed one of only two glass-nosed Me 262A-2a/U2s (V555) at a field occupied by the USAAF's 439th Troop Carrier Group at war's end. The Luftwaffe jet pilot gave an impromptu air show performance before landing, recalled Joe Obendorf, who took the snapshots. Whether or not this belly-landing was deliberate, it has been recorded that some Luftwaffe pilots intentionally crash-landed or ground-looped their aircraft as a last act of defiance when landing to surrender at the close of hostilities. Obendorf said the first American officer to approach the German pilot in the jet did so with his service .45 pistol drawn as a precaution. (*Photos by Joe Obendorf*)

41: The line of deliberately damaged Me 262s at Lager-Lechfeld must have dismayed as well as intrigued the Americans who surveyed these crippled examples of turbojet warriors in 1945. Interestingly, no two paint schemes seem to be the same on the Lechfeld gaggle of Me 262s. (*USAAF via Gary Boyd*)

42: Technicians of the 28th Air Disarmament Squadron unload German bombsights at their squadron area, circa June 1945. The bombsights were about to be converted to scrap. (*USAAF*)

43: When the USAAF inspected abandoned Ju 88s at Villacoublay airfield, just southwest of Paris, they encountered fairly typical examples of souvenir-hunting, like the removal of the trophy swastika panel from the vertical fin of the aircraft in the center of this vintage Kodachrome transparency. (*Brown Collection/USAFA*)

44: Ramshackle Ju 88s at Villacoublay outside Paris were abandoned in haste by the Germans in the face of Allied advances in August 1944. Ravaged airframes show indications of extensive cannibalization by the Germans to keep others flying. Evaluations of abandoned aircraft could reveal intelligence details about the ongoing strength or weakness of the operational Luftwaffe. (*Brown Collection/USAFA*)

45: Le Bourget airfield yielded this dappled He 111 for inspection by American military personnel. (*Brown Collection/USAFA*)

46: Notes for this color transparency say the airmen peering from a well-scavenged Luftwaffe bomber at Le Bourget are "Lt. Col Fredricks and Capt. Love in He 111". (*Brown Collection/USAFA*)

47: This ravaged Bf 109 fuselage caught the attention of visiting USAAF officers at Le Bourget airfield in 1944. (*Brown Collection/USAFA*)

48: Looking weary and perhaps distrustful, Hermann Göring faced American officers and reporters in the summer of 1945. Göring was interrogated by American officers on May 10, 1945, and his answers to military questions were shared with "Hap" Arnold. (*NARA via Stan Piet*)

49: Luftwaffe aircraft at Brunswick-Waggum airfield in Germany at war's end included two Fw 190s, a Ju 188, and Ju 88 nightfighter. For every machine harvested by the Allies, many more had to be summarily scrapped. (*Brown Collection/USAFA*)

50: American troops and civilians pushing a baby buggy visited a lone Fw 200 patrol bomber at Brunswick-Waggum airfield in Germany, its war having ended when its crew flew in from Norway to surrender. (*Brown Collection/USAFA*)

51: Me 262s were sheltered in forests near roads, with cut boughs adding to the camouflage effect. American troops assessed a number of abandoned Me 262s in 1945, shipping some to the US and scrapping others in Germany. (AAF)

52: The huge Ju 290 dominated the foreign-aircraft display at Wright AAF for a public event late in 1945. This German bomber was scrapped in December 1946. Nicknamed by the Americans who appropriated it in 1945, it symbolizes the fate of the wartime Luftwaffe. (*Photo by Ned Schultz via Richard P. Lutz*)

53: Ju 388 FE-4010 made the trip to America aboard HMS *Reaper*. This bomber flew for evaluations and demonstrations in the US, spending time at Freeman AAF and Wright AAF, where this photo was taken in 1945. It subsequently became part of the National Air and Space Museum Collection. (*Photo by Ned Schultz via Richard P. Lutz*)

54: This repainted Me 262 (FE-111) was viewed by visitors to an event at Wright AAF in late 1945. By July 1946 it was in storage at Park Ridge, Illinois. It went on to become part of the National Air and Space Museum in Washington, D.C., being meticulously restored to its wartime condition in the 1970s. (*Photo by Ned Schultz via Richard P. Lutz*)

55: A V2, looking crimped and a bit worse for wear, towers over a Ju 388 at a postwar event at Wright Field in late 1945. People near the base of the V2 give an idea of its size. (*Photo by Ned Schultz via Richard P. Lutz*)

56: This Fw 190G (wartime Evaluation Branch serial EB-104; later T2-125) was studied at Wright Field in flight tests commencing in late February 1944. This color photo was taken during a postwar event at Wright AAF in 1945. (*Photo by Ned Schultz via Richard P. Lutz*)

57: Of several He 162 jet fighters that migrated to the United States after the war, this example's subsequent history is unknown; it probably was scrapped sometime after 1946. (*Photo by Ned Schultz via Richard P. Lutz*)

58: V2 tailfin assemblies, recently delivered from Nordhausen, await assembly with rocket bodies at White Sands, New Mexico, on May 10, 1946. Photographed on large-format 4 in. x 5in. Kodachrome transparency film, this image is preserved in the US National Archives. (*NARA*)

59: Color photography was still the exception when this yellow and black V2 was photographed during launch at White Sands. This is probably the first V2 launched in the United States, on April 16, 1946. (*NARA*)

60: The earth at Freeman Field yielded this corroded and bent tail section from a war-booty Fw 190 when searchers excavated in 1997. The Freeman AAF Museum preserves the activities of this storied base in buildings on the field, now the civilian airport serving Seymour, Indiana. (*Author Photo*)

61: Restored and repainted in the bold yellow and black test markings of the first V2 launched from White Sands in 1946, the V2 displayed at the White Sands Missile Range Museum, New Mexico provides close-up inspection of this iconic shape. This photo was taken in April 2013 by the author.

62: The National Air and Space Museum's German V1 (Fi 103) was dappled with sun and shadows in the museum's immense rocket gallery. Acquired from USAF holdings in the 1940s, it was restored in 1975 and 1976 for display. (*Author Photo*)

63: A brood of incomplete Dornier Do 335 pusher-puller fighters was photographed at Oberpfaffenhofen, Germany at war's end. One Do 335 that had been shipped to the United States was later refurbished by Dornier, who had the aircraft on loan from the National Air and Space Museum. (*AFHRA*)

64: German PoWs, wearing remnants of German uniforms, were tasked with dismantling this Me 262 for scrap in a small town southeast of Wurzburg, Germany in August 1945. They labor under the watchful eye of a G.I. carrying an M-1 carbine. The rapid disappearance of the Luftwaffe reinforced the totality of the Allied victory. (*USAAF via AFHRA*)

65: Fw 190D, *sans* tail, rested on one extended and one folded main gear at Straubing, Bavaria, after war's end. (*Photo by Ralph Nortell*)

66: This late-model He 111 with dorsal power turret was hastily overpainted with US star insignia in 1945; this can be seen with the reflection of the German cross under the wing, possibly from the sheen of paint used to obliterate the cross. (*Photo by Harry Fisher*)

67: This Ju 290 was acquired by US forces. The extant literature gives this Ju 290 the same initial USAAF/RAF acquisition number (022) as that given to a Ju 290 known by the German codes A3+HB instead of P1+PS, as seen in this photo. The aircraft probably had both letter codes in its career. (*Photo by Harry Fisher*)

68: The Americanization of Ju 290 P1+PS included the hasty marking of an outline star in place of the Luftwaffe insignia on the fuselage. (*Photo by Harry Fisher*)

69: Crowds thronged to see wreckage and airframes of Japanese and German war prizes at Wright Field in the early postwar period. (*Warburton Collection*)

70: At Villacoublay, France, where most of the German aircraft were destroyed, this mostly intact Ju 88 nightfighter looked suspicious to the first Americans on scene, who feared it might be booby-trapped. They called in an emergency ordnance disposal team just in case. (*Ninth Air Force photo by Warrant Officer Scheuerman*)

71: This overpainted Ju 88 tail at Lechfeld in May 1945 featured a very non-standard improvised US star surmounting the swastika, signifying the new owners of this German bomber. (*AFHRA*)

72: The Messerschmitt experimental hangar at Augsburg housed intriguing large-aircraft assemblies when visited by the 54th Air Disarmament Squadron in May 1945. The parts may be unfinished remnants of the canceled Me 264 long-range bomber project. (*AFHRA*)

73: The Siebel Si 204 light twin-engined Luftwaffe transport aircraft was of scant technological interest to the USAAF in 1945. As a result, photos of these German transports are scarce. A number of these twins were pressed into service by the British on the Continent in the summer of 1945, and postwar France re-equipped its air force with some Si 204s. (*Photo by Ralph Nortell*)

74: Opposite side view of the Siebel Si 204 transport in the accompanying photo (DG+PH) shows the general form of the aircraft as the Americans encountered it. (*Photo by Ralph Nortell*)

75: Bf 109 fuselages and wings stretch into the distance in this photo depicting German aircraft at the 28th Air Disarmament Squadron's Scrap Collecting Point, Wertheim am Main, Germany, on August 31, 1945. (*AFHRA*)

76: First contact between the crew of this Ju 188 and the Americans came when the Junkers developed problems en route from Norway and Denmark in May 1945 and landed at the 29th Air Disarmament Squadron base instead of their intended surrender site. (*AFHRA*)

77: An American officer looks into the cockpit of an appropriated He 162 jet fighter near Kassel, Germany in the summer of 1945. (*AFHRA*)

78: German pilot Hans Padell flew this Do 335 to the 30th Air Disarmament Squadron's airfield in June 1945. It is believed this Do 335 made it to Freeman AAF as FE-1012, but its ultimate disposition is not known. (*AFHRA*)

79: This Do 335 was flown by a German pilot to a US airfield in June 1945; here it is shown parked on the grass behind the massive Ju 290 bomber. (*AFHRA*)

80: The trophies of Allied victory included this Fw 190 wing panel that formed the sign at the entry to Freeman Field during the heyday of foreign technology work at this Indiana air base. (*AFHRA*)

81: The Me 262 pilot is identified as USAAF Maj Russ Schleeh; the mock P-38 attack happened over the farms of the midwestern United States, not Germany. The patchy finish on Me 262 number 711 shows evidence of gap filler applied to unpainted metal. (*USAAF via Peter M. Bowers*)

82: The original caption reads: "Part of the German Air Ministry library starts on its way to Paris," as 30th Air Disarmament Squadron G.I.s use a forklift to hoist crates of printed materials into a C-47 in July 1945. The squadron was based at Roth in Bavaria, with a PSP steel-mat runway serving their needs. (*AFHRA*)

83: The pantheon of American aeronautical genius was represented at Maastricht, Holland in May 1945 by Theodor von Kármán, left, and NACA's Hugh L. Dryden, as photographed by their peer George Schairer from Boeing. The three specialists were invited to inspect German aeronautical technologies in Europe and interrogate their German counterparts. Though civilians, they wore uniforms with no rank and an abundance of US lapel insignia. (*Photo by George Schairer via Museum of Flight*)

84: An excursion off the Cherbourg runway on July 6, 1945 led to a nose-down stance for the captured Me 262B nicknamed "Willie," after Messerschmitt pilot Willie Hoffman who assisted USAAF pilots. The flames appear to be emitting from the gasoline tank for the turbojet starter motor. This jet was repaired and displayed in the US for years at NAS Willow Grove, Pennsylvania. (*Will Riepl Collection*)

85: Sleeved in protective cloth, a Horten flying wing panel is hefted by US military members into the bed of an American truck as an unidentified woman in the truckbed looks on. The scene was near Kempten, Germany. (*AFHRA*)

86: Alexander Lippisch's thick-winged DM 1 research glider was a triangular enigma when discovered in a partially finished state in 1945. The design was shipped to NACA's facility in Langley, Virginia for wind-tunnel evaluations that would include modifications to the design. (*AFHRA*)

87: In the German summer of 1945, G.I.s manhandle Fw 190 wings into the bed of a US Army truck, to be carried away as salvage. (*USAAF/10th Disarmament Group*)

88: The unusual twin pulsejet-powered Me 328 bomber concept was documented with artwork and a photograph in intelligence files maintained by the USAAF in the summer of 1945. (*AFHRA*)

decades in storage awaiting restoration. It was given American numbers FE-490 and T2-490, and underwent static restoration at Freeman AAF, Indiana in 1946. (*Author Photo*)

100: The rudimentary cockpit of the Bachem Ba 349 Natter was stored at a right angle to the rest of the disposable fuselage of this desperation aircraft that captured the imagination of reporters when displayed at Freeman AAF and elsewhere in the 1940s. It was photographed at NASM's Silver Hill facility in August 1979. (*Author Photo*)

101: The tattered wings of one of the Horten flying wing sailplanes awaiting restoration at Silver Hill in 1979. Two Horten Ho III and one Horten Ho VI all-wing gliders were lent to Northrop for study; none were flown in the United States. (*Author Photo*)

102: A bug-nosed Ju 388L fuselage (W.Nr. 560049) resting in wooden cradles at Silver Hill, Maryland in 1979. Derived from the ubiquitous Ju 88, the Ju 388L had a service ceiling above 44,000ft. It included tail-warning radar, and a wooden gondola for reconnaissance cameras and fuel. It was stored at Park Ridge, Illinois before NASM. (*Author Photo*)

103: On a bleak January day in 1957, one of Watson's Me 262 war prizes sat semi-derelict at the US Naval Research Lab in Washington, D.C. Its disposition is clouded, but it almost certainly was scrapped. (*Photo by Robert F. Dorr*)

104: The unrestored patina of age added character to the Me 163B photographed at NASM's Silver Hill in August 1979. Bearing US number T2-500, this Komet migrated to Muroc AAF in California in April 1946. Consideration was given to powering the Me 163 for some Muroc tests, but it was only released as a glider behind a B-29. (*Author photo*)

105: This Me 410A at Silver Hill in 1979 originally carried US identification EB-103; this was later changed to FE-499, then T2-499. A wartime acquisition taken intact on Sicily in 1943, this fighter arrived at Wright AAF in January 1944, undergoing several months of reassembly there. (*Author Photo*)

106: The travels of this Fw 190D-13 began following its surrender to the British, who gave it to the Americans for transport on HMS *Reaper* to the US. After a stint at Freeman AAF, it moved to Georgia, then Santa Barbara, California, where it was photographed in August 1967. Doug Champlin bought it and shipped it to Germany for thorough restoration in the 1970s. Subsequently it became part of the Paul Allen Collection in Everett, Washington. (*Author Photo*)

APPENDICES

APPENDIX 1:

THE 1945 VON BRAUN NEGOTIATIONS WITH THE UNITED STATES

Wernher von Braun's unshakable belief and vision in the future of rocketry for space exploration began before the Nazis came to power and lasted long after the fall of the Third Reich. Whatever his talents as a rocket scientist may have been, he was also the necessary entrepreneur and champion of such a mission and the team he believed could make it become a reality. When he led a large contingent of his colleagues toward the American lines in May 1945, von Braun acted as their agent, trying to broker the best possible deal for the greatest number of scientists to export the German rocket program to America. An original memorandum in the Air Force Historical Research Agency holdings at Maxwell AFB in Montgomery, Alabama is signed simply "v. Braun," and articulates concerns and demands of the assemblage of German scientists. Though not the final word in the matter, this rare document captures a fleeting moment in June 1945 when the victorious Americans and the vanquished Germans were still sizing each other up, and maneuvering for best perceived advantage. The text of that memorandum is presented in its entirety here, including possible spelling and usage errors. The use of English led to misspelled and sometimes misapplied words, and the syntax is decidedly not in the American vernacular. But the urgency is palpable.

Garmisch-Partenkirchen, June 13, 1945.

The commission had convened those employees of the EW [probably a reference to the rocket development works] and other institutes relatet to the matter concerned – in as far as they are now in Garmisch-Partenkirchen -, who are necessitated for an evacuation of a devellopping institute of rockets and the erection of corresponding plants of manufacturing, to a meeting at 11.30 a.m.

At the beginning of this meeting the representative of the commission gave nearly the following explanations:

"You aggreed to continue your experimental work with rockets as a group in bulk. This is possible only under the auspices of the governments of the United Nations. The government of the USA is considering the idea to allow you to work over there. The conditions under which the work has to be performed, the lodging, payment, and nourishment are constituted exclusivly by the government of the USA. The American authorities will possibly endeavour to settle the families in the territory occupied by the US forces. Those, who want to join in under these conditiones, may sign a form of declaration being now distributed. That concerns a voluntary signature to which none of you shall be compelled. There is no obligation of the US government on account of the declaration given by you."

In addition the representative of the commission declared, that the declaration is requested, in order to prevent, that those who undersigned are in the position of claiming anything later on. Those who undersigned have however to stick to the declaration given by them.

Following to the declaration the representative of the commission demanded immediately the decision of the assembled, if they want to sign the declaration or not.

Before going into questioning those present, if they are willing to sign, the representative of the commission was asked the following questions by men from the assemblage:

I.1.) About the state of employment and the resulting questions:

a.) Does the possibility exist to withdraw the offer of entering a state of employment given to the US government by signing the declaration?

Reply: No.

b.) Will there be concluded a contract of employment between those employees willing to emigrate and the US government?

Reply: No. The conditiones for the state of deployment are settled exclusivly by the government of the USA.

c.) Will there be granted to us the same rights with respect to labour and social conditions as to the American employees?

Reply: Principally not.

2.) About the endurance of the state of employment.

Question: What time will run the state of employment?

Reply: At least six months, for more than that no obligation of the US government.

3.) About the lodging for the time of the state of employment.

Question: Will there be granted full freedom of movement or is there considered a concentration in a working-camp?

There happened no reply to this question.

II.) The representative of the commission was asked the following questions which arose from the care for the families of the men going to USA, because they were excluded from going with them immediately.

1.) Is it possible to take our families with us?

Reply: No.

2.) Is it possible to result with our families about addressing an application to the US goverment before we give an obliging declaration?

Reply: No.

3.) Is it possible to visit our families before the crossing?

Reply: It is not possible to give an obliging answer about that. The commission will see what can be done about such a visit.

4.) Will there be possible an emigration of the families subsequently?

Reply: There are very few chances in that. (*Die Aussichten dazu sind sehr dunn* [Probably translates as 'The views in addition are very much weak'.]).

5.) What will be done with the families remaining in Germany?

Reply: We will try to move these families to the territory occupied by the US-forces. There cannot be given an obliging [obligatory penciled in] declaration on that matter.

6.) Will there be, too, evacuated the Families from the territory occupied by the Red Army?

Reply: We will try, but there are few chances in performing it.

7.) How will be supported the families remaining in Germany?

Reply: It will be possible to transfer part of your payment to your families in Germany, but there cannot be given any garantee to it.

The number of the aforesaid questions recorded from our memory and the Replies given, made seeming desirable, to delay somewhat the signing of the prepared declaration. A corresponding proposal, to deliver the signed declaration to the commission at 3 o-clock p.m., was refused. The signature was said to be given at once before leaving the room, a later delivery not more to be possible, and a withdrawal of the application not to come into question.

The subsequent questioning of the people present proved, that only an extraordinarily small part of the employees convened was willing to sign the declaration, before clearing the pending questions.

The reasons of their refusal have to be seen above all in the following:

The version of the declaration:

"I herewith apply voluntarily for an employment by the government of the US. The employment may be finished by the US government at any time. I will dispose [illegible pencil note inserted here] my full working power without any restriction in case of acceptance of my application.

signature."

makes the offer to the USA of entering into a state of employment seeming voluntary, but does not contain any hint, whatsoever, respecting to the in the verbal amendments expressly given explanation, that the state of employment is regulated exclusivly by the government of the USA. On account of that the one signing the declaration renounces any possibility, to influence the tenor of the state of employment on his part. The express confirmation of the one-sidedness of appointing the state of employment follows from the declaration of the representative of the commission in the verbal amendments to the form, saying: "The declaration is requested, in order to prevent, that those who undersigned are in the position of claiming anything later on."

A further supposed reason for the refusal of signing the prepared declaration follows from the unsatisfying regulation of the situation of the families remaining in Germany. The explanations, which the representative of the commission gave concerning this point made recognizable that, besides just their willingness to help those families, the American authorities are not willing to take upon themselves any obligation concerning a garantee of the necessary requirements of life of those families, nothing to say about a fulfilment of the justified desire, to transport those families to the environments of the field of operation of their bread-winners.

At last a further reason for the refusal of giving the signature must be found in the fact, that the representative of the commission showed himself unable, to give any reference to the shaping of the state of employment and the performance of the intended evacuation.

If the commission should be of the opinion, that the government of the USA will continue in caring to pursue further the research of rockets on the basis created by the EW and to make use of the coworkers proposed by the EW to that purpose, the points are given in the following, which can form, in the opinion of the direction of the EW and of outstanding men of the employeeship, a basis for further negotiations:

The government of the United States made recognizable, that it is occupied with the idea, further to develop the principle of rocket-propulsion on the basis, thus far created in Germany by the EW, by the help of voluntary cowork of its members.

The EW is principally inclined to cooporate in this task by placing to its disposal its experiences in this field and the working power of its employees. The EW therefore will – under the aspect, that the continuance of building rockets is to be performed in the US – recommend its employees to immigrate to USA and to cooperate in the field of work referred to, if the government of the USA on its part is willing to assume obligatorily the following suppositions and its fulfilment: [Emphasis added]

1.) It is garanteed to the employee to carry with him his family (wife and children) and the necessary luggage, and to board for the crossing and to perform it together with his family. It is to be garanteed in the same way, that the employee can stay with his family in America during his employment.

2.) The government of USA will conclude, a contract of work either generally with the EW or with the single employees which will regulate the reciprocal rights and duties on the usual basis of such contracts in the USA.

3.) Irrespective of the conditions of employment which still have to be agreed upon in its single points the following conditions are to be considered as essential part of the in § [section] 2 aforesaid contract:

a.) The type of work concerned will correspond to the professional education of the employee referred to; likewise his payment to comparable states of employment in USA.

b.) The least time of employment will be three years. In the case that the contract will be annihilated onesidedly by the government of the USA the agreed payment for the rest of the time must be paid without shortening.

c.) Outside of the working hours the employee will enjoy full freedom of movement. The same will be valid for the families.

d) In case of finishing the state of employment – irrespective if ['of the fact that' penciled in place of 'if'] the end of the state of employment ends by not renewing the contract or by a premature and onesided action of the government of the USA – the means for returning to Germany for the employee and his family will be placed to the disposal of the employee without putting them to the account of his ordinary salary. The means for the crossing have to be of the same amount as that granted to an American state official or employee of the same social position.

4.) By a frame contract the aforesaid points are on the part of the government of the USA to be assured obligatorily by a fully authorized representative before boarding for the crossing to the USA.

(Signatures)

Appendix 2:

He 162 GERMAN PILOT COMMENTARY, AUGUST 16, 1945

Among the thousands of pages of documentation concerning German aircraft performance, the following transcribes a German test pilot's comments on the He 162, given to American R. A. Fleischer during a trip to German aircraft plants in the summer of 1945. The pilot, listed as Engineer Gerhard Gleuwitz, prepared his remarks in English. They are presented here as the 1945 report recorded them; some interpretation of syntax may be required.

Engineer Gerhard Gleuwitz   Kassel-Wilhelmshoehe

August 16th, 1945

Details regarding the German jet pursuit plan[e]
<u>He 162 (Volksjaeger) with BMW-TL-003 drive.</u>

1. <u>Introduction.</u>

For nearly ten years I have been employed as engineer-pilot with several plants of the German Aircraft Industry and during this period I was entrusted with the task of testing planes. For some years I was chief-pilot and worksmanager of the Gerhard Fieseler plant in Kassel. In this capacity I was responsible for the fulfil[l]ment of the "Jäger-Program", and managed flying and shop affairs on two airdromes. After the fatal crash of the chief-pilot of the Ernst Heinkel-Werke in Vienna (2nd test flight He 162) I became his successor in January 1945.

2. <u>General remarks.</u>

I may assume that the general appearance and the construction details of the He 162 are well known. Up to my joining Heinkel's the following was the general history of the He 162. As the result of the more and more pressing shortage of fuel and materials, a cheap and easy to be manufactured fighter, preferable from wood, was asked to be manufactured in big series and brought to the front in the shortest time possible. This plane was to be powered by one BMW TL power plant (pushing power, Schuhkraft 800 kg). Begin of construction summer 1944. According to the favourable critic of the at that time chief-pilot, Mr. Peter, and the assurance of the firm of Ernst Heinkel to the Air Ministry that planes of this type built in series could be delivered to the front in great numbers already during the months of February/March 1945, the Air Ministry ruled that the manufacture of this type had to be taken up by several German aircraft plants. At the same time designs of other manufacturers were shelved. Towards the middle of December 1944 the chief-pilot crashed fatal[l]y during the second test flight with this type. This fatal test flight took place in the presence of many German experts and Air Force specialists called together to demonstrate in their presence this new type. The crash occur[r]ed in low altitude whilst going with high speed as result of wing failure. Supposed reason: The speed whilst making a roll was too great. I am of the opinion that this excessive rolling speed was due to slight rudder forces with consequent excessive wing overload or a sudden instability. After the skin-plating had been increased from 4-5 mm to 6 mm thickness, the plane was again put through flight tests. During this time, however, the manufacture in big series went on at the Heinkel Works in Rostock as well as at Junkers in Bernburg and, if I am rightly informed, in other plants too. About at this stage I joined Heinkels in Vienna.

3. Further course of the flight-performance tests of the He 162 in Vienna-Schwechat.

I regarded it as too big a risk to go on with the manufacture in big series of this plane, especially when I took into consideration that the manufacture of all other German types of planes was virtually stopped. I was of the opinion that the deficiencies of this plane as p.o. instability in the transversal axis, to great rudder efficiency with consequent wing overload, frequent fires in the power plant, failures of the power plant in high altitudes were too numerous and too dangerous in the hand of an unexperienced pilot. Under no circumstances could these planes therefore in the stipulated period of time and in the demanded big numbers be delivered to the front. I am of the opinion that the continuance of this manufacturing programme would have developed to a major catastrophe unprecedented in the German aircraft industry as well as in the German Air Force. Whilst in Rostock and Bernburg the first planes manufactured in series were flown, a proofed final judgment regarding performance in altitude flight, endurance tests, sufficient firing tests, radio tests and so on was not available. All this was especially due to the nearly daily heavy air-raids in the Vienna districts.

My personal criticism of the He 162: Without regard to the opinion that this plane would not have accomplished the guaranteed performances and surely would have been about 100 km (about 60 m) slower than the Me 262 the following has to be remarked:

a) Controls.
The wing flaps were not quite as they should have been. (Wing flap position indicator was not provided for). But with the exception of this deficiency the control of the plane after, of course, sufficient training, was simple and easy to survey. Starts and let-downs were easier as with the Focke-Wulf or the Heinkel pursuit plane due to nose wheel arrangement (starting distance fully loaded on a concrete runway, dead calm, about 1200 to 1300 mtr.). The let-down speed was about 20 km/hr (about 13 m) higher as with the Focke-Wulf or Messerschmitt pursuit plane. The let-down preparations required considerable more time (killing of the high speed) and the acceleration after the start was as the result of the power plant properties and nature less than that of the planes Me 109 and FW 190. Both these facts endangered the He 162 during starts and let-downs when attacked by enemy pursuit planes at that moment. The control of the turbine and the display of the instruments was for the pilot more handy as with gasoline engines.

b) Length of flying time.
Planes were constructed with fuel tank capacities for 20 to 45 minutes. But also flying times of 45 minutes I regard as fully insufficient for turbine-fighters.

c) Armament.
I regard 2 3cm guns as sufficient, provided these small planes launch their attack in mass-formation.

d) Flight performance during turns.
Tests had been arranged to compare these performances with those of other planes. I myself, however, regard them as "good".

e) Chances to bail out in emergency.
A seat catapulted out by a charge to be detonated by the pilot in emergency was provided for. A successful bailout during the test-flight period did not occur, unfortunately, however several fatal crashes.

f) Stressing of the pilot.

A special physical stressing of the pilot compared with other plane types was not experienced.

Conclusion.

I am convinced that the He 162 could not have brought about a decisive change in the air-war developments, even if this plane had been thoroughly tested and tried out and even if a sufficient number had been available. Against bomber formations bombing through clouds with instruments as often performed, the turbine pursuit plane He 162 had no operation-possibilities and could not been sent up to attack. I believe, however, that it would be worthwhile to go on with the development of this plane for special purposes and combat tasks. But to begin with the construction should principally be altered in some regards.

APPENDIX 3:

INTERROGATION OF HERMANN GÖRING, MAY 10, 1945

What follows is a transcribed copy of the interrogation with Hermann Göring that Lt Gen Spaatz gave to Gen Arnold with a note saying: "Believe you will find this most interesting."[1]

Interrogation of Reich Marshal Hermann Göring

Ritter Schule, Augsburg
1700 to 1900 hours
10 May 1945.

(Because Lt Gen Alexander Patch is personally responsible for the safe custody of the prisoner, it was necessary for Lt Gen Spaatz' party to go from Headquarters Ninth Air Force to Headquarters Seventh US Army).

Reich Marshal Göring was standing in a small office of the school wearing grayish wool, no medals but epaulets of a Field Marshal; (that is, a large eagle, a small Swastika, and crossed batons.) He had a silver ring on the third finger of his right hand. Blue eyes, ruddy not unpleasant face, big thighs, tan boots.

Interpreter provided by the Seventh Army.

Those present were:

Reich Marshal Hermann Göring
Lt Gen Spaatz, CG, USSTAF
Lt Gen Alexander Patch (part of the time) CG, 7th Army
Lt Gen Vandenberg, CG, Ninth Air Force
Brig Gen E. P. Curtis, C/S, USSTAF
Brig Gen Paul Barcus
Maj Alexander de Seversky, Special Consultant to Secretary of War.
Dr. Bruce Hopper, Historian, USSTAF.

Spaatz: Would you tell us something of the organization of the Luftwaffe and the plans, especially the factors which went into the non-fulfillment of those plans?

Göring: In the early years when I had supreme command of the Luftwaffe, I had definite plans, but in 1940 Hitler began to interfere, taking air fleets away from our planned operations. That was the beginning of the breakdown of the Luftwaffe efficiency.

Spaatz: In the Battle of Britain why did you maintain such rigid formations of fighters and bombers?

Göring: It was necessary to cover the bombers because their fire power was low (not like your bombers). It was also necessary for our fighters to closely cover each other. You see, it was a question of equipment.

Spaatz: Was the JU 88 designed for the Battle of Britain?

Göring: The JU 88 was primarily a commercial airplane which had to be adapted for the Battle of Britain along with the HE 111 because we had nothing else. I was not in favor of engaging in the Battle of Brtain at that time. It was too early. The HE 177 was late in development. The HE 177 was a development from the original Stuka with two propellers on four motors. It was a failure; it wasted two years. That is why we had no large bombers in the Battle of Britain.

Spaatz: When did you know that the Luftwaffe was losing control of the air?

Göring: When the American long range fighters were able to escort the bombers as far as Hannover, and it was not long until they got to Berlin. We then knew we must develop the jet planes. Our plan for the early development of the jet was unsuccessful only because of your bombing attacks.

Spaatz: Did our attacks affect your training program?

Göring: Yes, for instance the attacks on oil retarded the training because our new pilots could not get sufficient training before they were put in the air where they were no match for your flyers.

Patch: Did the Luftwaffe have priority in the distribution of manpower?

Göring: Yes, the Luftwaffe had first priority and thus had the cream of Germany, the U-boats were second, and the panzers third. Even at the end the best of German youth went into the Luftwaffe. Only the Waffen SS sometimes held back personnel. All other organizations surrendered personnel to the Luftwaffe on application.

Spaatz: Did the jet airplane really have a chance to win against us?

Göring: Yes, I am still convinced, if we had only four to five months more time. Our underground installations were practically all ready. The factory at Karla (?) had a capacity of 1000 to 1200 jet airplanes a month. Now with 5000 to 6000 jets the outcome would have been different.

Vandenberg: But could you train sufficient jet pilots, considering your shortage of oil?

Göring: Yes, we would have had underground factories for oil, producing a sufficient quantity for the jets. The transition to jets was very easy in training. The jet pilot output was always ahead of the jet aircraft production.

Spaatz: Could Germany have been defeated by air power alone, using England as a base, without invasion?

Göring: No, because German industry was going underground, and our counter measures could have kept pace with your bombing. But the point is, that if Germany were attacked in her weakened condition as now, then the air could do it alone. That is, the land invasion meant that so many workers had to be withdrawn from factories' production and even from the Luftwaffe.

Patch: Was that also true of England?

Göring: To me, this is a difficult question. Germany was prepared for war and England wasn't. I was forced by Hitler to divert air forces to the East (which I always opposed). Only the diversion of the Luftwaffe to the Russian front saved England. She was unable to save herself and unable to bomb Germany.

Spaatz: When you conquered France in 1940, why didn't you go on through to Spain and Gibraltar?

Göring: Germany had saved Spain from the Bolsheviks. Spain was in the German camp. I insisted on going to Spain but to no avail. We could have bottled the British Fleet in the Mediterranean, but no – the Führer wanted to go to Russia. My idea was to close both ends of the Mediterranean, "*Und dann die sache ist in ordnung*". I am positive we could have taken Gibraltar. The Luftwaffe was ready and we had two divisions of parachutists ready and trained, but Mussolini objected. Part of our pain – the Italians. Also there was the complication of the relations between France and Spain.

Spaatz: Did you know anything of our movement to Africa as to time and place?

Göring: Well, I presumed it, but if the Germans had only held Morocco and the Canaries as I wanted, the going would have been difficult for you.

Spaatz: Your best attack on us was at Poltava, at the airfield. Why was that so successful?

Göring: Those were wonderful times. We had an observation ship flying with you. You did not know it. It was a 177 which fortunately developed motor trouble and indicated it couldn't land on the field with only one motor. So it was able to return to give the information on your landing at Poltava. As we had an attack planned on a railway nearby we merely diverted it to your airfield.

Vandenberg: Will you tell me why you bombed cities in England instead of concentrating on aircraft and engine factories.

Göring: My intention at first was to attack only military targets and factories, but after the British attacked Hamburg the people were angry and I was ordered to attack indiscriminately.

Spaatz: Which had the more effect in the defeat of Germany, the area bombing or the precision bombing?

Göring: The precision bombing, because it was decisive. Destroyed cities could be evacuated but destroyed industry was difficult to replace.

Spaatz: Did the Germans realize that the American Air Forces by intention did only precision bombing?

Göring: Yes. I planned to do only precision bombing myself at the beginning. I wanted to build a wall of contact mines around Britain and close the ports but again I was forced to do otherwise by political Diktat.

Curtis: Was our selection of targets good, particularly oil?

Göring: Yes, excellent. As soon as we started to repair an oil installation you always bombed it again before we could produce one ton.

Vandenberg: Why didn't you attempt to cut us off in Africa and send the Luftwaffe, which was then superior in the air, against our shipping and the concentration of our airplanes at Gibraltar?

Göring: We had too few long range airplanes and then, later, when you got to Algiers the airfields in Italy were inadequate. You have no idea what a bad time we had in Italy. If they had only been our enemies instead of our Allies we might have won the war.

Spaatz: Why did you use your bombers to haul gas to Rommel instead of bombing the line of communications from Algiers to Constantine to Tunisia?

Göring: Higher Hq. orders;

Vandenberg: Why did you attack our airdromes on January 1, 1945?

Göring: Because every airdrome was loaded with airplanes.

Vandenberg: Well, why didn't you come back?

Göring: Orders from higher headquarters. Hitler said it was no good to bomb American planes because more of them would come like bees.

Vandenberg: But why did you concentrate on RAF airfields more than on ours?

Göring: Because the RAF airfields were closer and otherwise more inviting targets. We used 2300 planes for that attack; what we did not allow for was the intense concentration of AA guns placed there against the V1.

Vandenberg: Would you contrast the Air Forces of the Allies.

Göring: Well, the Russians are no good, except on undefended targets. You need only three or four Luftwaffe airplanes to drive off a 20-plane Russian attack. The Americans are superior technically and in production. As for the personnel, the English, German and American are equal as fighters in the air.

Spaatz: Have you any knowledge of a proximity fuse?

Göring: Yes, in three or four months there would have been production.

Spaatz: Has Japan the designs of this fuse?

Göring: I do not think so because it was not yet in production and we never gave them anything unless it was in production. The Japanese have had the designs of the ME 262 for some time.

Göring then talked for several minutes, the gist of which emphasized our successful use of radar and counter radar measures to which he attributes much of the success of our operations.

Spaatz: If you had to design the Luftwaffe again, what would be the first airplane you would develop?

Göring: The jet fighter and then the jet bomber. The problem of speed has been solved. It is now a question of fuel. The jet fighter takes too much. The jet bomber, ME 264, designed to go to America and back, awaited only the final solution of the fuel consumption problem. I might add that according to my view the future airplane is one without fuselage (flying wing) equipped with turbine in combination with the jet and propeller.

Seversky: In view of your diminishing manufacturing resources, who made the decision to divert a large portion of your national effort to manufacture of V1 and V2 weapons instead of building up the Luftwaffe?

Göring: Well, there was great confusion of thought in Germany. Prior to the invasion the V1 would have been effective. After the invasion our effort should have been concentrated on the ME 262 (jet). The decision on the V2 project was made at higher headquarters.

Vandenberg: In the tactical operations of our Air Force, what attacks on what targets were most damaging to you?

Göring: Before D-Day it was the attacks in Northern France which hurt the most because we were not able to rebuild in France as quickly as in Germany. The attacks on marshalling yards were most effective, next came the low level attacks on troops and then the attacks on bridges. The low flying airplanes had a terror effect and caused great damage to our communications. Also demoralizing were the umbrella fighters which after escorting the bombers would swoop down and hit everything including the jet planes in process of landing.

Spaatz: Did you have a three-inch gun for the jet?

Göring: The 5.5 centimeter machine gun, only now going into production, would have made a great difference in the jet. While waiting for that we used the 5.5 centimeter rocket. You might find around Germany some jet airplanes equipped with anti-tank guns. Don't blame me for such monstrosities. This was done on the explicit orders of the Führer. Hitler knew nothing about the air. He may have known something about the Army or Navy, but absolutely nothing about the air. He even considered the ME 262 to be a bomber; and he insisted it should be called a bomber.

Seversky: I know that four-engine Focke-Wulf planes were in production in 1939. When you found out after the Battle of Britain that your planes did not have sufficient fire power and bombing power why didn't you concentrate on these four-engine planes as a heavy bomber?

Göring: Instead of that, we were developing the HE 177 and tried to develop the ME 264 which was designed to go to America and return. We did use the Focke-Wulf against shipping from Norway. Because our production capacity was not so great as that of America we could not produce quickly everything we needed. Moreover, our plants were subject to constant bombing so that is was difficult to carry out our plans for heavy bomber production.

Seversky: The reason why I asked the previous question was because I wanted to establish whether you failed to build the big bombers because you did not believe in strategic air power or because your productive capacity was restricted to the production of tactical aircraft for the Russian campaign.

Göring: No, I always believed in strategic use of air power. I built the Luftwaffe as the finest bomber fleet, only to see it wasted on Stalingrad. My beautiful bomber fleet was used up in transporting munitions and supplies to the army of 200,000 at Stalingrad. I always was against the Russian campaign.

APPENDIX 4:

"GERMAN AVIATION" – JULY 20, 1945

This paper was written by George S. Schairer as a consultant to the US Scientific Advisory Board headed by Dr. Theodore von Kármán. It illuminates some perceptions about the Luftwaffe and the German aircraft industry and provides an interesting perspective on the swept-wing data development issue, the value of which Schairer recognized as he studied German documents that summer.

20 July 1945

Subject: German Aviation.

To: Dr. Theodore von Kármán, Director Scientific Advisory Group

1. During the recent European tour various phases of German aviation were observed primarily to determine those events in recent years which would throw some light on future planning requirements in this country as covered by the Scientific Advisory Group directive. The majority of information obtained was from various key personnel of German aircraft manufacturing industry, although some of it comes from intelligence reports, publications, and German research men. The sources of information were quite limited and hence many of the conclusions may have to be changed when the intelligence work in Germany is completed.

2. German aviation during this war was based primarily on work of those German scientists who had been permitted, after the last war, to either continue their interest in aviation or to be trained into the arts of aviation. The majority of these personnel were interested in aviation as such without reference to military uses or the future of Germany, although these same people were quite willing to utilize their efforts in such directions when war became imminent even though originating among their own political leaders. The majority of these aviation leaders appeared to be former glider manufacturers and pilots who had then graduated into small civil airplanes and only in recent years had turned towards either large airplanes or high performance military airplanes.

Apparently the Germany Air Forces never seriously considered the use of air power for strategic purposes, such as strategic bombing, etc. The airplane was conceived of primarily as a device to be used with the ground forces as in the early Panzer Divisions with Stuka dive-bomber cover and attack.

3. Use of the fighter as an interceptor against the bomber was undoubtedly always of interest but apparently not of primary interest even at the end of the war. The Germans had many airplanes in the fighter-bomber and medium bomber class which were used for bombing purposes primarily. The Germans built larger airplanes in the pre-war period for transport use and continued to spend a small amount of effort on them throughout the war, but these airplanes were nearly always intended for special purposes where only limited numbers would be required. None of them was developed sufficiently to be considered suitable for mass production. The Germans did use one of their civil types as a cargo airplane to great advantage in the earlier years of the war.

4. The above policy, with respect to use of airplanes, undoubtedly derives from several important factors. Germany does not have any adequate fuel supply for maintaining a large active air force and therefore it has been necessary for them to concentrate only on a few types which they consider most important and even on these production is liable to be limited by fuel availability. In addition to this fundamental limitation in their air force, the German General Staff consisted of men trained in the traditional methods of fighting wars which did not include the use of aircraft. This was undoubtedly one of the greatest handicaps that German aviation had to put up with. A number of comments made by German airplane designers indicated a belief among them that the Battle of Britain was lost entirely as a result of misunderstandings and clashes between the German Air Force and the German General Staff. The German Air Force was not prepared for such a battle either in aircraft types or crew training and had expected to use the concentration of aircraft at that time to assist in an invasion of England by water and not as a strategic bombing attempt. The failure of this battle and the subsequent success of Allied aircraft flying unchecked over Germany produced a rift in government circles which resulted in a great reduction of expectations from aircraft. This resulted in a major attempt on the part of the aircraft procuring and designing people to design aircraft suitable for intercepting Allied bomber attacks. The fundamentals necessary for such a program had long since been laid in the development of turbojet engines dating back to 1935 and the subsequent development of several partially successful jet-propelled aircraft. Contracts were given to all parties interested to develop any conceivable means of intercepting bombers. All types of devices were in the process of being tried in the hope that someone would be

successful. Obviously a large number of the devices had been sold on the basis of pretty pictures and fast talk and very few of the efforts were being sufficiently well coordinated to give much chance of success. Great reliance was being placed on invention and practically none upon sound engineering treatment of the problem at hand. This was to a great extent caused by the lack of understanding of engineering development processes by Hitler and his immediate advisors. It does not appear, however, that the projects most likely to succeed were greatly hampered by the many projects of lesser probable importance. A very free hand was given with respect to manpower and materials and money was readily available to the various investigators.

5. The relationship between industry and research organizations was very similar to that in other countries. There was no assurance that research advancements would become known and used by those directly concerned with the design of the actual production articles. The sweepback problem was quite typical of this. The value of sweepback at high speeds became known to research people throughout the world as far back as 1935. This information, however, was not transmitted to airplane designers until very recently. Apparently in Germany, as well as in all other countries throughout the world, the men designing the airplanes were not sufficiently advanced in aerodynamic training to have followed closely the finer points being studied in the research laboratories. They were not even familiar with the publications which contained this information. At the time that high Mach number problems became serious in Germany various industrial aerodynamicists searched actively for a solution to their problems, and only after considerable discussions with Busseman and Betz did they learn from these two men that "possibly sweepback might help a little bit." It was then that active experimental work to prove the value of sweepback was undertaken. Apparently German industry was as greatly disconcerted over their lack of knowledge of sweepback two years ago as American and English people are at this time. It would appear that the practical utilization of sweepback resulted from the "need" and not from the "knowledge" and without question sweepback would have become known as an important variable in the United States during the year 1945, even if no information concerning this had arrived from Germany.

6. As in the case of sweepback, there is every reason to believe that the relationships between German industry and German research, the Air Ministry, etc. were essentially identical to the same relationships in this country and the same problems were being encountered. In general, the differences between the various countries lie only in degree.

7. It is evident that much progressive thinking had been occurring in Germany during the peacetime years. To what extent this was general is not

known but in some manner or other sufficient interest was aroused in the more capable engineers to develop ideas and devices such as the V1 engine, the rocket projectile such as V2, the turbojet engine, engines such as that used in the 163 airplane, and many other similar developments. The majority of these were well developed at the start of the war but only came into prominence in the last year. This was partially due to prejudice against the new devices, although mostly to lack of sufficient development.

8. As mentioned above, German aircraft industry appears to have sprung from the glider development. Herein lay its start but also its greatest weaknesses. Some of the concerns, such as Junkers, date back to the last war and are quite substantial industries, but in most cases the companies were relatively new and inexperienced. This was as intended by the Versailles Treaty. Without doubt the many years the Germans lived under the terms of the Versailles Treaty paid great dividends to the Allies in this war. The Germans did not have as well established an industry and as large a background of experience and backlog of trained men as was available in the United States and England. In general, German aviation was a small-scale operation even up to the end of the war. Great difficulties had been encountered and were still being encountered with the expansion of personnel. In the last year or two this had been further aggravated by dispersal of locations. Nearly every successful aircraft device seen by the undersigned in Germany stemmed directly from the abilities and knowledge of men who had been active in German aviation for ten or more years. Undoubtedly these devices could not have been nearly as successful if the experience of these men had been more limited. It is believed that further investigation of this phase of the German problem can lead to certain very definite recommendations as to the future limitations to be placed on Germany with respect to aviation matters. If the training of these men had not been permitted and their experience with aircraft matters even in the form of small gliders had not been permitted, they would have been unable to catch up with aviation in sufficient time to have used the airplane successfully in this war.

George S. Schairer
Consultant

65

66

67

68

73

74

75

76

77

78

79

82

83

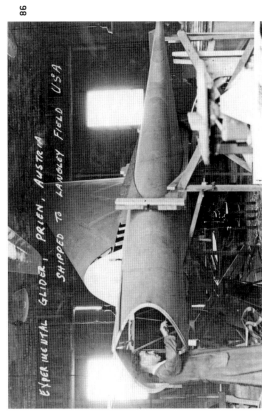

84

85

86

87

EXPERIMENTAL GLIDER, PRIEN, AUSTRIA
SHIPPED TO LANGLEY FIELD USA

Me 328 B

Me 328 A

89

90

91

92

93

94

95

102

103

104

105

106

APPENDIX 5:

INTERROGATION OF GENERAL KARL KOLLER, 1945

This fascinating 1945 interrogation with German General der Flieger Karl Koller revealed early insights into issues faced by the Luftwaffe in wartime Germany. A copy of the interrogation is retained at the Air Force Historical Research Agency at Maxwell AFB, Alabama.

Subject: OKL Screening Interrogation Report.
To: See distribution.

General der Flieger Koller, Chief of Staff

1. Gen. KOLLER though at first very reserved and formal, can be drawn out when subjects are touched upon relating to the mismanagement of the German Air Force due to Party politics, about which he is very bitter. He will then become exceedingly excited and the statements then made by him are positive, clear and illuminating. He gives the impression of speaking truthfully and without reservations.

2. He is very much interested in Anti-Aircraft Artillery, and appears to have considerable knowledge on this subject on a high level plane. According to him one of the grave mistakes was in the way manufacturers of AA guns were allowed to build the pieces with static mounts (Lafetten). The manufacturers, anxious to show production figures counted gun barrels, and had brought pressure to bear to have mobile mounts eliminated, on the charge that they required more material to manufacture. The Luftwaffe General Staff opposed this right from the start, and finally succeeded in Spring 1944 to get approval on a simple mobile cross mount (Kreuzlaffette), which was ultimately used on the Eastern front. However, this came too late, and Allied offensives on both the Western and Eastern front, resulted in the capture and the destruction of thousands of Flak pieces, whose immobility rendered them useless in retreat, and with resultant ever-increasing reduction of AA batteries available for the home-defense.

3. Although prisoner was not in charge at the start of the Russian campaign, he was very much concerned with GAF tactics after he became Chief of Operations 24 August 1943, a post he held until he was temporarily retired 4 September 1944. Gen. KOLLER worked very closely with Gen. KORTEN who had taken over the post of JESCHONNEK after the latter's suicide in August 1944.

4. During the campaigns of Poland, Norway, the Lowlands and France, the theory of using Air Force solely in support of the army, a theory stoutly adhered to by HITLER, JESCHONNEK and VON RICHTHOFEN, had worked with apparent success. The infantry, in fact demanded: "Tanks in front, Artillery behind, and Aircraft overhead".

5. However, prisoner, a bomber pilot, maintained that it was necessary to split the GAF into a Tactical and Strategical Air Force, and constantly made himself unpopular by pointing out that, aside from Stukas (Ju 87) GAF aircraft was not intended for such purposes. With Gen. GUDERIAN he had worked out the whole crossing of the river Maas at SEDAN, using his bombers to immobilize French reinforcements and to deny them access to the threatened point of attack.

6. When the Russian campaign started the GAF estimated their strength at 10,000 aircraft, a figure which was then considered excessive, but which later on proved below the actual Russian strength, now estimated to have been nearly 15,000 aircraft. However, the GAF was qualitatively superior, and after the initial attacks on Russian airfields behind the front lines, the Russian aircraft did not prove aggressive and avoided combat when GAF fighters were sighted. The GAF flew many sorties per day and obtained a tremendous volume of victories.

7. The use of the GAF as "extended Artillery" in support of the Army, was, according to prisoner, definitely finished during the Russian winter, and after a careful study it was proposed to use the bomber units for concerted attacks on Russian industries. Since the actual manufacturing centers in the Ural Mountains were out of range, the power stations of the Upper Volga, MOSKOW and near STALINGRAD were to be the targets. These plans were prepared in close collaboration with Prof. Dr. STEINMANN, Ministerialdirigent whose extensive knowledge on RUSSIA was used. STEINMANN was believed to be at present in the Northern part of GERMANY. Scale models were prepared and crews were re-trained for the job on hand. The Russian offensive caused a switch again to Army support, in spite of two months training and extensive preparations for the planned bombing attack.

8. KOLLER never gave up the idea, but started training the personnel of IV Flieger Korps (then under Gen. MEISTER) for long range missions with all

sorts of auxiliary equipment. Again models were built, showing targets in snow and without snow. Besides Dr. STEINMANN, Gen. ASCHENBRENNER former air attaché in MOSKOW supplied details. Just before the attacks on Russian power stations were about to begin, demands came from Army that railroad lines had to be cut behind the enemy front. HITLER promised personally that after a few of such attacks the bomber units would be released to carry out the attack on power stations. However, this promise was broken, as the Army demanded continuance of bombing communications. The IV Flieger Korps suffered heavy losses and as the German Army was pushed back further, the power stations fell out of operational range, and the plan was again abandoned.

9. With tenacity KOLLER stuck to his ideas, and after experiments the "MISTEL" aircraft, the so-called "Father-and-Son" pickaback aircraft, were prepared in November 1944 to carry out the plan. KOLLER by this time had the help of SPEER and both were very worried that the Western Allies would attack the fields of ORANIENBURG and RECHLIN. But even the third attempt was spoiled by the Russian offensive, and these composite aircraft were ordered to be used against bridges on the Oder [river] and at REMAGEN with poor results and vast losses.

10. At the end of the war prisoner estimated that the Russian Air Force had about 17,000 aircraft. He stated that the GAF admired the exceedingly efficient ground organization of the Russians. Air strips were immediately laid down in newly won territory. German intelligence never quite understood why the Russian Air Force would fly a large number of sorties for 2 or 3 days and suddenly lapse into a pause for several days. The most plausible theory prisoner could give was that this was perhaps due to lack of sufficient fuel.

11. While describing the desperate attempts against RUSSIA, prisoner was led to talk of the ramming of Allied four-engined aircraft, an idea he had fathered. Though it would mean almost sure death some 1500 pilots volunteered for the job. For a time a mass assault of these suicide pilots was planned, but then it became clear that it would have Germany without any pilots since there was no reserve, it was rejected. Prisoner then proposed to do it piecemeal, in about fifty at a time, always aiming for the leading Allied aircraft in a formation. First, he explained, he would get all the leaders. When, as a result of these tactics, the Allies would change formation and fly the leaders in the rear, he would still attack only the leaders, hoping thereby to cause a break in morale to the point that tight formations would be broken up at the approach of German fighters. This plan was never carried out.

12. Prisoner was visibly moved when he talked of his difficulties with HITLER, whom he described as "an infantry man, and a poor one at that".

He was very bitter about the manner in which HITLER blamed everything on the Luftwaffe, without giving them the chance they needed. As an example he cited how KREIPE (successor to KORTEN, who was killed in the abortive bomb-plot against HITLER'S life, 20 July 1944) came from a stormy interview with HITLER in August 1944. "What shall we do?" KREIPE was reported to have said, "HITLER wants to scrap the whole Luftwaffe and make only cannon. He said that he has always hated aircraft – the most hateful weapon – and if he would become Supreme in the world, that he would forbid all use of aircraft…" Prisoner was able to point out to HITLER the fallacy of using only cannon to defend the country.

13. Towards the last month HITLER showed increasing mistrust towards everybody, and accused all and sundry of treason and lies. An instance of this was when Prisoner showed HITLER where Allied aircraft was superior to German, with a chart illustrating differences point by point. When HITLER subsequently demanded from GOERING why he had not built better aircraft, and wanted KOLLER to produce the chart, the latter could not find it in his briefcase whereupon HITLER accused him of not daring to show it to GOERING. Asked in which respect he thought the German aircraft were weak in comparison to the Allied, Prisoner stated that the greatest weakness of German aircraft lay in their poor endurance.

14. On HITLER, Prisoner blamed the erroneous decision that the new Me-262 jet aircraft should be used as a bomber. KG 51 was given the first Me-262's for such purposes, with HITLER insisting that they would be used in support of the Army.

15. Prisoner gave an interesting sidelight on the attack by the GAF on 1 January 1945 on Allied airfields. The plan for this attack had been approved by HITLER and ordered by GOERING. First results showed losses to be 100 GAF aircraft, as against 500 Allied aircraft believed to have been totally damaged on the ground. These results brought forth immediate rage from HITLER. Subsequently German losses were tabulated to have been 200. Even then, KOLLER explained, that attack was very successful, because GERMAN losses in the air had been 5, 6, or even 7 to 1 Allied aircraft shot down. He explained to HITLER that even a one-to-one loss would have been far more of a profitable rate than under ordinary conditions.

16. Prisoner's possible contributions of interest for local intelligence purposes appear to be very small. His views and intimate connection with overall GAF tactics, as well as his relationships with leading military and Party officials qualify him for immediate evacuation to ADI(K) for detailed interrogation.

17. Since Prisoner relies in large part on the collaboration of his aide Oberst WOLTER, the latter-named officer has been evacuated with him.

18. Details of Prisoner: General der Flieger KARL KOLLER, born 22.2.1898 (10 yrs)...... P/W.

M. van Rossum Daum,
Major, AC.

APPENDIX 6:

INTERROGATION OF LIPPISCH AND VON LATSCHER, 1945

This 1945 interrogation with German designer Alexander Lippisch and von Latscher and a colleague, conducted by Allied aviation subject matter experts, reveals some of the rationale that went into the evolving design of the Me 163 Komet. Some typographical errors in this interrogation have been corrected; some words appear with more than one spelling. Lippisch's name has been misspelt throughout, but this has not been corrected. The Dr. H. S. "Taein" referred to is probably a misspelling of Tsien. Some numbers are blurred sufficiently on the copy to bring their quantities into question. Nonetheless, the overall document has historical value still.

Copy
Office of the Director
AAF Scientific Advisory Group

Memo: Assistant Chief of Staff A-2
Subject: Interrogation of Lippish & von Latscher.
Lippish was questioned on June 10, 1945 at St. Germaine by Dr. H. S. Taein and Mr. G. Schairer concerning the aerodynamics of tail-less airplanes and rocket motors. The rocket motor work will be reported by Dr. Taien.

Lippish indicated that the later stages of his developments of flying wings were mostly related to the ME 163 series. This airplane exists in three arrangements. The 163A had zero moment coefficient sections and obtained stability by washout. The 163B superseded this with a wing of nearly identical planform but with an airfoil with positive moment coefficient at the center. The tips were symmetrical and had 5.7° of aerodynamic washout. The leading edge was sweptback 29° and a 40% span fixed slot was used. The wing of the 163C differed from that of the 163B primarily in that the twist was removed.

A fixed slot was used to prevent tip stalling with attendant bad rolling characteristics as well as longitudinal instability. Lippish used fixed slots because he felt that the drag of a properly designed fixed slot was no greater than the actual drag of a moveable slot when manufacturing tolerances and flight deflections were considered. His fixed slots were designed to have low drag by connecting points of equal pressure. He estimated the local section drag was increased by 30% by the slot.

Lippish said that the most serious stall problems were encountered upon recovery from turns. This was due to the use of down elevons at high lifts in this condition. This is not a steady state condition but a maneuvering condition.

The 163B airplane was rocket powered. It had 1500Kg thrust and weighed 4100Kg initially. 2100Kg of fuel were carried and all but 500Kg were consumed in the climb which took 3 minutes to reach 10,000 meters. The remaining fuel was used for cruising and combat. Due to the inertia of rotating parts the engine required one minute to reach full power.

At high mach numbers a diving moment was obtained. The airplanes were placarded against exceeding M - .75 by a Mach meter. Recovering from excessive speed could be made by cutting power. Wind tunnel experiments indicated critical stability Mach numbers of M - .85 for 163 B and M - .92 for 163 C.

A CG location of about 21% MAC was used. CG limits of 17 to 22% are normal. The elevons are specially designed. They have 26.3% [note: manuscript is smudged; number appears to be 26.3%] of their area ahead of the hinge line and have a rounded nose. There is a large gap between the elevons and the wing and the wing ahead of the elevon is terminated in a radius. The elevons do not cause much instability due to upfloating. The leading edge slot which has as exit gap of 1.2% chord prevents serious upfloating near the stall.

Lippish has done much work on lateral stability. Very little dihedral is used and roll due to yaw is kept as small as possible but still positive. Sufficient vertical tail is added to keep a conventional ratio of rolling moment due to yawing moment due to yaw. Lippish desires to have a lateral center of pressure about 40% MAC aft of the CG. He considers it necessary to use a vertical tail on tail-less airplanes. He does not believe that these tails should be located on the wing tips because of flutter problems and effects of the tip vortex on the rudders.

Lippish has obtained a maximum value of lift of 01 – 1.25. The lift drag ratios of his airplanes are 163A – 1:18, 163B – 1:16, 163C not measured. These airplanes have an aspect ratio of 4.4.

Appendix 7:

LIST OF GERMAN AND AUSTRIAN SCIENTISTS IN THE UNITED STATES, JANUARY 2, 1947

This roster is culled from a Joint Intelligence Objectives Agency list of approximately 1,600 German and Austrian scientists, and represents only those with an indicated location in the United States when the list was compiled in January 1947. While it may not represent all German scientists, engineers and technicians who came to the US after World War II, the 250+ names and specialties on this list nonetheless provide an interesting snapshot that shows the breadth and depth of expertise the United States gained in the immediate postwar years. In addition to specialties of direct interest to the Air Force (Parachutes, Jet Engines, Guided Missiles, for example) the roster includes some who aided non-aerospace efforts as well. Several were listed as experts in Oil Shale, a petroleum discipline that remains in the news.

Name and address	Field
Gerhard E Aichinger, Wright Field, Ohio	Parachutes
Dr. Leonard Alberts, Army War College, Washington, D.C.	Hydro-Carbons
Dr. Rudolph Maria Ammann, Wright Field, Ohio	Jet Engines
Wilhelm Angele, Fort Bliss, Texas	Guided Missiles
Dr. Gottfried Max Arnold, Wright Field, Ohio	Supersonic Measures
Dr. Carol Aschenbrenner, Wright Field, Ohio	Aerial Photography
Herbert Feliya Axter, Fort Bliss, Texas	Guided Missiles
Erich K. A. Ball, Fort Bliss, Texas	Guided Missiles
Dr. Adolf Baumker, Wright Field, Ohio	Air Facilities
Oskar Bauschinger, Fort Bliss, Texas	Guided Missiles
Hermann F. Bedverftid, Fort Bliss, Texas	Guided Missiles
Heinz Beer, Wright Field, Ohio	Jet Engines
Rudi Beichel, Fort Bliss, Texas	Guided Missiles

Anton Beier, Fort Bliss, Texas	Guided Missiles
Ing. Herbert Bergeler, Fort Bliss, Texas	Guided Missiles
Hans Otto Berkner, Wright Field, Ohio	Diesel Engines
Dipl. Ing. Rudi Berndt, Wright Field, Ohio	Production Parachutes, Inspection A4
Hans Bielstein, Wright Field, Ohio	Chemist
Walther Gustav Carl Boccius, Wright Ficld, Ohio	Plane Tests
Dr. Otto Heinrich Bock, Wright Field, Ohio	Supersonics
Joseph Maria Boehm, Fort Bliss, Texas	Guided Missiles
Ing. Hermann Bottenhorn, Wright Field, Ohio	Rolling Mill Designer
Dr. Gerhard Winfried Braun, Wright Field, Ohio	Motor Research
Magnus von Braun, Fort Bliss, Texas	Guided Missiles
Werner von Braun, Fort Bliss, Texas	Guided Missiles
Ing. Hans Brede, Wright Field, Ohio	Jet Propulsion
Dr. Bruno Wolf Bruckmann, Wright Field, Ohio	Jet Propulsion
Erhardt Bruenecke, Fort Bliss, Texas	Guided Missiles
Prof. Theodore Buchhold, Fort Bliss, Texas	Guided Missiles
Walter W. B. Burose, Fort Bliss, Texas	Guided Missiles
Kurt Daniels, Wright Field, Ohio	Aircraft Designer
Ing. Konrad Dannenberg, Fort Bliss, Texas	Guided Missiles
Gerd Wilhelm De Beek, Fort Bliss, Texas	Guided Missiles
Dr. Ing. Kurt DeBus, Fort Bliss, Texas	Guided Missiles
Guenther Dellmeir, Wright Field, Ohio	Wind Tunnels
Hans Deppe, Fort Bliss, Texas	Guided Missiles
Frederick Dhom, Fort Bliss, Texas	Guided Missiles
Dr. Bernard Dirksen, Wright Field, Ohio	Structures and Materials
Mr. Frederick Doblehoff, Wright Field, Ohio	Jet-Propelled Helicopters
Herbert Dobrick, Fort Bliss, Texas	Guided Missiles
Dr. Philipp von Doepp, Wright Field, Ohio	Guided Missiles Aero Design
Gerhard Drawe, Fort Bliss, Texas	Guided Missiles
Bernhard Duell, Army War College, Washington, D.C.	Bio-Climatology
Gertraud (Mrs. Bernhard) Duell, Army War College, Washington, D.C.	Bio-Climatology
Friedrich Duerr, Fort Bliss, Texas	Guided Missiles
Gerhard Eber, Navy Yard, Washington, D.C.	Supersonics
Ernst Rudolf Eckert, Wright Field, Ohio	Aerodynamics
Hans Ulrich Eckert, Wright Field, Ohio	Wind Tunnels
Dr. Rudolf Edse, Wright Field, Ohio	Rocket Fuels

Hermann P. Ehrhardt, Wright Field, Ohio	Rockets
Otto K. Eisenhardt, Fort Bliss, Texas	Guided Missiles
Willy Elias, Wright Field, Ohio	Test Engineer
Rudolph Engelmann, Navy Yard, Washington, D.C.	Chemist
Kurt Erfurth, Wright Field, Ohio	Aircraft Designer
Hans Joachim Oskar Fichtner, Fort Bliss, Texas	Guided Missiles
Johannes Finzel, Fort Bliss, Texas	Guided Missiles
Eduard Martin Fischel, Fort Bliss, Texas	Guided Missiles
Dr. Hans Fischer, Aberdeen Proving Ground, Maryland	Cold Processing of Steel
Dr. Heinz Fischer, Wright Field, Ohio	Aerodynamics Flow Visualization
Dr. Karl A. Fischer, Army War College, Washington, D.C.	Oil Shale
Carlotto Fleischer, Fort Bliss, Texas	Guided Missiles
Heins Fornoff, Wright Field, Ohio	Jet Engines
Dr. Anselm, Wright Field, Ohio	Jet Engines
Dr. Erich Frese, Army War College, Washington, D.C.	Oil Shale
Hans Rudolph Friedrich, Fort Bliss, Texas	Guided Missiles
Herbert Walter Fuhrmann, Fort Bliss, Texas	Guided Missiles
Dipl. Ing. Heintz Gartmann, Wright Field, Ohio	Jet Rockets
Ernst Geissler, Fort Bliss, Texas	Guided Missiles
Bernard August Goethert, Wright Field, Ohio	Aerodynamics
Dr. Ernst Graf, Army War College, Washington, D.C.	Oil Shale
Dieter Grau, Fort Bliss, Texas	Guided Missiles
Lambert Graulich, Wright Field, Ohio	Jet Propulsion
Reinhold Gross, Wright Field, Ohio	Parachutes
Dr. Phil Erich Groth, Wright Field, Ohio	Aerodynamics
Hans Gruene, Fort Bliss, Texas	Guided Missiles
Heinz Ernst Reinhard Gruner, Army Map Service, Washington, D.C.	Photogrammetry
Dr. Gottfried Guderley, Wright Field, Ohio	High-Speed Aerodynamics
Herbert Hans Guendel, Fort Bliss, Texas	Guided Missiles
Werner Kurt Gengelbach, Fort Bliss, Texas	Guided Missiles
Karl Franz Hager, Fort Bliss, Texas	Guided Missiles
Dr. Georg Hass, Fort Belvoir, Virginia	Infra-red
Gunther Haukohl, Fort Bliss, Texas	Guided Missiles
Alfons Hegele, Wright Field, Ohio	Parachutes
Karl Ludwig Heimburg, Fort Bliss, Texas	Guided Missiles
Dr. Hans Heinrich, Wright Field, Ohio	Fuel Systems

Dr. Helmut Heinrich, Wright Field, Ohio	Parachutes
Wilfried Hell, Navy Yard, New York	Remote Control System
Emil A. H., Hellebrand, Fort Bliss, Texas	Guided Missiles
Gerhard Heller, Fort Bliss, Texas	Guided Missiles
Bruno Helm, Fort Bliss, Texas	Guided Missiles
Alfred H. Henning, Fort Bliss, Texas	Guided Missiles
Dr. Rudolf Herman, Wright Field, Ohio	Supersonics
Dipl. Ing. Albrecht Herzog, Wright Field, Ohio	Material Structures
Bruno Heusinger, Fort Bliss, Texas	Guided Missiles
Willi Hermann Heybey, Navy Yard, Washington, D.C.	Supersonics
Mathias Hickertz, Wright Field, Ohio	Jet Propulsion
Guenther Hintze, Fort Bliss, Texas	Guided Missiles
Otto Heinrich Hirschler, Fort Bliss, Texas	Guided Missiles
Otto August Hoberg, Fort Bliss, Texas	Guided Missiles
Rudolf Franz Maria Homlker, Fort Bliss, Texas	Guided Missiles
Adolph von Hobemann, Fort Hunt, Virginia	Diesel Engines
Sighard Hoerner, Wright Field, Ohio	Aeronautical Engineer
Rudolf Friedrick Hoffman, Port Washington, New York	Torpedoes
Dipl. Ing. Siegfried Hoh, Wright Field, Ohio	Wind Tunnels
Mr. Bernhard Hohmann, Wright Field, Ohio	Guided Missiles
Oskar F. Holderer, Fort Bliss, Texas	Guided Missiles
Helmut Horn, Fort Bliss, Texas	Guided Missiles
Leo Horrec, Wright Field, Ohio	Jet Propulsion
Hans Henning Hosenthin, Fort Bliss, Texas	Guided Missiles
Dipl. Ing. Franz Huber, Wright Field, Ohio	Aerodynamics
Dr. Ing. Otto Hubmann, Army War College, Washington, D.C.	Petroleum
Josef Hubert, Wright Field, Ohio	Aerodynamics
Hans Hueter, Fort Bliss, Texas	Guided Missiles
Dieter K.F. Huzel, Fort Bliss, Texas	Guided Missiles
Richard Johann Jacob, Fort Hunt, Virginia	Diesel Engines
Walter Jacobi, Fort Bliss, Texas	Guided Missiles
Dr. Wunibald Kamn, Wright Field, Ohio	Power Plants
Peter Kappus, Wright Field, Ohio	Jet Engines
Erich Kaschig, Fort Bliss, Texas	Guided Missiles
Rudolf Kassner, Wright Field, Ohio	Jet Engines
Dr. Wolfram Kerris, Wright Field, Ohio	Instruments
Ernst E. Klaus, Fort Bliss, Texas	Guided Missiles

Johann Klein, Fort Bliss, Texas	Guided Missiles
Georg Klingler, Wright Field, Ohio	Aerodynamics
Dipl. Ing. Theodor Knacke, Wright Field, Ohio	Parachutes
Wilhelm F. H. Knackstedt, Wright Field, Ohio	Supersonic Flow
Georg Knausenberg, Port Washington, New York	Electronics
Eugen Knoernschild, Wright Field, Ohio	Thermodynamics
Hermann Koehl, Wright Field, Ohio	Turbines
Axel Kolb, Wright Field, Ohio	Aerodynamics
Heinrich Anton Karl Kopp, Aberdeen Proving Grounds, Maryland	Cold Processing
Karl Peter Krack, Washington Navy Yard, DC	Submarine Installations
Dr. Max Kramer, Wright Field, Ohio	Rocket Bombs
Gerhard Krause, Wright Field, Ohio	Hydraulic Presses
Gustav Kroll, Fort Bliss, Texas	Guided Missiles
Heinrich Kuhper, Port Washington, New York	Bomb Fuzes
Werner Koers, Fort Bliss, Texas	Guided Missiles
Dr. Hermann H. Kurzweg, Navy Yard, Washington, D.C.	Supersonics
Reinhard Lahde, Navy Yard, Long Island	Remote Control Systems
Dr. Wolfgang Lang, Fort Hunt, Virginia	Diesel Engines
Herman E. Lange, Fort Bliss, Texas	Guided Missiles
Richard Lehnert, Navy Yard, Washington, D.C.	Supersonics
Hans Josef Lindenmayer, Fort Bliss, Texas	Guided Missiles
Kurt A. Lindner, Fort Bliss, Texas	Guided Missiles
Dr. Alexander Lippisch, Wright Field, Ohio	Tailless Aircraft
Hannes Gunther Leuhrsen, Fort Bliss, Texas	Guided Missiles
Georg Madelung, Port Washington, New York	Bomb Torpedo Research
Carl Heinz Mandel, Fort Bliss, Texas	Guided Missiles
Frank Matossi, Navy Yard, Washington, D.C.	Infra-red
Heinz Matt, Wright Field, Ohio	Supersonics
Hans Hermann Maus, Fort Bliss, Texas	Rocket Power Units
Hans Ferdinand Mayer, Wright Field, Ohio	Acoustic Homing Devices
Ernst Helmut Merk, Aberdeen Proving Grounds, Maryland	Guided Missiles
Dr. Ludwig Meyer, Wright Field, Ohio	Magnetrons
Josef Martin Michel, Fort Bliss, Texas	Guided Missiles
Hans Walter Milde, Aberdeen Proving Grounds, Maryland	Guided Missiles

Heinz Albert Millinger, Fort Bliss, Texas	Guided Missiles
Rudolf Friederich Franz Minning, Fort Bliss, Texas	Guided Missiles
Dipl. Ing. Ferdinand Mirus, Wright Field, Ohio	Aerodynamics
Willi Mrazek, Fort Bliss, Texas	Guided Missiles
Joachim Wilhelm Muehlner, Fort Bliss, Texas	Guided Missiles
Hans Fritz Mueller, Fort Hunt, Virginia	Propellers
Heinz Mueller, Wright Field, Ohio	Bomb Sights
Erwin Naumann, Wright Field, Ohio	Power Plants
Hermann Nehlsen Wright Field, Ohio	Rolling Mills
Erich Walter Neubert, Fort Bliss, Texas	Guided Missiles
Franz Josef Neugebauer, Wright Field, Ohio	Aerodynamics
Kurt Kunibert Karlmann Neuhoefer, Fort Bliss, Texas	Guided Missiles
Wolfgang O. Noeggerath, Wright Field, Ohio	Rocket Fuel
Max Ernst Nowak, Fort Bliss, Texas	Guided Missiles
Werner von der Nuell, Wright Field, Ohio	Superchargers
Mr. Rudolph Opimz, Wright Field, Ohio	Rocket Planes
Robert Heinrich Karl Paetz, Fort Bliss, Texas	Guided Missiles
Hans Rudolf Palagro, Fort Bliss, Texas	Guided Missiles
Albert Karl Patin, Wright Field, Ohio	Jet Engines
Kurt Paul Erich Patt, Fort Bliss, Texas	Guided Missiles
Hans Paul, Fort Bliss, Texas	Guided Missiles
Willi Peter, Port Washington, New York	Electrical Fuzes
Max Peucker, Navy Yard, Washington, D.C.	Supersonics
Dr. Karl Pohlhausen, Wright Field, Ohio	Aerodynamics
Theo Anton Poppel, Fort Bliss, Texas	Guided Missiles
Heinrich Ramm, Wright Field, Ohio	Supersonics
Otto Oskar Rudolf Ratz, Army Map Service, Washington, D.C.	Photogrammetry
Eberhard Fritz Michael Res, Fort Bliss, Texas	Guided Missiles
Heinrich Reindorf, Wright Field, Ohio	Power Plants
Gerhard Herbert Richard Reisig, Fort Bliss, Texas	Guided Missiles
Heinz Richter, Wright Field, Ohio	Jet Engines
Dr. Georg Rickhey, Wright Field, Ohio	Guided Missiles
Walther Johannes Riedel, Fort Bliss, Texas	Guided Missiles
Franz Georg Rinecker, Wright Field, Ohio	Textiles
Friedrich Otto Adolf Ringleb, Wright Field, Ohio	Aerodynamics
Hans Joachim Rister, Wright Field, Ohio	Aerodynamics

Herbert Rosin, Wright Field, Ohio	Jet Engines
Werner Kurt-Otto Rosinski, Fort Bliss, Texas	Guided Missiles
Prof. Theodor Rossmann, Wright Field, Ohio	Weapons
Ludwig Roth, Fort Bliss, Texas	Guided Missiles
Ing. Heinrich Rothe, Fort Bliss, Texas	Guided Missiles
Arthur Louis Hugo Rudolph, Fort Bliss, Texas	Guided Missiles
Martin Ruhnke, Wright Field, Ohio	Jet Engines
Eugen Iwanowitsch Ryschkewitsch, Wright Field, Ohio	Carbides
Erich Sarapuu, Army War College, Washington, D.C.	Oil Shale
Hans Sauerland, Wright Field, Ohio	Jet Engines
Otto Friedrich Schaper, Port Washington, New York	Guided Missiles
Heinz Ludwig Schnarowski, Fort Bliss, Texas	Guided Missiles
Helmut Rudolf Schelp, Wright Field, Ohio	Jet Power Units
Klaus Eduard Schufelen, Fort Bliss, Texas	Guided Missiles
Martin Schilling, Fort Bliss, Texas	Guided Missiles
Dr. Heinz Schlicke, Port Washington, New York	Electronic Research
Rudolf Karl Hans Schlidt, Fort Bliss, Texas	Guided Missiles
Helmut Wilhelm Emil Schlitt, Fort Bliss, Texas	Guided Missiles
Helmut Heinrich Schmid, Fort Bliss, Texas	Guided Missiles
Heinz Eugen Schmitt, Wright Field, Ohio	Jet Engines
Dr. Ing. Josef Schugt, Wright Field, Ohio	Bombsight Equipment
Albert E. Schuler, Fort Bliss, Texas	Guided Missiles
August Schulze, Fort Bliss, Texas	Guided Missiles
Ludwig Schuster, Abderdeen Proving Ground, Maryland	Cold Processing Steel
Friedrich Wilhelm Schwarz, Fort Bliss, Texas	Guided Missiles
Walter Hans Schwidnetsky, Fort Bliss, Texas	Guided Missiles
Karl Sendler, Fort Bliss, Texas	Guided Missiles
Werner Sieber, Fort Bliss, Texas	Guided Missiles
Ernst Sielaff, Wright Field, Ohio	Aircraft Construction
Dietrich E.G.F. Singelmann, Wright Field, Ohio	Guided Missiles
Alexander Smakula, Fort Belvoir, Virginia	Guided Missiles, Infra-red
Hans Guenther Snay, Port Washington, New York	Underwater Explosives
Eberhard Julius Spohn, Fort Bliss, Texas	Guided Missiles
Ernst August Wilhelm Steinhoff, Fort Bliss, Texas	Guided Missiles
Wolfgang Hermann Steurer, Fort Bliss, Texas	Guided Missiles
Edmund Stollenwerk, Navy Yard, Washington, D.C.	Supersonics
Kurt Strohmeyer, Wright Field, Ohio	Aerodynamics

Adolf Strott, Wright Field, Ohio	Chemist
Ernst Stuhlinger, Fort Bliss, Texas	Guided Missiles
Theodor Friedrich Sturm, Port Washington, Long Island, NY	Guided Missiles
Dr. Ottmar Stutzer, Wright Field, Ohio	Short-Wave Radar
Bernhard Tessmann, Fort Bliss, Texas	Guided Missiles
Adolf Karl Thiel, Fort Bliss, Texas	Guided Missiles
Arthur Tiller, Fort Hunt, Virginia	Small-Boat Designer
Ing. Werner Tiller, Fort Bliss, Texas	Guided Missiles
Walter Trockel, Army War College, Washington, D.C.	Oil Shale
Johann Gustav, Fort Bliss, Texas	Guided Missiles
Fritz Vandersee, Fort Bliss, Texas	Guided Missiles
Ludwig Karl Vogel, Wright Field, Ohio	Fighter Planes
Karl Voll, Wright Field, Ohio	Electrical Research
Carl Wilhelm Wagner, Long Island Navy Yard, NY	Structures and Jets
Dr. Hendric Wahl, Army War College, Washington, D.C.	Shale Oil
Prof. Otto Walchner, Wright Field, Ohio	Supersonics Aerodynamics
Emil Johann Walk, Wright Field, Ohio	Wind Tunnels
Peter Paul Wegener, Navy Yard, Washington, D.C.	Supersonics
Hermann Joachim Weidner, Fort Bliss, Texas	Guided Missiles
Carl Werner Weihe, Wright Field, Ohio	Infra-red
Friedrich Stefan Weimig, Wright Field, Ohio	Turbines
Hans Johann Wiedemann; returned to Germany (Port Washington, New York)	Guided Missiles
Walter Fritz Wiesemann, Fort Bliss, Texas	Guided Missiles
Albert Franz Zeiler, Fort Bliss, Texas	Guided Missiles
Philipp Wolfgang Zettler-Seidel, Navy Yard, Washington, D.C.	Supersonics
Theodor Wilhelm Zobel, Wright Field, Ohio	Aerodynamics
Helmut Max Arthur Zoike, Fort Bliss, Texas	Guided Missiles

APPENDIX 8:

INTERROGATION OF VON DOEPP AND FRENGL [sic], JUNE 11, 1945

The experienced American aeronautical specialists invited to travel to Germany in the summer of 1945 exploited German documents and key personnel in interrogations that opened some new possibilities for postwar developments. The following is a transcript of an interrogation with Junkers personnel. The interrogators had some leading American engineers including Boeing's George Schairer and NACA's Hugh Dryden. Dr. Phillip von Doepp's name shows up at Wright Field after the war. This interrogation probed fertile technical fields including Junkers' use of high-speed wind tunnels in the transonic region, benefits of specific jet-engine nacelle placements on airframes, and the challenges and rationale for using forward swept-wing designs. Von Doepp's acknowledgment that the forward swept wing as used on the experimental Junkers Ju 287 bomber was important because it gave the aircraft better stall characteristics was a harbinger of things to come three decades later when that characteristic became one of the design tenets for the Grumman X-29 tested by NASA. It remained for composite aircraft lay-up technologies and computer fly-by-wire capabilities to be developed before the high-speed promise of forward swept-wing design could be realized in the X-29. Chronologies for the X-29's development typically include acknowledgment of the World War II Ju 287 for its pioneering role in exploring forward swept-wing designs. The Ju 287 and some members of its design team were exploited by the Soviet Union after the war.

Office of the Director
AAF Scientific Advisory Group

Memorandum for Director of Intelligence:
Subject: Interrogation of von Doepp & Frengl on June 11, 1945.

Von Doepp and Otto Frengl of the Junkers Company in Dessau were interrogated at St. Germain on June 11, 1945 by Mr. G. Schairer, Dr. H. L.

Dryden, Dr. H. S. Tsien, Dr. F. Wattendorf, and Mr. A. M. O. Smith of Douglas-El Segundo who is attached to the Naval Technical Mission. The interrogation was conducted with the assistance of the complete wind tunnel data files of Junkers Co. Von Doepp has been with Junkers since the last war and is director of the department for flow research. Frengl is in charge of the Junkers high speed wind tunnel.

Junkers have three wind tunnels. The first is 90 cm X 110 cm Eiffel type tunnel built in 1915 and driven by a 100 HP centrifugal fan. This tunnel could also be operated with a 70 cm diameter throat. The speeds were 30 and 55 meters per second.

The second tunnel is a medium size open throat tunnel with a 12 sided jet adjustable between 2½ and 4 meters width. It was built in 1934. The tunnel was driven by a 600 HP motor and had speeds from 40 to 65 meters per second. This tunnel has a 6 component balance.

Junkers also have a high speed wind tunnel driven by steam. This tunnel was started in 1939 and was designed with the aid of a 100mm dia model tunnel. This tunnel was provided with three different test sections: (1) open throat .3 X .284 meters. (2) 2 sides open – 2 sides closed .35 X .35 meters and (3) closed throat .35 X .35 meters. The tunnel was driven by suction and had no return. It was intended to heat the intake air to minimize condensation shocks but neither this nor air drying was accomplished.

The suction to drive the tunnel was supplied by a steam operated induction system. The steam was used to induce a flow at critical speed through a channel followed by a diffuser. This channel was attached to the test section by a channel which had adjustable bleed shutters. It was understood that the inducer was always run at critical speeds and the test speed controlled by adjusting the bleed shutters. The test section could be operated at speeds up to .98 Mach No. The steam was supplied by a steam storage system wherein a large boiler of pressurized water was heated by steam from a smaller continuously operated boiler. The storage system was operated at 12 atmospheres.

It is understood that all data obtained in these tunnels since 1924 is available.

Junkers use conventional wind tunnel wall corrections at low speeds. Nearly all their high speed tests were run in the ½ open tunnel. Since the corrections for such a tunnel are zero at low speeds Junkers has applied no corrections for either tip effects or blocking to their high speed data. The speed is determined from the test section chamber pressure.

The effect of wing sweep on drag at high Mach Nos. was measured by Junkers. Very favorable results were obtained. Pressure distribution tests appeared to confirm the approximate validity of a simple angular shock theory to explain the gains. A number of different planforms were tested.

Junkers has done extensive wind tunnel testing to determine the optimum location of a turbojet nacelle on a wing. At low speeds the drag of the combination was not greatly affected by location. However, at high Mach Nos. the drag of the combination was greatly affected by arrangement at speeds where large Mach No. effects on the individual items would not be expected. The best location tested was with the nose of the nacelle at the trailing edge of the wing. As the nacelle moved forward the drag increased until a maximum was obtained when the leading edges of both bodies were together. The drag dropped off again as the nacelle moved further forward. More complete tests on this are necessary.

Junkers have also run extensive tests on turbo jet nacelles added to the sides of fuselages near their nose. Good results were obtained from most standpoints. The low speed drag was similar to that when the nacelles were added to a wing. The high speed results can be good or bad. The good results are obtained when additional velocities from the nacelles and fuselages do not add to large values. It was Junkers opinion that most results could be predicted as good or bad by merely considering the amount and location of maximum thicknesses of the bodies both when considering wings and fuselages.

Junkers made tests to determine the effect of the turbo jet slipstreams on the airplane. Tests were run with hot and cold jets. The jets on the nose of the fuselage were studied for their heating effect on the fuselage and wing. For the position tested, no fuselage heating could be measured. Some wing heating was found. The jet simulation system was important in this problem. The amount of deflection of the jet by an airstream at an angle to it was greatly affected by the jet temperature. It was necessary to exactly simulate jet conditions if results in agreement with flight tests were desired. Large effects of the jets on stability were sometimes found. In one case these were eliminated by putting the tips of the stabilizer in the jets.

Junkers simulated power in half models by pumping air out the jet nozzle. This air is heated by an oxygen-acetelyne [sic] torch inside the model. The jet temperature is measured by a thermocouple at the aft tip of the turnip in the jet exit. Body and wing heating were measured by thermocouples set into plaster placed in holes in metal models. If surface conduction was to be simulated, a piece of screen was imbeded [sic] in the plaster.

Junkers have made extensive use of the half model technique. On the whole the results have been satisfactory. Many end plate and boundary layer problems are encountered. Tests were conducted in a slow tunnel to investigate half model errors. The only important errors found were in longitudinal stability where small but noticeable differences were found.

Von Doepp was asked about methods for calculating lift distributions on sweptback wings. He said that reports had been written and published by both Multhopp and Weissenger and that the latter's work was best.

Von Doepp said that there was much concern over dihedral problems on airplanes with sweptforward wings. These had not been encountered in flight on the JU-287 but this airplane had not been flown over 550 km/hr and difficulties were expected only at higher speeds. The JU-287 had not been flown faster because of flutter and strength worries. Systematic shake flight tests were planned.

Von Doepp said that the sweptforward wing was desired because of its good stall characteristics. He was asked about longitudinal control problems when flaps are deflected on such a wing. He said that these problems had been suitably solved in the JU-287 but admitted that they were serious. He has suggested the use of a retractable wing on the nose of the fuselage which is extended when the flaps are deflected. This would reduce the stability somewhat but could be compensated for by the aft movement of the aerodynamic center which is found on Fowler or similar flaps. He has not tried this.

The interrogation was terminated for lack of time. Much additional information of great value is undoubtedly available from this same source.

G. Schairer

APPENDIX 9:

DESCRIPTION OF *WASSERFALL*

Had the German military been able to stretch the war into 1946, the specter of *Wasserfall*, a proximity-fuzed surface-to-air missile, held the potential to wreak havoc with Allied strategic bombers. Inspectors of German equipment, papers, and technicians prepared the following overview of *Wasserfall* as an appendix to a postwar 1945 Combined Intelligence Objectives Subcommittee report on areas of interest identified as "Group 2 Targets in Nordhausen Area." It is noteworthy that one of the persons interrogated is identified as "Direktor Rees," no doubt referring to Eberhard Rees, Wernher von Braun's trusted deputy from Peenemünde in the 1940s to NASA in the 1960s and beyond. Also notable is *Wasserfall's* reliance on the then-unperfected proximity fuze, the cause of so much concern for "Hap" Arnold of the USAAF. The arrangement of warhead explosives within the *Wasserfall* shell was intended to fragment the entire rocket upon detonation – a consideration when the size of fragments raining down on Germany could affect the amount of collateral damage such fragments would cause. The projected economy of using *Wasserfall* as opposed to traditional flak is explored in this document. While sobering, this must remain conjectural since the war ended before this missile could be made operational.

C.2 (Wasserfall)
Ground to Air Guided Anti Aircraft Rocket
Sources of Information
The information given below is based on a preliminary examination of the Wasserfall components and the interrogation of Direktor Rees, Direktor Fleischer, Dr. Groettrop, Herr Riedel III, Herr Temesvary, Herr Gengelbach and Herr Kagerer, senior members of the E.W. In no case was the evidence of the above contradictory except in small details and further confirmation of the information was obtained from certain documents found at Volkenrode. Copies of these are given in Appendix 10.

General

Work on Wasserfall was started at Peenemunde two years ago and it was hoped to have it in operational use by May 1946. It has obviously been designed for very large scale production and the non-availability of certain materials and lack of certain production capacity has obviously influenced the design considerably.

The whole rocket is fabricated from mild steel. Compressed gas is used for fuel expulsion, while it was admitted that on a projectile of this size a turbine with pumps would have been lighter. Ground control was chosen primarily because of the economy of electrical components which resulted.

It was expected to shoot down one aircraft with every two projectiles each costing 7,000 to 10,000 marks which compares favourably with standard flak which requires 4,000 projectiles at 100 marks each per aircraft shot down.

It was stated that until recently Wasserfall did not have the highest priority as Professor Wagner had more influence with the Air Ministry than Professor von Braun and even in his own organisation Professor von Braun gave higher priority to the larger rockets in spite of their lower military value as he always hoped ultimately to fire a rocket to the moon!

Brief Specification

Total weight of projectile	7700 lb.
Weight of warhead	520 lb.
Weight of propellant	4100 lb.
Overall length	25' 7"
Diameter of body	3' 0"
Overall diameter (across fins)	8' 2 ½"
Maximum slant range	29,000 yards
Maximum height	58,000 feet
Velocity	2,500ft./sec.
Thrust	17,500 lb.
Burning time	40 seconds
Initial acceleration	1.2 g.
Final acceleration	4 g. approx.

Propulsion System

The propulsion system was developed at Peenemunde and provides a thrust of 17500 lb. for 40 seconds. The propellant used consists of Mischsaure (10% H_2SO_4 + 90% HNO_3) and Visol (Vinyl compounds) in the ratio 5 : 1 respectively by weight. It is said to be auto-igniting and to be very satisfactory. The acid is used to cool the combustion chamber.

Further information concerning the general design of the combustion chamber was obtained from Herr Riedel III and is given in Appendix 9.

The propellant is expelled by nitrogen or air stored at 2900 lb./sq.in. and reduced to about 290 lb./sq.in. in the fuel tanks; the combustion chamber pressure is 220 lb./sq.in. The problem of removing the fuel from the tanks when subject to lateral acceleration has been solved by the use of a swinging exit pipe, which, being subject to the same acceleration as the propellant, remains flooded. It is interesting to note that a prize was awarded for the best solution to this problem, the competition being open to all members of the Establishment. The piston solution was discarded on account of increased weight and production difficulties.

Propellant is admitted to the combustion chamber by the simultaneous opening of three solenoid operated valves, bursting discs being incorporated in the valves to prevent leakage.

The projectiles were filled at the factory and by the use of special treatment of the internal surface of the tanks satisfactory storage up to 6 months had been achieved. It was hoped to increase this time to 1 year in the near future.

It was stated that the specific impulse of the fuel was 180 and that a thrust of 8 tons was developed for 40 seconds. This indicates a fuel load of 1.78 tons and this figure agrees with the estimation from a preliminary measurement of tank size and the documentary evidence given in Appendix 10. The initial acceleration was stated to be 1.2 g. when fired vertically and this indicates a total weight of 3.5 tons, and this also agrees with the documentary evidence. The ratio of the fuel weight to total weight on this figure works out at 0.51 and this tallies with an independent statement that it was 0.50. It will be possible to obtain the final check on this figure after detailed examination of the components. The final velocity fired vertically was stated to be between 2500 and 3000ft./sec. dependent on the yaw and this also agrees with the documentary evidence obtained at Volkenrode. The passage through the sonic barrier will therefore be very slow but it was stated emphatically that no trouble had been experienced due to this factor.

Control System

The projectile is fitted with four small bi-convex wings at the C. of G. and four stabilising fins at the rear, these being fitted with control surfaces. Four further control surfaces (normally on the same axes as the above) are situated in the gas stream.

The projectile is roll-stabilised and ground control is used. The reasons given for the adoption of ground control were

(1) The equipment in the projectile was simpler and this had to be handled by troops in the field. It would also be more economical to produce.

(2) The experience with the A.4 rocket showed that the beam control in azimuth was badly upset by stray reflections from A/C. It was agreed that with a shorter wave-length this trouble might not be experienced.

During the early trials optical manual control was used with a small joy-stick similar to that used to control HS 117. A total of 30 rounds had been fired – 20 without, and 10 with manual control. The response of the projectile had been satisfactory although no attempt had been made to guide the projectile to a target.

Operationally it was intended to have one beam locked on the projectile and another on the target and to arrange by manual control for these beams to be made to coincide. Eventually this control would be automatic although two beams would always be used. The wave-length intended was 25 cms.

Three position gyros (kurskreisel) were fitted, one for roll stabilisation, the other two being monitored by the output of the "mischgerat" for control in pitch and yaw. It was understood that the position gyros were shortly to be abandoned in favour of rate gyros (wendezeiger).

The servo control had been developed in three stages. On the early models a cylinder of oil pressurised by nitrogen at 590 lb./sq.in. had been used to operate simple pistons connected to the control vane spindles through an electrically operated valve arrangement. This system was discarded in favour of self-contained electrically operated hydraulic torque motors, each unit being fitted with its own electric drive and circulating pump. A.4 units were used initially for this purpose but they developed insufficient torque and a new and much neater unit was later adopted.

Finally it was decided to use all-electric servos and these were stated to be much more satisfactory from the points of view of manufacture, reliability and response. Each unit consisted of a motor the armature of which was made to oscillate at 50 cycles/sec. by a trembler device, the mid-point of the oscillation being monitored by the output from the "mischgerat". By this means it was claimed that back-lash was eliminated in the reduction gearing.

Four servos are employed each driving one external and one jet control vane. The ratio between these was stated to be ideally 2 : 1 respectively, but 1 : 1 (same axis) had been found to be adequate and simplified the mechanical design. Roll stabilisation was applied through all four sets of controls, it being stated that this gave better results in practice than stabilisation through two sets.

As the gas vanes were only necessary in the early stages of control and in the later stages they caused trouble due to asymmetrical burning, they were jettisoned after 10 to 20 secs. by explosive bolts. It was stated that the gas vanes might ultimately be dispensed with altogether, although it is difficult to see how this would be possible in view of the low initial acceleration.

A time switch of the type used on A.4 is employed to increase the amplification of the radio receiver as the range increases. It is also used to jettison the gas vanes at the appropriate moment. The main power supply for the servos was to be from lead/acid batteries. These were high load, short-life batteries which had been specially developed for the job and were said to be a big improvement on the A.4 batteries which were required for some time before launch and could not therefore be of the short-life type. The batteries for Wasserfall were considerably lighter than a corresponding generator and turbine. Actual figures could not be obtained.

Launching Arrangements
Wasserfall is fired vertically like the A.4 and may be fired from mobile equipment. In order to prevent the rocket being blown over by the wind before launching it is fastened down by four explosive bolts, which are blown one second after ignition of the fuels. As soon as the rocket is launched the controls are moved hard over in the direction in which the projectile is required to move.

This is important since it is essential for the turn to be made while the velocity is low. The maximum lateral acceleration of which the projectile is capable was stated to be 4.4. g. (20 per cent better than that which a pilot is capable of sustaining), and this figure agrees with that obtained from an approximate calculation of wing strength; the radius of curvature at maximum velocity must therefore be very high. Even commencing the turn immediately after launch the minimum height at which it would be possible to engage a stationary target at 60° Q.E. was stated to be 3300 feet. With fast moving targets, the "dog and master" effect of the pursuit curve further increased the minimum effective range and it was not intended to use the weapon at ranges of less than 3 miles. A diagram showing the shape of the effective zone is given in Appendix 10.

For long range weapons the above method of launching appears to be very satisfactory, and given lower axial acceleration and more robust wings it should be possible to extend the technique to shorter ranges. The method has the added advantage of dispensing with the boost, although the lower acceleration must always increase the time of flight. In the case of Wasserfall, this effect is off-set by the very high final velocity.

Warhead
No example of the warhead was found but it was stated that it was originally intended to weigh 330 lb., but that it had been increased to 520 lb. This increase may well have been due to the fact that it was intended to distribute

H.E. throughout the projectile thus fragmenting the whole body and reducing the damage to property on the ground. The casing of the warhead proper was stated to be 0.2 in. thick.

Fuzing

It was intended to use a radio proximity fuze set to operate at a distance of 80-160 feet from the target, the exact distance to be determined later by trials. This fuze was stated to be not yet reliable.

APPENDIX 10:

GERMAN SINGLE-JET FIGHTER PROJECTS

The prolific production of reports treating captured German technologies formed a catalog of ideas shared by the British and the Americans. Reproduced here is the text of a seminal report produced by the British on German single-engined jet fighter projects in some stage of development when the Allied victory terminated them. A copy resides in the USAF Historical Research Agency holdings at Maxwell AFB, Alabama. In addition to ever more sleek, semi-tailless types, the report chronicles the Messerschmitt P 1110, looking presciently like the Hawker Hunter of the 1950s. Some pragmatic ideas surface in this recap of German fighters near the end of the war – they feature frontal protection for the pilot against 12.7mm gunfire, but heavier protection from the rear. That frontal armament expressed in millimeters equates to the standard US M-2 .50 caliber aircraft machine gun, expectedly the only armament such jet fighters would expect to face in frontal attacks on bombers, while attacks from the rear might include fighters with larger-bore weapons.

A.I.2.(g) Report No. 2369

German Single-Jet Fighter Projects

1. At the request of the EHK (Chief Development Commission) and the TLR (Technical Air Equipment Branch), designs for single-jet fighter aircraft were submitted during 1945 by Focke-Wulf, Messerschmitt, Heinkel, Junkers and Blohm and Voss. The projects were to be discussed at a meeting on 27th and 28th February and a decision was to be made "concerning the completion of these designs". For use at this meeting a paper summarising the particulars of the projects was prepared and the present report is based on this document. The eight designs dealt with (they are known only by their project designations) are:-

Focke-Wulf I
Focke-Wulf II
Messerschmitt P.1101

Messerschmitt P.1110
Messerschmitt P.1111
Heinkel P.1078
Junkers EF.128
Blohm and Voss P.212

2. Reference is made in the paper to the difficulties experienced in its preparation on account of bad communication facilities. It was not possible to obtain a written DVL [Deutsche Versuchsanstalt für Luftfahrt, or German Aeronautics Research Institute] report on general performance and characteristics nor could the DVL compare the Heinkel P.1078 and the Messerschmitt P.1101 and P.1111. These last three designs were not, apparently, included in an earlier list of projects.

3. For the Messerschmitt P.1110, an increase in wing and fuselage size was contemplated.

4. It is pointed out that the performance figures quoted were provided by the firms and were not to be considered as "absolute estimates". They were to serve only for comparison.

5. The following brief descriptions give an idea of the main characteristics of the eight projects. Technical data are set out in the attached tables and three-view general arrangement drawings are also included. Re-drawing has not been attempted in view of the small size of the original prints and the amount of detail depicted. The original prints, together with additional data on certain of the projects are available at A.I.2.(g).

FOCKE-WULF I

6. This project (See Sheet I) is a shoulder-wing monoplane with swept-back wing, fin and tailplane. The 2-piece wing which accommodates the main fuel supply is of composite construction with steel spars and wooden ribs and skin. Landing flaps are fitted.

7. The main structural members are in the upper portion of the fuselage, which accommodates the pilot's cockpit, instruments and equipment and a small fuel tank. In the lower rear portion of the fuselage is housed the turbojet unit with straight-through intake extending forward to the nose. The armament comprising either 2 x or 4 x MK 108 30 mm. guns is disposed in the lower part of the nose beneath the intake. For the 2-gun installation 200 rounds are carried, and with four guns the quantity of ammunition is increased to 320 rounds.

8. A sharply swept-back fin with the swept-back tailplane at its upper end gives the aircraft an unusual appearance. The fin is of wood construction and

is built around a box spar. The rudder is identical with the ailerons and the tailplane has pronounced dihedral.

9. The main wheels (700 x 175 mm.) are carried on Fw 190 oleo legs and retract forwards and inwards into the fuselage. The nose wheel is 465 x 165 mm.

10. Armour protection is provided against 12.7 mm. fire from the front.

FOCKE-WULF II

11. Project II is generally similar to project I as regards wing and fuselage arrangement but the tail unit is considerably modified (Sheet 1). Sweepback on both fin and tailplane has been retained, but the tailplane is set only moderately high and the fin and rudder occupy the conventional position above the horizontal surface.

12. The duralumin fuselage is equipped with a pressure cabin and accommodates two self-sealing tanks of 66 and 110 gallons capacity. The wing tanks increase the total capacity to 462 gallons. Normal armament comprises 2 x MK 108 (100 rpg) mounted one on each side of the intake. A third MK 108 can be fitted above the intake at the expense of the forward fuselage fuel tank.

13. The main undercarriage wheels which may be either 700 x 175 mm. or 740 x 210 mm. have oleo pneumatic suspension and hydraulic retraction.

MESSERSCHMITT P.1101

14. The Messerschmitt P.1101 is also a shoulder-wing monoplane (See Sheet 2). The 2-piece wing has steel spars with wooden ribs and skin and is swept back at 40 deg. There are leading-edge slots and plain camber-changing landing flaps.

15. The pressure cabin is located well forward in the upper part of the fuselage followed by the fuel tanks, undercarriage retraction space and tail cone housing the equipment. Underneath is the central intake leading to the turbojet unit at the rear. The armament disposed on each side of the cockpit comprises 2 or 4 x MK 108 with 100 rpg.

16. The nose wheel (500 x 180 mm.) retracts with a 90 deg. turn into a space beneath the intake. The main undercarriage wheels (740 x 210 mm.) retract rearwards and inwards into the upper portion of the fuselage.

17. The pilot is protected by armour plate against 12.7 mm. fire from the front and 20 mm. fire from the rear.

MESSERSCHMITT P.1110

18. The P.1110 (Sheet 2) has the same wing as the P.1101 but the fuselage arrangement differs considerably from that of any of the projects so far

described. It is of all-metal construction and the elimination of the nose intake has permitted a slender design of approximately circular cross-section to be obtained. The armament of 3 x MK 108 guns (2 x 70 + 1 x 100 rounds) is housed in the nose immediately in front of the pressure cabin. Two more MK 108's can be fitted as optional equipment. Behind the cabin is the main fuel tank followed by the turbojet unit. The latter is mounted far back so that the tailpipe terminates beneath the tailplane. The air intakes are far back along the sides of the fuselage above the wing and just forward of the trailing-edge fillets. A suction fan driven from the turbine draws in the boundary layer from the forward part of the fuselage through slots in the intakes.

19. Initially a tailplane and rudder of wood construction with 40-deg. sweepback was proposed, but it was planned later to substitute a vee tail.

20. The nose wheel is retracted into the lower portion of the gun compartment while the main wheels retract forwards into the wing roots.

21. Armour protection is provided for the pilot against 12.7 mm. fire from the front and 20 mm. fire from the rear.

MESSERSCHMITT P.1111

22. The P.1111 (Sheet 2) is characterized by the elimination of the tailplane although the swept-back fin and rudder are retained. The deep-chord swept-back mid wing contains the whole of the fuel supply (330 gallons). The ailerons also serve as elevators and leading-edge slots extend over the outer portions of the wing.

23. Two MK 108 guns (100 rpg) are housed in the slender nose and there is an additional MK 108 (100 rounds) in each wing root. The fairing behind the pressure cabin extends to the end of the fuselage where it is blended with the fin. The air intakes are located at the roots of the wing leading-edge and are connected with the turbine inlet by slightly curved ducts passing on either side of the cockpit. Between the cockpit and the turbo-jet unit there is a space for the radio equipment.

24. The nose wheel, which is mounted very far forward, retracts into the lower part of the gun compartment, while the main wheels (465 by 165 mm) of the wide-track undercarriage are stowed in the wing roots. Protection for the pilot is the same as on the P.1110 and P.1111.

HEINKEL P.1078

25. Still less conventional is the Heinkel P.1078 (Sheet 3). This is a shoulder-wing monoplane of the true tail-less type with a pronounced inverted-gull wing which contains the whole of the fuel supply (320 gallons). The air intake is in the nose of the fuselage and is flattened to provide space

for the pilots cockpit above and the retracted nose wheel below. Two MK 108's (100 rpg) are mounted one on each side of the cockpit. The main undercarriage (660 by 190 mm.) retracts forwards and inwards and the rear of the fuselage is occupied by the turbo-jet unit.

JUNKERS EF.128

26. Another tail-less design with double-spar all-wood shoulder wing is the EF.128 (Sheet 3). There are lateral control surfaces above and below the wing just inboard of the ailerons.

27. The pressure cabin with catapult seat is located well forward with space for the nose wheel beneath and the armament of 2 or 4 x MK 108 (100 rpg) at the side. Aft of the cabin are the fuselage fuel tanks (226 gallons) and the turbo-jet unit. The intakes are at the sides of the fuselage under the wing at about the mid-chord position and provision is made for diverting the boundary layer flow to a vent outlet aft of the cockpit fairing. In addition to the fuselage fuel tanks there are wing tanks with a capacity of 119 gallons.

28. The main wheels (710 mm. x 185 mm.) retract backwards and inwards into the lower portion of the fuselage.

29. Armour protection is provided for the pilot against 12.7 mm. fire from the front and 20 mm. fire from the rear.

BLOHM AND VOSS P.212

30. The Blohm and Voss P.212 is also tail-less. It has a swept-back inverted-gull wing with lateral control surfaces near the tips. These control surfaces do not extend below the wing as on the EF.128. The control surface on the downward-sloping wing tip serves as an elevator and also partially fulfils the functions of rudder and aileron. In addition there is a small vertical rudder and a small aileron inboard of the vertical fin. The wings are of steel skin construction with built-in fuel tanks. Landing flaps of unusual depth are provided at the trailing-edge and there are "nose flaps" which slide into the leading-edge.

31. From the intake in the nose a curved tubular steel duct leads to the compressor inlet. This duct forms part of the fuselage structure being attached to two longitudinal beams which in turn carry the wing attachments and turbo-jet mounting points. The pressure cabin is above the inlet duct and between the cabin and the turbo-jet unit at the rear there is a fuselage fuel tank which, with the wing tanks, gives a total capacity of 330 gallons

32. Two MK 108 guns (100 rpg) are mounted in the nose one on each side of the air duct. A third MK 108 can be fitted above the duct immediately in front of the cabin. If required two supplementary Mk 108's (60 rpg) can be mounted low down in the sides of the fuselage.

33. The nose wheel (465 by 165 mm.) retracts forwards and is stowed flat in the nose. The main wheels (710 by 185 mm.) also retract forwards into the fuselage.

A.I. 2.(g)
D. of I. (R)
30th August, 1945

(H. F. King)
Squadron Leader
For Wing Commander.

Distribution[2]

U.S. FORCES

D. of I., H.Q., U.S.S.T.A.F.	20
The Commander, U.S. Naval Forces France.	1
Chief U.S. Naval Technical Mission in Europe	1
A-2 Sect.H.Q., 8th Air Force	6
U.S. Naval Air Attache	4
Int. Branch, Air Division, U.S. Group C.C.	2

APPENDIX 11:

MESSERSCHMITT Me 328B LIGHT HIGH-SPEED BOMBER

Presented is the text of a British-generated report from August 29, 1945 that was shared with the United States (and preserved in the Air Force Historical Research Agency holdings at Maxwell AFB, Alabama). It details the abortive development of the Me 328, intended as a twin pulse-jet propelled manned bomber, originally conceived for coastal defense against the eventual Allied invasion. Remarkable high speeds at low altitude were promised, but pulse-jet vibrations posed one hurdle to successful implementation.

A.I.2.(g) Report No. 2371

Me 328B Light High-Speed Bomber

1. The Me 328B was developed from the Me 328A, a front view of which is shown herewith. The design is of interest because it represents the first serious attempt to apply Argus 014 impulse duct propulsion units to a piloted aircraft. Although full specifications had been drawn up by the end of 1942 the Me 328B never went into production. It is known that damage to the tail resulted from the pulsations of the jet units and that the first prototype crashed for this reason.

2. The aircraft, shown in the sketch (top), was intended to be used as a light, high-speed bomber for daylight operations against strongly defended targets and more particularly as "flying coastal artillery" for defence against Allied landings. Virtual immunity from fighter interception was to be ensured by high speed at low altitude which would also make it a difficult target for ground defences, particularly in view of its small size. The design is simple throughout to ensure cheap and rapid production.

Fuselage

3. The wood fuselage is of circular cross-section throughout with a maximum diameter of 3ft. 11 in. It is made in four parts, namely nose; cylindrical centre section; rear fuselage; and conical tail end. On assembly bulkheads are interposed between the various sections. The upper portion of the centre-section is recessed to receive the one-piece spar for the shoulder

wing, and on the underside of this section are fitted the retractable landing skid and bomb carrier.

4. Two self-sealing tanks of equal capacity occupy the whole of the nose space and two identical tanks, but in reverse positions, are housed in the rear fuselage. The pilot's cockpit is in the centre-section together with most of the instruments and equipment. There is a space beneath the pilot's seat which could be utilised for additional fuel or for the stowage of anti-personnel bombs.

5. There is a 15 mm. armour bulkhead between the two nose fuel tanks and an armour ring 10 inches wide and 15 mm. thick between the nose and centre-sections. Further protection for the pilot is afforded by an 80 mm. bullet-proof windscreen. The cockpit cover is hinged on the starboard side and the wood fairing as shown in the general arrangement drawing is extended as far as the rear of the fuselage where it blends with the fin. A balloon cable-cutter is fitted to the nose.

Landing Skid

6. The aircraft is landed on a central skid of composite wood and steel construction which incorporates a braking arrangement. Part of the skid surface at the rear is cut away to accommodate the bomb carrier. Landing shock is absorbed by a modified Fw 200 oleo leg fitted with a roller which runs on a track on the upper surface of the skid. At take-off the skid is retracted and locked against the underside of the fuselage so that although the bomb is carried by the skid the load is transferred to the main structure. The skid can only be lowered after the bomb has been dropped.

7. The aircraft is supported on the jettisonable undercarriage (employed for take-off) on two spherical sockets in the wings and a third point at the rear of the fuselage. There are three alternative methods of take-off:-

(1) Borsig rocket-propelled rail carriage.

(2) Three-wheel carriage and cable-type catapult.

(3) Three-wheel carriage and towing aircraft.

Wing and Tailplane

8. The tapered wing is of wood construction throughout, including the single spar. The camber-changing flaps are cut away to clear the propulsion units. They can be deflected through a maximum angle of 50 degrees. Outboard of the propulsion units are fixed leading-edge slots, and balloon cable-cutters extend along the full length of the leading-edges.

9. Long-span and short-span versions were proposed, the long span being shown in the drawing. The short span is identical except that the wing-tip sections are omitted and the fairings of the wind-driven generators form the end caps. The spans are 28ft. 2 ½ in. and 22ft. 7 ½ in. and the corresponding wing areas 101 sq.ft. and 91.5 sq.ft. respectively.

10. Adjacent to the power units the undersurface of the wing is protected by asbestos-covered plates.

Power Units

11. Two Argus 109 014 propulsion units are flexibly suspended under the wing and are quickly interchangeable. In emergency they can be jettisoned by explosive bolts. For added strength the jet tubes are enclosed in outer tubes at the mounting points. Initially it was proposed to instal[l] units of 660 lb. static thrust and units of 880 lb. thrust were to be substituted when available. It is stated that the thrust varies directly with atmospheric density and falls to zero at 35,600ft.

12. Fuel is delivered to the units by electrically driven pumps, the current supply being taken from an accumulator on the undercarriage until the wind-driven generators come into operation. Special Argus regulators meter the fuel in accordance with the speed and altitude.

Emergency Exit

13. On account of supply difficulties a catapult seat was not to be fitted. Instead there was to be an arrangement whereby the whole of the rear portion of the fuselage behind the pilot's seat could be jettisoned by explosive bolts to facilitate baling out.

Performance

14. The accompanying Tables I and II give the maker's estimated performances with the alternative power unit installations.

Other Me 328 Fighter and Bomber Projects

15. In addition to the unarmed Me 328B bomber several other versions of this aircraft were projected. Among these were the following:

a. Fighter with 2 x 660 lb. or 4 x 330 lb. thrust.

Span	21ft.
Length	22.4ft.
Armament (nose)	2 x MG 151/20 (200 rpg.)
Landing skid	
Max. speed at S.L.	468 m.p.h.

b. Fighter-bomber with 2 x 660 lb. thrust.

Span	21ft. (leading-edges swept back 36 deg.)
Length	22.4ft.
Armament (nose)	2 x MG 151/20 (200 rpg.)
Multi-wheel retractable undercarriage	
Max. speed at S.L.	422 m.p.h. with 500 kg. bomb

c. Fighter-bomber with 2 x 660 lb. thrust

Span	15.1ft. (leading edges swept back 45°)
Length	22.4ft.
Armament (nose)	2 x MG 151/20 (200 rpg.)
Landing skid	

d. Fighter with 4 x 660 lb. thrust.

Span	27.85ft. (leading-edges swept back 36 deg.)
Length	26.65ft.
Armament	
Nose	2 x MG 151/20 (200 rpg.)
wing roots	2 x MK 105 (50 rpg.)
tail (fixed)	1 x MG 151/20 (200 rounds)
Multi-wheel retractable undercarriage	
Max. speed at S.L.	571 m.p.h.

e. Bomber-Reconnaissance aircraft with 4 x 660 lb. thrust.

Span	27.85ft. (leading-edges swept back 36 deg.)
Length	26.65ft.
Armament (nose)	2 x MG 151/20 (200 rpg.)
Bombs	2 x 500 kg. carried under wing roots.
Multi-wheel retractable undercarriage	
Max. speed at S.L.	With 2 x 500 kg. bomb 497 m.p.h.
	Reconnaissance version 576 m.p.h.

TABLE I. Me 328B. PERFORMANCE DATA WITH 2 x 660 lb. THRUST

	Without bomb	1 x 500 kg. bomb	1 x 1000 kg. bomb
Flying wt. lb. (440 gall. of petrol)	7125	8230	9330
Max. speed			
S.L., m.p.h.	434	372	329
6500ft. m.p.h.	402	312	–
Range	-	-	-
S.L. miles	391	360	338
Outward at S.L., return at 16,400ft., miles	466	422	391

Endurance			
S.L., hrs.	0.9	0.9	0.9
Outward at S.L., return at 16,400ft., hrs.	1.24	1.19	1.16
Service ceiling			
Max. flying wt.,ft.	13,100	7,220	3,610
At 4,400 lb. wt.,ft.	22,300	–	–
Rate of climb			
(at max. flying wt.) S.L.ft./min.	2105	1103	492
6,500ft.,ft./min.	1024	197	–
Landing speed, m.p.h.	113	113	113
Wing Loading			
Max. flying wt., lb./sq.ft.	78	90	102
Landing wt., lb./sq.ft.	42.5	42.5	42.5

TABLE II. Me 328B. PERFORMANCE DATA WITH 2 x 880 lb. THRUST

	Without bomb	1 x 500 kg. bomb	1 x 1000 kg. bomb
Flying wt. lb. (547 gallons of petrol)	7125	8230	9330
Max. speed			
S.L., m.p.h.	502	434	391
9800 ft. m.p.h.	453	375	283
Range			
S.L. miles	329	304	289
Outward at S.L., return at 16,400ft., miles	407	368	345
Endurance			
S.L. hrs.	0.65	0.65	0.65
Outward at S.L., return at 16,400ft., hrs.	0.92	0.88	0.86

Service ceiling			
At max. flying wt.,ft.	16,000	13,100	9,200
At 4,400 lb. wt.,ft.	23,300	–	–
Rate of Climb (at max. flying wt.)			
S.L.ft./min.	3720	2340	1650
6,500ft.,ft./min.	2260	1140	530
Landing speed, m.p.h.	115	115	115
Wing Loading			
Max. flying wt.,lb./sq.ft.	78	90	102
Landing wt., lb./sq.ft.	42.5	42.5	42.5

A.I.2.(g) D. of I. (R).

29th August, 1945.

(H.F. King) Squadron Leader

For Wing Commander

Appendix 12:

MUSEUM AIRCRAFT IDENTIFIED FOR PRESERVATION, MAY 9, 1946

A significant lot of aircraft intended for the USAAF museum collection including specimens from Germany, Japan, Great Britain and the USAAF was identified for movement to Orchard Place, Illinois in May 1946. This would protect aircraft inside the former Douglas C-54 assembly plant there. Subsequently, the list was clarified to send some of the larger aircraft that required outdoor storage to the USAAF's burgeoning desert storage facility at Davis-Monthan AAB in Tucson, Arizona. This list, preserved as an attachment to the Freeman Field historical report for January–June 1946, is especially useful for the serial numbers included with the vast majority of aircraft. Some icons, such as the venerable B-24D Liberator (42-72843) and the Ju 88D (T2-1598) survive to this day in the national Museum of the United States Air Force in Dayton, Ohio. Others, such as Fw 190s T2-116 and T2-125, subsequently disappeared from the scene, probably to salvage. Still others, like the B-32, went extinct. The XP-51 (41-38) slumbered at Orchard Place before being transferred to the National Air and Space Museum's legendary storage complex at Silver Hill, Maryland. In 1975, it was released to the Experimental Aircraft Association (EAA), refurbished for flight, and operated for a time before being placed in the EAA Museum in Oshkosh, Wisconsin where it is on display at the time of writing. This list is notable for what it does not include; the high-interest German jets, rockets, and exotic aircraft like the Do 335, many of which were preserved, do not show up on this document.

AIRCRAFT TO BE SHIPPED BY RAIL OR TRUCK

1.	PQ-14A	43-44217
2.	L-5	42-14798
3.	L-1A	41-19015
4.	PT-13	36-19
5.	UC-61A	43-14506

6.	PT-19A	43-33842
7.	L-4B	43-1074
8.	L-3B	43-26889
9.	XR-4	41-18874
10.	XP-55	42-78846
11.	XO-60	42-13610
12.	XR-5	43-47954
13.	JB-10	
14.	O-47A	37-273
15.	P-40N	44-47959
16.	XP-75	44-32166
17.	XP-47J	42-46952
18.	XP-75	44-44553
19.	XCG-14	44-90989
20.	Typhoon	

FLIGHT DELIVERY PRIORITY FOR RELOCATION OF AIRCRAFT IS AS FOLLOWS:

1.	JU-88	T2-1598
2.	FW-190	T2-125
3.	FW-190	T2-116
4.	TP-40N	44-7084
5.	BT-13A	41-22124
6.	O-47A	37-279
7.	C-45A	41-11864
8.	C-82N	45-25437
9.	PT-26	42-14299
10.	B-17G	44-83504
11.	P-51D	44-74939
12.	P-47D	44-32691
13.	P-61B	42-39608
14.	TB-29-15	42-6364
15.	A-20H	44-306
16.	TB-29-90	45-21728
17.	XP-47H	42-23298
18.	XBQ-3	43-25253
19.	RB-17E	41-2407
20.	B-25J	45-8813

21.	XB-26	44-68221
22.	TB-26C	41-35784
23.	P-59A-1	44-22627
24.	C-54A	41-37295
25.	RP-63A	42-70255
26.	B-32	42-108474
27.	P-38J	42-14406
28.	XA-38	43-14406
29.	A-26C	44-35933
30.	XC-53A	42-6480
31.	C-47	41-38734
32.	YP-61	41-18878
33.	B-24D	42-72843
34.	UC-64	42-5046
35.	RP-47B	41-5917
36.	C-60A	42-55995
37.	AT-6	40-718
38.	C-87	41-77608
39.	XP-51	41-38
40.	AT-7	41-1144
41.	XCG-15	43-37082
42.	XPG-2A	42-77062
43.	CG-A4	45-13883
44.	XCG-16	44-76193
45.	Zeke	
46.	Spitfire	T2-492
47.	FW-190	T2-125 [listed twice on original]

ACRONYMS AND ABBREVIATIONS

AAB   Army Air Base.

AAF   Army Airfield.

AAFSAG   Army Air Forces Scientific Advisory Group.

ACR   Advance Confidential Report.

ADRC   Air Documents Research Center.

ADS   Air Disarmament Squadron.

AFHRA   Air Force Historical Research Agency. Located at Maxwell AFB, Alabama, AFHRA is the repository for official Air Force histories and supporting documents, including many dealing with German technologies.

AFSC   Air Force Service Command.

AFTC   Air Force Test Center.

AMG   Allied Military Government.

ATI   Air Technical Intelligence.

ATSC   Air Technical Service Command.

AWPD   Air War Plan Division.

CIA   Central Intelligence Agency.

CIOS   Combined Intelligence Objectives Subcommittee.

CMR   Confidential Memorandum Report.

CSDIC   Combined Services Detailed Interrogation Centre

DTIC   Defense Technical Information Center.

DVL   Deutsche Versuchsanstalt für Luftfahrt – German Aeronautics Research Institute.

EAA   Experimental Aircraft Association.

EOU   Enemy Objectives Unit.

ETO   European Theater of Operations.

FEAF   Far East Air Forces.

FIST   Flugtechnisches Institute Stuttgart, or Flight Institute of the Technical University/ Stuttgart.

GAF   German Air Force. Wartime American documents seldom referred to it as the Luftwaffe.

ICBM   Intercontinental ballistic missile.
JATO   Jet-assisted takeoff.
JIOA   Joint Intelligence Objectives Agency.
MAAF   Mediterranean Allied Air Forces.
MSFC   Marshall Space Flight Center (part of NASA).
MTO   Mediterranean Theater of Operations.
NACA   National Advisory Committee for Aeronautics (the predecessor organization to NASA).
NAIC   National Air Intelligence Center.
NARA   National Archives and Records Administration.
NASA   National Aeronautics and Space Administration.
NASM   National Air and Space Museum. This museum in the Smithsonian Institution family of museums has preserved and restored a number of iconic Luftwaffe aircraft and missiles.
NMUSAF   National Museum of the United States Air Force.
NRL   Naval Research Laboratory.
RAF   Royal Air Force.
SDAM   San Diego Aerospace Museum.
SHAEF   Supreme Headquarters Allied Expeditionary Forces.
USAAC   United States Army Air Corps.
USAAF   United States Army Air Forces. The separate United States Air Force (USAF) did not come into being until after World War II, on September 18, 1947.
USAFA   United States Air Force Academy Special Collections.
USSBS   United States Strategic Bombing Survey.
USSR   Union of Soviet Socialist Republics (the Soviet Union).
USSTAF   United States Strategic Air Force, or US Strategic Air Forces in Europe. Outgrowth of Eighth Air Force, USSTAF came into being on February 22, 1944, ultimately exercising some operational control over both Eighth and Fifteenth air forces, and some administrative control over both Eighth and Ninth air forces. It served with occupation forces in Europe after the war.

SELECT
BIBLIOGRAPHY

Bolton, Robert and Mindling, George, *US Air Force Tactical Missiles 1949–1969: The Pioneers*, Lulu.com, Raleigh, 2011

Boyne, Walter J., *Messerschmitt Me 262: Arrow to the Future*, Smithsonian Institution Press, Washington DC, 1980

Butler, Phil, *War Prizes: An Illustrated Survey of German, Italian and Japanese Aircraft Brought to Allied Countries During and After the Second World War*, Midland Counties Publications, Leicester, 1994

Chambers, Joseph R. and Chambers, Mark A., *Radical Wings and Wind Tunnels: Advanced Concepts Tested at NASA Langley*, Specialty Press, North Branch, 2008

Dressel, Joachim and Griehl, Manfred, *The Luftwaffe Album: Fighters and Bombers of the German Air Force, 1933–1945*, Arms and Armour, London, 1999

Green, William, *Warplanes of the Third Reich*, Doubleday, Garden City, 1976

Held, Werner, *Fighter! Luftwaffe Fighter Planes and Pilots*, Prentice-Hall, Englewood Cliffs, 1979

Jenkins, Dennis R., *Messerschmitt Me 262 Sturmvogel*, Specialty Press, North Branch, Minnesota, 1996

Kennedy, Gregory P., *The Rockets and Missiles of White Sands Proving Ground, 1945–1958*, Schiffer Publishing, Atglen, 2009

Kreis, John F. (ed.), *Piercing the Fog: Intelligence and Army Air Forces Operations in World War II*, Air Force History and Museums Program, Washington, D. C., 1996

Merrick, K.A., *German Aircraft Markings, 1939–1945*, Sky Books Press, New York, 1977

Miller, Jay, *Convair B-58*, Aerograph 4, Aerofax, Arlington,1985

Scutts, Jerry, *Messerschmitt Bf 109*, Motorbooks, Osceola, 1996

Ward, Bob, *Dr. Space: The Life of Wernher von Braun*, Naval Institute Press, Annapolis, 2005

ENDNOTES

CHAPTER 1

1. From notes in the Murray Green collection of papers pertinent to "Hap" Arnold in the USAFA.
2. Dr. Richard P. Hallion, *Observation in Context: Reconsidering Lindbergh's Interwar Assessments of German Aviation*, National Air and Space Museum, Washington, D.C., 2007 (copyright 2007 R.P. Hallion, reproduced with permission).
3. "Truman Smith: 1893–1946 – The Facts of Life – A Narrative with Documents" in the Hoover Institution collection at Stanford University.
4. Letter, Maj Truman Smith, Military Attaché, American Embassy, Berlin, to Col Charles A. Lindbergh, November 2, 1937, in the Hoover Institution collection at Stanford University.
5. "General Estimate as of Nov. 1, 1937," M.I.D. Report, by Truman Smith, Major, G.S., Military Attaché.
6. *Ibid.*
7. *Ibid.*
8. *Ibid.*
9. Hallion (2007) op. cit.
10. Smith, "General Estimate" op. cit.
11. *The United States Strategic Bombing Survey – Summary Report – (European War), September 30, 1945*, reprinted by Air University Press, Maxwell AFB, Alabama, October 1987.
12. Hallion (2007) op. cit.
13. Smith, "General Estimate" op. cit.
14. *Ibid.*
15. *Ibid.*
16. Title page from "Air Intelligence Activities – Office of the Military Attaché, American Embassy, Berlin, Germany, August 1935 – April 1939" by Col Truman Smith, USA, (Ret.), prepared between September 1954 and September 1956.
17. Report, "Estimate of Germany's Present and Potential Capacity to Produce Airplanes," by Truman Smith, Lieutenant Colonel, Infantry, September 16, 1940.
18. William Green, *Warplanes of the Third Reich,* Doubleday, Garden City, 1976.
19. Citation for Distinguished Service Medal for Col Truman Smith.

CHAPTER 2

1.   Bruce Ashcroft and Robert L. Young, *A Brief History of Air Force Scientific and Technical Intelligence*, National Air Intelligence Center (NAIC) History Office.
2.   *Ibid.*
3.   "Crash Report #2," Intelligence Service, US Army Air Forces, Washington, D.C., December 28, 1942.
4.   *Ibid.*
5.   *Ibid.*
6.   Another contemporary USAAF document says it was due to a collision with an attacking P-39.
7.   "Crash Report #2" op. cit.
8.   The designation format represents the way it appears in Gen Carroll's 1944 letter, using "Me" instead of "Bf" for the Messerschmitt 109s.
9.   Letter, Brig Gen Frank O. Carroll, Chief, Engineering Division, to Commanding General, Army Air Forces Proving Ground Command, Eglin Field, Florida; subject: Disposition of Captured Enemy Aircraft, March 10, 1944.
10. *Ibid.*
11. *Ibid.*
12. Letter, Lt Col J.B. Martin, Liaison Officer, Materiel Command, Eglin Field, Florida, to Commanding General, Materiel Command, Wright Field, Dayton, Ohio; subject: Informal Progress Report on Operations of Foreign Aircraft, Proving Ground Command Headquarters, April 8, 1944.
13. *Ibid.*
14. "Aircraft Evaluation Report – German Messerschmitt-109F," prepared by Materiel Command, Engineering Division, Wright Field, Dayton, Ohio (Report No. 110), printed July 2, 1943.
15. Frederick A. Johnsen, *P-40 Warhawk*, Motorbooks/MBI, Osceola, 1998.
16. "Aircraft Evaluation Report – German Messerschmitt-109F" op. cit.
17. Conversation between the author and Col Ralph Hoewing, USAF (Ret.), June 20, 1998.
18. Memorandum, Headquarters, Twelfth Air Force, to Commanding General – All Subordinate Commands and Wings, Twelfth Air Force; subject: Technical Intelligence and C.S.D.I.C., April 12, 1944. (In AFHRA holdings.)
19. Memorandum, Headquarters MATAF, to A-2, XII TAC, *et al*; subject: Interrogation of Air Prisoners of War and Handling of Captured Enemy Air Equipment, May 4, 1944. (In AFHRA holdings.)
20. Chronology, "Progress of MX-544 – Chinese Copy of German V1 Buzz Bomb," from the papers of Col Ezra Kotcher, USAAF, circa. September 1944. ("Chinese Copy" is a term used to reference an item that is reverse-engineered from an existing article.)
21. *Ibid.*
22. See also Richard Hallion, "The American Buzz Bombs," *Aeroplane Monthly*, November 1976, pp. 566–71.
23. *Ibid.*
24. From notes in the Murray Green "Hap" Arnold collection at the US Air Force Academy.
25. *Ibid.*
26. *Ibid.*

27. Memorandum for the Commanding General, Army Air Forces; subject: Report of Col L.W. Sweetser's Recent Mission to England on *Crossbow*, March 16, 1944, by Brig Gen Thomas D. White, Assistant Chief of Air Staff, Intelligence.
28. Interview, Murray Green with Gen Samuel Anderson, Los Angeles, California, August 17, 1970, in the Murray Green "Hap" Arnold collection at the US Air Force Academy.
29. From notes in the Murray Green "Hap" Arnold collection at the US Air Force Academy.
30. *Ibid.*
31. *Ibid.*
32. *Ibid.*
33. *Ibid.*
34. *Ibid,* referencing a letter from Gen Kuter to Gen Arnold, January 28, 1945.

CHAPTER 3

1. From notes in the Murray Green collection of papers pertinent to "Hap" Arnold in the US Air Force Academy.
2. *Ibid.*
3. *Ibid.*
4. Wartime American documents seldom referred to the German Air Force as the Luftwaffe.
5. From notes in the Murray Green collection of papers pertinent to "Hap" Arnold in the US Air Force Academy.
6. *Ibid.*
7. Letter, Carl Spaatz, Lieutenant General, to ("Hap"Arnold) Commanding General, US Army Air Forces, September 3, 1944 in the Murray Green collection at the US Air Force Academy.
8. *Ibid.*
9. From notes in the Murray Green collection of papers pertinent to "Hap" Arnold in the US Air Force Academy.
10. Interview transcript, Lt Gen Barney Giles, May 12, 1970, in the Murray Green collection at the US Air Force Academy.
11. Kenn C. Rust, *Fifteenth Air Force Story*, Historical Aviation Album, Temple City, California, 1976.
12. Letter, Ira C. Eaker, Lieutenant General, to Lt Gen Barney M. Giles, Chief of the Air Staff, Headquarters, Army Air Forces, October 4, 1944 in the Murray Green collection at the US Air Force Academy.
13. From notes in the Murray Green collection of papers pertinent to "Hap" Arnold in the US Air Force Academy.
14. W.W. Rostow, *The Beginnings of Air Targeting*, CIA Historical Review Program, September 22, 1993.
15. From notes in the Murray Green collection of papers pertinent to "Hap" Arnold in the US Air Force Academy.
16. Rostow (1993) op. cit.
17. Kit C. Carter and Robert Mueller, *Combat Chronology, 1941–1945: US Army Air Forces in World War II*, Center for Air Force History, Washington, D.C., 1991.
18. *Ibid.*
19. J. Richard Smith, *The Messerschmitt Me 262*, Profile 130, Profile Publications Ltd., Surrey, 1971.

20. Rostow (1993) op. cit.
21. *The Intelligence Exploitation of Germany*, Report of Combined Intelligence Objectives Subcommittee, G-2 Division, SHAEF, September 15, 1945 (AFHRA).
22. Rostow (1993) op. cit.
23. *Ibid.*
24. Report; subject: A Counter Air Force Program for the Fighters, from: Embassy of the United States of America, Enemy Objectives Unit, Economic Warfare Division, London, (Irwin Nat Pincus), to: Col L. K. Callahan, A-2 Eighth Fighter Command, Pinetree, via Widewing, October 28, 1944 (AFHRA collection).
25. Richard P. Bateson, *Arado Ar 234 Blitz*, Profile 215, Profile Publications Ltd., Berkshire, 1972.
26. *Ibid.*
27. From notes in the Murray Green collection of papers pertinent to "Hap" Arnold in the US Air Force Academy.
28. *Ibid.*
29. Letter, Barney M. Giles, Lieutenant General, to Lt Gen Carl Spaatz, Commanding General, US Strategic Air Forces in Europe, January 26, 1945, in the Murray Green collection at the US Air Force Academy.
30. Interview transcript, Lt Gen Henry Viccellio, May 13, 1970, in the Murray Green collection at the US Air Force Academy.
31. Interview transcript, Maj Gen Donald J. Keirn, September 25, 1970, in the Murray Green collection at the US Air Force Academy.
32. Interview transcript, Lt Gen Barney Giles, May 12, 1970, in the Murray Green collection at the US Air Force Academy. The emphasis given to the P-80 hedged this a bit, without impeding ongoing production of P-51s.
33. Table, "Monthly Production of Major German Jet Types" derived from the United States Strategic Bombing Survey by Kenn C. Rust and William N. Hess for "The German jets and the US Army Air Force," *American Aviation Historical Society Journal*, Vol. 8, No. 3, Third Quarter 1963.
34. Interview transcript, Gen Earle E. Partridge, December 6, 1969, in the Murray Green collection at the US Air Force Academy.
35. From notes in the Murray Green collection of papers pertinent to "Hap" Arnold in the US Air Force Academy.
36. *Interrogation of Reich Marshal Hermann Göring*, Ritter Schule, Augsburg, May 10, 1945 (in the Murray Green collection of papers pertinent to "Hap" Arnold at USAFA).
37. Memorandum, "Occupation Period Requirements of US Air Forces in Europe," Headquarters, United States Strategic Air Forces in Europe, March 15, 1945.
38. "Directives and Recommendations Concerning German Ministries and Central Agencies, Part II: Military," prepared by Planning Coordination Section, US Group CC, status of March 22, 1945 (at AFHRA).
39. "Report on German Flying Helmet," Headquarters, Air Disarmament Command, United States Strategic Air Force in Europe, USAAF Station 549, in a package dated December 9, 1944 (AFHRA collection).
40. John F. Kreis (ed.), *Piercing the Fog: Intelligence and Army Air Forces Operations in World War II*, Air Force History and Museums Program, Washington, D.C., 1996.
41. *Ibid.*
42. *Ibid.*

43. *Ibid.*
44. *Ibid.*
45. *Ibid.*
46. *Ibid.*
47. *Ibid.*
48. *Ibid.*

CHAPTER 4

1. *Interrogation of Reich Marshal Hermann Göring*, Ritter Schule, Augsburg, May 10, 1945 (in the Murray Green collection pertinent to "Hap" Arnold at USAFA).
2. *History of the Air Disarmament Division, IX Air Force Service Command, October 1944 to March 1946*, published by the IX AF Service Command, Erlangen, Germany, May 1946.
3. *Ibid.*
4. *Ibid.*
5. *Ibid.*
6. *The Intelligence Exploitation of Germany*, Report of Combined Intelligence Objectives Subcommittee, G-2 Division, SHAEF, September 15, 1945 (AFHRA).
7. *Ibid.*
8. *Ibid.*
9. *Ibid.*
10. *Ibid.* See also Chapter 6 of this work.
11. *Ibid.*
12. *History of the Air Disarmament Division* (May 1946) op. cit.
13. Headquarters 54th Air Disarmament Squadron (Provisional), Unit History for month of April 1945 (AFHRA).
14. 54th Air Disarmament Sq (P), Office of the Operations Officer; subject: Unit History, to: Commanding Officer, 2nd Air Disarm. Wing, October 6, 1945 (AFHRA).
15. *Ibid.*
16. Headquarters 54th Air Disarmament Squadron (Provisional), Unit History for month of May 1945 (AFHRA).
17. 54th Air Disarmament Sq (P), Office of the Operations Officer; subject: Unit History, to: Commanding Officer, 2nd Air Disarm. Wing, October 6, 1945 (AFHRA).
18. *Ibid.*
19. Headquarters 54th Air Disarmament Squadron (Provisional), Unit History for month of May 1945 (AFHRA).
20. Headquarters 54th Air Disarmament Squadron (Provisional), Unit History for month of June 1945 (AFHRA).
21. 54th Air Disarmament Sq (P), Office of the Operations Officer; subject: Unit History, to: Commanding Officer, 2nd Air Disarm. Wing, October 6, 1945 (AFHRA).
22. Headquarters 54th Air Disarmament Squadron (Provisional), Unit History for month of June 1945 (AFHRA). See also the section entitled "Watson found the good stuff" that follows.
23. 54th Air Disarmament Sq (Prov), Office of the Squadron Commander, Unit History for Month of August 1945 (AFHRA).
24. Points were accumulated for service, and were a way of prioritizing which troops were to be sent home.

25. 54th Air Disarmament Sq (Prov), Office of the Squadron Commander, Unit History for Month of August 1945 (AFHRA).
26. *Ibid.*
27. 54th Air Disarmament Sq (P), Office of the Operations Officer; subject: Unit History, to: Commanding Officer, 2nd Air Disarm. Wing, October 6, 1945 (AFHRA).
28. *History of the Air Disarmament Division* (May 1946) op. cit.
29. Russell Lee, "Dissecting an Air Force – Air Disarmament Division's Role in Neutralizing the Luftwaffe and Plundering its Secrets," *American Aviation Historical Society Journal,* Spring 1999.
30. *History of the Air Disarmament Division* (May 1946) op. cit.
31. *Ibid.*
32. *Ibid.*
33. *Ibid.*
34. *Ibid.*
35. *Ibid.*
36. *Ibid.*
37. *Ibid.*
38. *Ibid.*
39. *Ibid.*
40. *Ibid.*
41. *Ibid.*
42. *Ibid.*
43. Phil Butler, *War Prizes: An Illustrated Survey of German, Italian and Japanese Aircraft Brought to Allied Countries During and After the Second World War,* Midland Counties Publications, Leicester, 1994.
44. *Ibid.*
45. Norman Malayney, "ATI and Operation Lusty, Part II," *American Aviation Historical Society Journal,* Summer 1995.
46. Jack Woolams, autobiographical sketch dated March 20, 1946, in the files of AFTC/HO.
47. *Ibid.*
48. Malayney (1995) op. cit.
49. Draft memo, "Draft of Foreign Aircraft Program," May 24, 1945, preserved in the US Air Force Museum research collection.
50. Memo, "German Conventional Type Aircraft," unsigned and undated, in the air disarmament papers at AFHRA.
51. *Ibid.*
52. *Ibid.*
53. United States Air Force Oral History Program, Interview #K239.0512-724 of Lt Gen Donald L. Putt, by Dr. James C. Hasdorff, April 1–3, 1974.
54. Interview transcript, Lt Gen Donald L. Putt with Murray Green, August 13, 1974, in the Murray Green collection at the US Air Force Academy.
55. United States Air Force Oral History Program, Interview #K239.0512-724 of Lt Gen Donald L. Putt, by Dr. James C. Hasdorff, April 1–3, 1974.
56. *Ibid.*, and Peter M. Bowers, *Boeing Aircraft Since 1916,* Putnam, London, 1966. See also detailed references in the Wikipedia entry for the B-47.
57. Interview transcript, Lt Gen Donald L. Putt with Murray Green, August 13, 1974, in the Murray Green collection at the US Air Force Academy.

58. *Ibid.*
59. *Ibid.*
60. *Ibid.*
61. From notes in the Murray Green collection of papers pertinent to "Hap" Arnold in the US Air Force Academy.
62. *Ibid.*
63. *Ibid.*
64. *Ibid.*
65. *Ibid.*
66. *Ibid.*
67. United States Air Force Oral History Program, Interview #K239.0512-724 of Lt Gen Donald L. Putt, by Dr. James C. Hasdorff, April 1–3, 1974.
68. *Ibid.*
69. From notes in the Murray Green collection of papers pertinent to "Hap" Arnold in the US Air Force Academy.
70. "HQ and HQ Squadron History for July 1945" 1st Air Disarmament Wing (Prov), August 7, 1945 (AFHRA).
71. Asif A. Siddiqi, *Challenge to Apollo: The Soviet Union and the Space Race, 1945–1974*, NASA SP-2000-4408, Washington, D.C., 2000.
72. From notes in the Murray Green collection of papers pertinent to "Hap" Arnold in the US Air Force Academy.
73. "Outline Plan for Disarmament of the German Air Force," undated and without authorship, but with references to Operation *Overlord* that indicate this document was drafted in 1944. Document in the AFHRA collection at Maxwell AFB, Alabama.
74. "Disarmament of the German Air Force," unsigned, probably dating from 1944. Document 553.164 at AFHRA.
75. Siddiqi (2000) op. cit.
76. *Ibid.*
77. Bob Ward, *Dr. Space: The Life of Wernher von Braun*, Naval Institute Press, Annapolis, Maryland, 2005.
78. Siddiqi (2000) op. cit.
79. *Ibid.*
80. Ward (2005) op. cit.

CHAPTER 5

1. Letter, George Schairer to Benedict Cohn, May 10, 1945 (courtesy The Boeing Company).
2. *Ibid.*
3. *Ibid.*
4. Walter J. Boyne, "Project Paperclip," *Air Force Magazine*, June 2007.
5. Report; subject: German Aviation, to: Dr. Theodore von Kármán, Director, Scientific Advisory Group, from: George S. Schairer, Consultant, July 20, 1945 (in the papers of George S. Schairer at the Museum of Flight, Seattle, Washington). See Appendix 4 for the full text of this document.
6. *Ibid.*
7. James R. Hansen, *Engineer in Charge*, NASA SP-4305, NASA, Washington, D.C., 1987.

8. *Ibid.*
9. *Ibid.*
10. Robert T. Jones, "Adolf Busemann, 1901–1986," in *Memorial Tributes: National Academy of Engineering*, Vol. 3, National Research Council, The National Academies Press, Washington, D.C., 1989.
11. Biography of Adolf Busemann from the website of the Busemann Advanced Concepts Laboratory at the University of Colorado.
12. Report, subject: German Aviation, to: Dr. Theodore von Kármán, Director, Scientific Advisory Group, from: George S. Schairer, Consultant, July 20, 1945 (in the papers of George S. Schairer at the Museum of Flight, Seattle, Washington.) See Appendix 4 for the full text of this document.
13. *Ibid.*
14. *Ibid.*
15. *Ibid.*
16. *Ibid.*
17. *Ibid.*
18. Memorandum for Director of Intelligence, subject: Interrogation of von Doepp and Frengl on June 11, 1945 (in the papers of George S. Schairer at the Museum of Flight, Seattle, Washington).
19. *Ibid.*
20. Summary report, untitled and undated, describing Bachem Natter historical details as of summer 1945, by Capt R.W. Bratt, US Army Air Force, and Flt Lt J. R. Ewans, RAF, in the AFHRA collection.
21. *Ibid.*
22. *Ibid.*
23. History, January through July 1948, 141st AF BU (Res Tng), Chicago Orchard Airport, Park Ridge, Illinois (report viewed at Air Force Historical Research Agency, Maxwell AFB, Alabama).
24. "High Speed Tunnel Measurements on the Natter," ATI 36861 (DTIC) August, 1946.
25. Ashcroft and Young op. cit.
26. Joseph R. Chambers and Mark A. Chambers, *Radical Wings and Wind Tunnels: Advanced Concepts Tested at NASA Langley*, Specialty Press, North Branch, Minnesota, 2008.
27. *Ibid.*
28. E-mail, from: Richard P. Hallion, to: Frederick A. Johnsen, November 5, 2013, subject: Re: Luftwaffe Technology Book Chapters.
29. Robert E. Bradley, "The Birth of the Delta Wing," *American Aviation Historical Society Journal*, Vol. 48, No. 4, Winter 2003.
30. E-mail, from: Richard P. Hallion, to: Frederick A. Johnsen, November 5, 2013, subject: Re: Luftwaffe Technology Book Chapters.
31. Alexander Lippisch, "Germany and the Delta Wing," *Aero Digest*, February 1951.
32. Jack Woolams, autobiographical sketch dated March 20, 1946, in the files of AFTC/HO.
33. *Interim Report No. 1 on Me-163*, by Lt Robert J. Ford, T-2 Technical Intelligence, Headquarters Air Materiel Command, Wright AAF, Dayton, Ohio. Date prepared: May 14, 1946; release date: June 11, 1946.
34. Memo (Routing and Record Sheet), subject: Flight Testing ME-163, to: TSDIN, attn: Col Putt, from: TSFTE (Col Albert Boyd, Chief, Flight Test Division), May 8, 1946.

35. *Ibid.*
36. *Ibid.*
37. *Ibid.*
38. News release, May 7, 1946, from Public Relations Office, Air Materiel Command, Wright AAF, Dayton, Ohio, untitled; topic: Me 163B tests at Muroc.
39. Memo (Routing and Record Sheet), subject: Flight Testing ME-163, to: TSDIN, attn: Col Putt, from: TSFTE (Col Albert Boyd, Chief, Flight Test Division), May 8, 1946. The typical desert winds at Muroc often abated at dawn, but kicked up with the increased heat of morning sun.
40. Letter, from unknown sender (signature undeciphered), Research Analysis Corp., McClean, Virginia, to Royal Frey, director, US Air Force Museum, May 3, 1968.
41. Letter, from: O. P. Echols, Major General, USA, Asst. Chief of Air Staff, Materiel and Services, Headquarters, USAAF, Washington, D.C., to: Director, USAAF, Air Technical Service Command, Wright Field, Dayton, Ohio, subject: Preservation in the U.S. of Enemy Items of Aeronautical Equipment, April 4, 1945 (from AFHRA).
42. *Ibid.*
43. Teletype (copy), undated, from: Arnold, Washington, D.C., to: Director ATSC, Wright AAF, Dayton, Ohio, attn: Engineers Division, AFDMA-4 54-20 Reference Letter from this HQ, subject: "Preservation in United States of enemy items of aeronautical interest" (from AFHRA).
44. Letter, from: TSEAL, Paul H. Kemmer, Colonel, USAAF, Chief, Aircraft and Physical Requirements Subdivision, Engineering Division, to: TSCON, subject: Portable Hangars for Foreign Aircraft Storage, April 28, 1945.
45. Letter, from: Paul S. Blair, Colonel, USAAF, Chief, Base Service Section, Personnel and Base Services Division, to: Commanding General, USAAF, Washington, D.C., subject: Request for Assignment, Freeman AAF, Seymour, Indiana.
46. *Ibid.*
47. Base History, Freeman AAF, Air Technical Services Command, Seymour, Indiana –June 15, 1945 to January 1, 1946 (at AFHRA).
48. *Ibid.*
49. *Ibid.*
50. *Ibid.*
51. *Ibid.*
52. *Ibid.*
53. *Ibid.*
54. *Ibid.*
55. *Ibid.*
56. Base History, Freeman AAF, Air Materiel Command, Seymour, Indiana –January 1, 1946 to June 30, 1946 (at AFHRA).
57. *Ibid.*
58. *Ibid.*
59. *Ibid.*
60. *Ibid.*
61. Letter, Lt Col C. H. Belvin, Jr., Director, Engr. Serv. Div., Headquarters, Freeman AAF, Air Materiel Command, Seymour, Indiana, to: All Concerned, subject: Relocation of Museum Aircraft, May 9, 1946 (in AFHRA).
62. Letter, Col Harold E. Watson, Chief, Collection Division, Intelligence (T-2),

Headquarters, Air Materiel Command, Wright AAF, Dayton, Ohio, to: Commanding Officer, Freeman Field, Seymour, Indiana, June 7, 1946 (in AFHRA).

63. USAAF Report of Major Accident, 500098 Me 262, date of accident August 19, 1945.

64. USAAF Report of Major Accident, FE-113 #1 Fw 190, date of accident September 12, 1945. See also Butler (1994) op. cit.

65. USAAF Report of Major Accident, FE-113 Fw 190, date of accident September 28, 1945.

66. USAAF Report of Major Accident, Foreign Equipment No. 119 Fw 190-D, date of accident September 22, 1945. See also Butler (1994) op. cit.

67. USAAF Report of Major Accident, FE-4600 Hs 129, date of accident July 24, 1946. See also Butler (1994) op. cit.

68. USAAF Report of Major Accident, T2-121 Fw 190-D9, date of accident August 2, 1946. See also Butler (1994) op. cit.

CHAPTER 6

1. Ashcroft and Young op. cit.

2. *Ibid.*

3. "Aircraft Weapons," Office, Director of Armament, Air Proving Ground, Eglin AFB, Florida, June 8, 1949.

4. Paper, "Technical-Historical Development of Parachutes and their Applications since World War I," Theodore W. Knacke, AIAA Ninth Aerodynamic Decelerator and Balloon Conference, October 7–9, 1986, Albuquerque, New Mexico.

5. *Ibid.*

6. *Ibid.*

7. *Ibid.*

8. *Ibid.*

9. James R. Hansen, *Engineer in Charge*, NASA SP-4305, NASA, Washington, D.C., 1987.

10. Kris Hughes and Walter Dranem, *North American F-86 SabreJet Day Fighters*, Warbird Tech Series, Vol. 3, Specialty Press, North Branch, Minnesota, 1996.

11. *Ibid.*

12. Green (1976) op. cit.

13. *Ibid.*

14. Dennis R. Jenkins, Tony Landis, and Jay Miller, *American X-Vehicles: An Inventory – X-1 to X-50*, NASA Monographs in Aerospace History No. 31, SP-2003-4531, Washington, D.C., June 2003.

15. Ward (2005) op. cit.

16. *Ibid.*

17. US Naval Research Laboratory website, accessed January 24, 2013 – http://www.nrl.navy.mil/accomplishments/rockets/v-2-rockets/

18. Gregory P. Kennedy, *The Rockets and Missiles of White Sands Proving Ground: 1945–1958*, Schiffer, Atglen, Pennsylvania, 2009.

19. Ruth P. Liebowitz, *Air Force Geophysics, 1945–1995: Contributions to Defense and to the Nation*, PL-TR-97-2034, Special Reports, No. 280, April 8, 1997, Geophysics Directorate, Hanscom AFB, Massachusetts.

20. Kennedy (2009) op. cit.

21. *Ibid.*
22. Robert Jaques, "From V2 to Saturn V – The Story of Dr. Eberhard Rees," *American Aviation Historical Society Journal*, Spring 1984.
23. *Ibid.*

CHAPTER 7

1. Butler 1994 op. cit.
2. *Ibid.*
3. Walter J. Boyne, *Messerschmitt Me 262: Arrow to the Future*, Smithsonian Institution Press, Washington, D.C., 1980.
4. *Ibid.*
5. Butler (1994) op. cit.
6. See also details of this aircraft at the NASM website.
7. Butler (1994) op. cit.

APPENDICES

1. Letter, Lt Gen Carl Spaatz, Commanding General, US Strategic Air Forces in Europe, to: General of the Army H. H. Arnold, Commanding General, USAAF, May 23, 1945, with attached Interrogation of Reich Marshal Hermann Göring, Ritter Schule, Augsburg, May 10, 1945; in the Murray Green collection at the US Air Force Academy.
2. The lengthy distribution list has been edited to show just the American recipients of this report.

INDEX

E

D

F

and disarmament 84
and technology 158
and V1s 41, 42
Freeman Army Airfield (Indiana) 118, 119, 120, 121–34
Frenzl, Otto 113, 208–11
fuel 31, 62, 77–78, 119

G

Ganzer, Vic 95
Gardner, Gen Grandison 37, 42
gas warfare 44–45
Geerlings, Capt Gerald K. 69
Gemini spacecraft 138
General Electric 98, 145–46
German Air Force *see* Luftwaffe
Germany:
    and aeronautics 16, 18–23, 94, 112, 157, 158–59, 160
    and aircraft 9
    and bombings 43–44
    and disarmament 70–74, 78–82, 84
    and jet fighters 48–49
    and surrender 55, 63–64
    and technology 10, 136, 155–56
    and USA 7–8
    see also Nazi Party
Giles, Lt Gen Barney 47, 51, 52, 59, 60–61
Glenn, John 147
Gleuwitz, Gerhard 179–82
Gluhareff, Michael 108, 117
Goddard, Dr. Robert H. 19
Goleta Airport (California) 148
Göring, Hermann 11, 15, 63, 70
    and interrogation 99, 183–88
Göttingen laboratories 19
Great Britain:
    and aircraft 8, 9, 21
    and defense 22
    and disarmament 84, 93, 95–96

and intelligence 66, 67, 68, 69
and Luftwaffe 71
and scientists 98
and technology 101, 102, 158
and USA 11, 41, 42
see also aircraft, British England
Great Depression 8, 108
Green, Larry 139
guided missiles 7, 75–76, 101, 146
    Henschel Hs 293; 87

H

hardware 7
Hegele, Alfons 137
Hitler, Adolf 17, 70, 104
    and Luftwaffe 8
    and nuclear weapons 76
    and technology 111
    and USA 23
Hoewing, Ralph 33–35
Holloman AFB (New Mexico) 99
Holt, Lt James K. 133
Horky, Ed 107
Hungary 22
Huntsville (Alabama) 141, 142, 145

I

Iceland 25, 26
infra-red night-vision 74–75
Institute of Aeronautical Sciences 127–28, 134
intelligence 11, 17, 36, 45, 65–69
    and bombardment 53
    and crashes 24–26
    and disarmament 72, 73–74, 79
    and scientists 99
    and V1s 41, 42

ABOUT THE AUTHOR

Frederick A. Johnsen is the author of more than 25 aviation books and monographs. His articles and photos have been published in hundreds of periodical issues worldwide.

He earned degrees in history and journalism at the University of Washington, where he worked his way through school at the Kirsten Wind Tunnel, testing projects ranging from early AWACS flutter models and Boeing 747s to remotely-piloted logging balloons.

Fred retired as Director of the Air Force Flight Test Center Museum at Edwards Air Force Base to gain time for writing, web, and video work. Previously, he was an award-winning USAF historian for more than 18 years, and public affairs director of NASA's Dryden Flight Research Center located on Edwards Air Force Base. He worked as the consulting curator to the Museum of Flight in Seattle during its development phase in the late 1970s and into 1980, after serving as editor of *Western Flyer* for several years. He was also the founding curator of the McChord Air Museum while he was historian at McChord Air Force Base in Washington state.